ANGLISTIK UND ENGLISCHUNTERRICHT

Herausgegeben von
Gabriele Linke
Holger Rossow
Merle Tönnies

Band 91

SARAH SCHÄFER-ALTHAUS
SARA STRAUß (Eds.)

Transient Bodies in Anglophone Literature and Culture

Universitätsverlag
WINTER
Heidelberg

Bibliografische Information der Deutschen Nationalbibliothek
Die Deutsche Nationalbibliothek verzeichnet diese Publikation
in der Deutschen Nationalbibliografie;
detaillierte bibliografische Daten sind im Internet
über *http://dnb.d-nb.de* abrufbar.

Herausgeber:
Prof. Dr. Gabriele Linke
PD Dr. Holger Rossow
Prof. Dr. Merle Tönnies

ISBN 978-3-8253-4663-8
ISSN 0344-8266

Dieses Werk einschließlich aller seiner Teile ist urheberrechtlich geschützt. Jede Verwertung außerhalb der engen Grenzen des Urheberrechtsgesetzes ist ohne Zustimmung des Verlages unzulässig und strafbar. Das gilt insbesondere für Vervielfältigungen, Übersetzungen, Mikroverfilmungen und die Einspeicherung und Verarbeitung in elektronischen Systemen.

© 2020 Universitätsverlag Winter GmbH Heidelberg
Imprimé en Allemagne · Printed in Germany
Druck: Memminger MedienCentrum, 87700 Memmingen

Gedruckt auf umweltfreundlichem, chlorfrei gebleichtem
und alterungsbeständigem Papier

Den Verlag erreichen Sie im Internet unter:
www.winter-verlag.de

Contents

Sarah Schäfer-Althaus and Sara Strauß
 Transient Bodies, Bodies in Transition: An Introduction   7

Sarah Schäfer-Althaus
 Dissecting Birth: Obstetrics, Bodily Transience and the
 Anatomist's Gaze in Eighteenth-Century Medical Atlases   23

Julia Schneider
 Birth without a Woman: Mary Shelley's *Frankenstein* in
 the Context of Eighteenth-Century Ideas on Birth,
 Motherhood and Midwifery   47

Sandra Dinter
 Child Bodies in the British Novel of the 1980s   69

Lena Schneider
 "It Was Her Own Body She Remembered":
 Female Bodily Experience in *Sunset Song*   89

Alexander Farber
 Love beyond Life's Boundaries: Transient Bodies in
 Matthew Lewis's *The Monk*   109

Lisa Ahrens
 Transient Bodies at the Threshold of Conversion:
 Physical Reflections of New Religious Identities   129

Alessandra Boller
 "It's Easier to Talk Like This in the Dark": The Body
 with AIDS in Colm Tóibín's *The Blackwater Lightship*   149

Christoph Singer
   The Body Suspended in Time: Transience and Memory
   in the Work of Elizabeth Bishop and Leah Kaminsky   169

Elise Brault-Dreux
   Who Cares for the Old? Old Age in Philip Larkin's Poems   187

Sara Strauß
   Ageing (Female) Bodies and Mortality in Eighteenth-
   Century Poetry   205

Contributors' Addresses   227

Sarah Schäfer-Althaus (Koblenz) and Sara Strauß (Paderborn)

Transient Bodies, Bodies in Transition: An Introduction

> I began to perceive more deeply than it has ever been stated, the trembling immateriality, the mist-like transience, of this seemingly so solid body in which we walk attired.
>
> Robert Louis Stevenson

1. Introduction

"Stop and consider! life is but a day; / A fragile dew-drop on its perilous way / From a tree's summit", John Keats muses in "Sleep and Poetry".[1] Life is transient and temporary. The frailty and instability of human existence as well as "anxieties over mortality, the body, soul, and the corpse"[2] have inspired artists, poets and writers throughout history. 'Transience', according to the *Oxford English Dictionary*, refers to "the quality or state of being transient, impermanent, or ephemeral" as well as "the action of passing from one state, place, etc., to another; transition, transference".[3] In this sense, 'transience' describes both the condition that life and every human existence is temporary and short-lived as well as the continuous experience of change and transition from one phase in life to another. In this respect, considerations of the transient human body not only concern the final days before passing away, but they also strongly focus on pivotal stages and rites of passage throughout one's lifespan. In *Ageing and Popular Culture*, Andrew Blaikie points to the long history of the conceptualisation of the individual life stages and their representation as processes of growth, transition and decline:

> [...] by medieval times the image of the ages of man as a series of steps ascending from infancy to a podium in early adulthood, plateau-ing through mid-life, followed by a descent through the later stages, had emerged to form a metaphor which persisted for centuries.[4]

In the Renaissance, artists symbolised the transience and fragility of human existence and its intimate connection to bodily frailty and decay by picturing the different ages of men and women. Among the most prominent examples of this era are paintings like *The Three Phases of Life and Death* (1509-1510), *The Ages of Woman and Death* (1541-1544) and *The Seven Ages of Woman* (1544) by Hans Baldung Grien[5] and *The Fountain of Youth* (1546) by Lucas Cranach the Elder, in which a rejuvenating bath restores female youth and beauty and thus prolongs life's ephemeral existence.[6] The works of eighteenth and nineteenth-century artists, then, are characterised by their portrayal of human vanity during central life phases and demonstrate people's naivety in ignoring the inevitability of life's transience. Thus, William Hogarth's series of paintings *A Rake's Progress* (1735) depicts the subject's rise and fall from adolescence through a hedonistic adult life to mental and physical impairment in old age.[7] Charles Allan Gilbert's *All is Vanity* (1892), by contrast, does not focus on the individual life stages but serves as a classic *memento mori*. Gilbert ironically plays with the *vanitas* motif when picturing a beautiful young woman at her dressing table, whose reflection in the mirror resembles a human skull.[8] Whereas nineteenth and early-twentieth-century impressionist painters were strongly concerned with the evanescence and transience of the moment,[9] the *vanitas* motif also resurfaces in contemporary art. For instance, in his artwork *For the Love of God* (2007), Damien Hirst decorated a human skull with 8,601 diamonds.[10] The combination of the skull, the original teeth and the abundance of diamonds creates an impression of decadence and reminds the viewer of the inevitability of mortality.

Apart from artistic *memento mori* and illustrations of the impermanence of time and its effect on life and the human body, metaphorical realisations of life's transience can also be found in literature. Two hundred years before Keats's "Sleep and Poetry" cited above, William Shakespeare wrote, for example, in Sonnet 60, "Like as the waves make towards the pebbled shore, / So do our minutes hasten to their end; / Each changing place with that which goes before".[11] Comparable to waves consistently trading places with one another when arriving at the "pebbled shore", so does each phase in life come and go in seamless transition and with unhesitating certainty, replacing childhood with adulthood, youth with old age, life with death, and thus one generation with the next.

Writers of the Romantic and Victorian periods like Matthew Lewis, Mary Shelley, Robert Louis Stevenson and Oscar Wilde paint a different and often darker picture of the transient human body. It is especially in the Gothic that the body becomes "the location of anti-social desire",[12] and cultural anxieties over mortality, decay and physical deterioration result in literary "fantas[ies] of preserving the body",[13] from necrophilic tendencies in Lewis's *The Monk*[14] to creating life out of dead matter, for example, in Shelley's *Frankenstein*. In response to people's desire to overcome life's boundaries, Shelley's novel warns against controversial medical experiments and critically reflects on eighteenth-century endeavours to manipulate the transient body.[15] In Stevenson's *Strange Case of Dr Jekyll and Mr Hyde*, which similarly engages with the manipulation of scientific methods, the human body is seen as "trembling immateriality", as a "seemingly [...] solid body"[16] that is nevertheless constantly in transition, continuously affected by change throughout the course of life and ultimately subject to transience. Wilde's *Picture of Dorian Gray*, in turn, is an aesthetic engagement with the impermanence of life. It portrays a society that hedonistically cherishes the ideal of decadence to counter its anxiety of death and decay.[17] As Briana Regelin asserts, "Dorian fears transience and loss", and while trying to thwart the evanescence of beauty and youth, "he ironically throws himself with abandon into a life that celebrates mortal, ephemeral and transient experiences".[18] Whereas Wilde himself explains that the portrayal of "a young man selling his soul in exchange for eternal youth [is] an idea that is old in the history of literature, but to which [he gave] new form",[19] Regelin observes that this practice "still remains, barely altered, in today's culture".[20]

2. Transient Bodies, Bodies in Transition: Conceptualisations and Theoretical Paradigms

What these examples show is the complexity, multiplicity and paradox of the transient body. Transient bodies are always bodies in transition. Embedded between birth and death, the human body continuously and inexorably passes through different stages in life – childhood and adulthood, youth and old age – all, in retrospect, as transient as life itself. Moreover, as Mariam Fraser and Monica Greco argue, the body is "something we have (the body as object), [...] something we are (the body as subject), and [...] something we become (the body as process and performativity)",[21] and it is particularly in the act of becoming that bodies face transience and transition.

Throughout history, the body – often simultaneously glorified and vilified – has been of central concern of many social, political, medical and gendered discourses and controversial academic debates. As a matter of fact, as David Hillman and Ulrika Maude remind us in *The Cambridge Companion to the Body in Literature*, "the body has always been a contested site [...] notoriously difficult to theorize or pin down, because it is mutable, in perpetual flux, different from day to day and resistant to conceptual definition".[22] In this respect, as Mary Douglas argues in "The Two Bodies", "the human body is always treated as an image of society and [...] there can be no natural way of considering the body that does not involve at the same time a social dimension".[23] Thus, as Elizabeth Grosz points out in *Volatile Bodies*,

> [t]he body must be regarded as a site of social, political, cultural, and geographical inscriptions, production, or constitution. The body is not opposed to culture [... ;] it is itself a cultural, *the* cultural product.[24]

Michel Foucault, furthermore, draws attention to the involvement of the body in the construction and retention of power relations. In *Discipline and Punish*, he explains that the study of the body needs to go beyond understanding it as a "purely biological base of existence":[25]

> Historians long ago began to write the history of the body. They have studied the body in the field of historical demography or pathology [...]. But the body is also directly involved in a political field; power relations have an immediate hold upon it; they invest it, mark it, train it, torture it, force it to carry out tasks, to perform ceremonies, to emit signs.[26]

Therefore, the body "needs to be understood as a performative construct, which operates within a distinct cultural, corporeal framework of [...] power".[27] Against this background, the body's agency in the construction and perpetuation of power relations has been an ongoing research interest within cultural studies, traditionally with regard to gender, class and ethnicity, but also in the context of new paradigms in interdisciplinary research, such as the medical humanities, intersectionality and ageing studies. With regard to bodily phases of transition and the experience of transience, the field of ageing studies, for example, focuses on old age as a rite of passage and examines the relationship between the (ageing) body and social agency. It is in its ageing process that the body ultimately draws attention to the transience of human existence. Hence, Chris Gilleard and Paul Higgs maintain that ageing "reinforces the experience of the transience of people's lives and their inherent corporeal vulnerability":[28]

> For most people, ageing remains a bodily affair. [...] [I]t is the ageing of bodies that remains the ineradicable concern of persons, confronting, in their own ageing bodies, the essential transience of their lives.[29]

While Gilleard and Higgs's study focuses predominantly on the perception of ageing during (later) adult life, the volume at hand addresses the experience of transience and bodily transformation throughout all stages of life, as in our understanding each phase in life consists in itself of a variety of minor and major rites of passages, such as coming of age and sexual awakening during adolescence and ceremonial and religious rituals, but also gendered rites of passage such as pregnancy and childbirth. Since the body and its performance are directly involved in the construction of identity, it is during these phases that physical transience and the resulting changes in a person's physique coincide with transformational processes that strongly shape one's identity.[30] Moreover, in recent years, as Hillman and Maude have observed, an "alternative way of understanding the body, supported by more recent discoveries in science, medicine and philosophy"[31] has emerged, which increasingly considers the significant role of the body "in thinking, feeling and the shaping of our personalities and that precisely for this reason, the body is in fact constitutive of what we call the self".[32]

Overall, the conceptualisation and theoretical paradigms concerning the body are as transient and continuously in transition as transience itself. However, the ongoing musings and theoretical reflections of what constitutes a body have come at least to three preliminary conclusions so far: First, there is no such thing as *the* body. According to Greco and Fraser, "it is commonplace now not to refer to *the* body but to *bodies* in the plural" and "to recognise that there is no body as such which is given and fixed for all time, and to recognise also that experiences rooted in different forms of embodiment may be radically incommensurable".[33] Second, even though the definition of the body is generally difficult, if not to a certain degree impossible, since

> there is no obvious way for the concrete materiality of the body to be fully present in or on the written page [... ,] over the last three or four decades, critics and theorists have found myriad ways of addressing the representation of the body and embodied experience in literature.[34]

Third, in spite of their conceptual impermanence and overall complexity, transience and embodied experiences of transience have been a permanent motif in literature and culture.

Interestingly, although attempts have been made to come to terms with the body and transience in current academic research, the representation of the transient body in Anglophone literature and culture has not been given the attention it deserves.[35] "It seems incontestable", Gilleard and Higgs assert, "that there are limits to every life span".[36] As such, it is not surprising that existing research on transient bodies has focussed predominantly either on old age and death or on specific life phases accompanied by corporeal transformations, such as childhood and coming of age. Because of the complexity of both the body and transience, the collection at hand cannot provide a conclusive overview of all facets of corporeal transience. However, "[i]t is in the biological materiality of the body that the 'cultural' approach towards understanding" transience and the life cycle in general "meets its greatest challenge"[37] and invites us to critically engage with literary and cultural but also historical representations of the transient body.

3. The Many Faces of Bodily Transience: The Contributions

Framed by discussions of the two poles of human existence, birth and death, coming to and going from this world, *Transient Bodies in Anglophone Literature and Culture* presents a wide array of case studies exploring not only bodily transience and the fragility of human existence but also bodies in transition from one phase of life to another. As such, the collection at hand focuses on bodily rites of passage between pregnancy and birth, childhood and adulthood, and old age and death. It combines historical perspectives on the transient body, from the eighteenth to the twenty-first century, and analyses "literature's ability to represent embodied experience" [38] of transience and with regard to cultural values and social norms. Therefore, the essays discuss narrative, poetic and aesthetic strategies employed to imagine and document the temporality of life, which can be "paradoxical, unstable, precarious, finite" and is often "in intimate company with death",[39] social anxieties and questions of morality.

The collection opens with Sarah Schäfer-Althaus's contribution, "Dissecting Birth: Obstetrics, Bodily Transience and the Anatomist's Gaze in Eighteenth-Century Medical Atlases", which explores the visual presentation of the transient gravid uterus in William Smellie's *A Sett of Anatomical Tables with Explanations, and an Abridgment of the Practice of Midwifery* (1754) and William Hunter's *The Anatomy of the Human Gravid Uterus* (1774). Schäfer-Althaus shows how both atlases' medico-scientific images of maternal anatomy and foetal development mirror the eighteenth century's transforming social, political and medical discourses on female (reproductive) sexuality and present the transient female body as a morbid, sometimes eroticised spectacle. By preserving life-in-death, as Schäfer-Althaus argues, these images not only aesthetically illustrate the fragility of human existence, but also claim medical and male authority over the female (reproductive) body.

The complex discourses surrounding midwifery, birth and motherhood are also the focus of Julia Schneider's contribution, "Birth without a Woman". Rather than analysing Mary Shelley's *Frankenstein* in terms of the medical methods anticipated in the novel, Schneider demonstrates that Shelley's text relies on and criticises historical debates and developments in medicine and science, such as the increasing intervention of 'male midwives' in childbirth, the frequent practice of dissections and the pseudoscientific theory of 'maternal imagination'. In her reading, Schneider argues that Victor Frankenstein's failed attempt to overcome corporeal transience, by replacing the female body's significance in childbirth with interventionist science, possesses the potential to undermine defamatory myths about female midwives and highlight the power of women's reproductive bodies.

Moving from birth to childhood and from the eighteenth to the twentieth century, Sandra Dinter explores the construction of the child's body in three literary examples: Iain Banks's *The Wasp Factory* (1984),

Ian McEwan's *The Child in Time* (1987) and Doris Lessing's *The Fifth Child* (1988). Dinter argues that not only is childhood a transient phase between infancy and adulthood but that critical and historical perspectives on the notion of the child's body are equally ephemeral and in flux. She illustrates how childhood studies witnessed a paradigm shift after the publication of Philippe Ariès's *Centuries of Childhood* (1960). After a discussion of the hegemonic notion of the child's body, Dinter shows how the child's transient body in the novels by Banks, McEwan and Lessing is produced and shaped by a constructivist agenda.

Focusing on a different set of social arrangements and theoretical paradigms, Lena Schneider's contribution, "'It Was Her Own Body She Remembered': Female Bodily Experience in *Sunset Song*", analyses how transient phases like sexual awakening, pregnancy and childbirth are linked to (female) embodiment and thereby connect past and current feminist concerns. Schneider demonstrates how Lewis Grassic Gibbon's novel parallels the transitoriness of agricultural life, as mirrored in the novel's four main sections – Ploughing, Drilling, Seed-Time and Harvest – with the major (bodily) transformations the protagonist, Chris, experiences – sexual maturity, pregnancy and childbirth.

Alexander Farber takes a rather different angle on bodily transience in his article, "Love beyond Life's Boundaries: Transient Bodies in Matthew Lewis's *The Monk*". Farber illustrates how Lewis's Gothic novel establishes the "negative aesthetics"[40] of the transient body as an object of (sexual) possessive desires often linked to domination, abuse of power and exertion of control. By comparing the text's juxtaposition of necrotic and necro-erotic scenes, Farber shows that acts of caressing the dead or supposedly dead body are a transgression of social taboos and as such a deviation from cultural norms.

The next contribution, "Transient Bodies at the Threshold of Conversion: Physical Reflections of New Religious Identities," by Lisa Ahrens, discusses the role of the transient body in the construction of religious identity. In this context, Ahrens considers religious conversion as a period of transience and examines the changing perceptions of the body throughout this rite of passage. For this purpose, her essay analyses the representation of embodied religious practices in twenty-first-century British Muslim writing, focusing on Robin Yassin-Kassab's novel *The Road from Damascus* and Leila Aboulela's *Minaret*.

The following two essays consider bodily transience as highlighted in the experience of disease and decay. In "'It's Easier to Talk Like This in the Dark': The Body with AIDS in Colm Toíbín's *The Blackwater Lightship*", Alessandra Boller examines Irish society's conservative attitudes towards homosexuality and AIDS during the 1980s and early 1990s. Through the analysis of the novel's narrative mode, which does not give a voice to the protagonist, as well as its multilayered imagery of corporeality, disease and decay, Boller demonstrates how Toíbín foregrounds the transient body with AIDS. She argues that Toíbín's overly graphic portrayal of the main character's body, while simultaneously silencing the homosexual protagonist himself, criticises the Irish code of silence about homosexuality and AIDS.

Christoph Singer's paper, "The Body Suspended in Time", focuses on the waiting room as a space which foregrounds the experience of transience and memory. In his comparison of Leah Kaminsky's novel *The Waiting Room* and Elizabeth Bishop's poem "In the Waiting Room", he shows that such waiting is a transient state per se that undermines the linear perception of time. Thus, it is especially during the practice of waiting that one becomes aware of the transience of the moment or of one's current stage of life.

The inevitable link between time, transience and the body is also the focus in the final two essays of the collection, which shed light on the body's ageing process and old age as the last phase of human existence before passing away. In her contribution about old age in Philip Larkin's poetry, Elise Brault-Dreux analyses how Larkin depicts the corporeality of ageing bodies. Seizing on Simone de Beauvoir's idea of the "abnormal normality" [41] of senescence, Brault-Dreux sketches the paradoxical condition that it is 'normal' for one's elderly body to look 'abnormal'. Against this background she shows that Larkin's poems depict old age not only as physical transience but also as a series of moments in which one ultimately becomes aware of one's transience.

The volume closes with Sara Strauß's exploration of "Ageing (Female) Bodies and Mortality in Eighteenth-Century Poetry". It examines lyrical works by Jonathan Swift and Anne Finch, Countess of Winchilsea, that link the passage of time and life's transience with sometimes satirical representations of bodily decay and loss of youthfulness. In a close reading of Swift's "A Lady's Dressing Room" and "A Beautiful Young Nymph Going to Bed" as well as Finch's "All

Is Vanity" and further selected poems, Strauß shows how both poets criticise the shallowness of society. They satirise people's vanity and their use of artificial means to prolong life and to uphold a utopia of longevity and immortality while the body, its beauty and health decay and eventually fade away.

As these chapters demonstrate, the transient body and thus "the inherent dialectics of life"[42] can be summarised as follows: "committed to itself, put at the mercy of its own performance, life must depend on conditions over which it has no control and which may deny themselves at any time".[43] Corporeal transience and transformation are dynamic processes, often operating inexorably in the shadows until they gradually become readable and visible on the body. In this "process, which must not cease" and which is "liable to interference",[44] life in general and the transient body in particular are influenced by and have to surrender to historical, social and political conditions and circumstances. Corporeal transience and transformation are also individual processes, as the contributions show, and yet, in the end, they are simultaneously united "in the straining of [life's] temporality always facing the imminent no-more".[45]

Acknowledgments

This project would not have been possible without our contributors, whose inspiring insights make up this collection and whom we would like to thank, first and foremost, for their time, commitment and patience in the genesis of this project.

The idea for this volume was born in the midst of lively and fruitful presentations and discussions at our conference "Transient Bodies in Anglophone Literature and Culture", held at the University of Koblenz-Landau in 2017. In this respect we are especially obliged to the Interdisziplinäres Promotionszentrum (IPZ) at the University of Koblenz-Landau for the generous funding of the project (Projekt NaWi) and particularly to Dr. Kathrin Ruhl, Solveig Schartl, and Anna-Maria Scherhag for their interest in the project from its early stages on. Furthermore, we wholeheartedly want to thank the series editors of *anglistik & englischunterricht*, Prof. Dr. Gabriele Linke, PD Dr. Holger

Rossow and Prof. Dr. Merle Tönnies for the possibility to publish our musings and reflections about transient bodies as part of the series.

To our former research and editorial assistant, Alexander Farber, we are thankful for his invaluable help in preparing the conference and for his unflagging support in spotting formatting errors in early stages of the manuscript. Special thanks, moreover, go out to our copy editor, Tim Feeney, whose magical editing skills and critical feedback improved the final version of this volume and who helped tirelessly with the technical side of preparing the manuscript for publication. Needless to say, all remaining errors are our own.

In the course of the project, the fragility of human existence and the transience of life have hit us more than once; we have entered new phases ourselves and left others behind; we welcomed new additions and mourned the loss of people dear to us. Transience, we learned, is omnipresent, and as Shakespeare concludes in Sonnet 73, we should not forget "To love that well which thou must leave ere long".[46]

Notes

[1] Keats, John (1905 [1816]). "Sleep and Poetry." *The Poems of John Keats*. Ed. Ernest de Sélincourt. New York: Dodd, Mead and Company, 40-49, 42, lines 85-87.
[2] Zigarovich, Jolene (2013). "Introduction." *Sex and Death in Eighteenth-Century Literature*. Ed. Zigarovich. New York: Routledge, 1-29, 19.
[3] "Transience." *Oxford English Dictionary*. Web. 1 April 2020. <www.oed.com/view/Entry/204787?redirectedFrom=transience#eid>.
[4] Blaikie, Andrew (1999). *Ageing and Popular Culture*. Cambridge: Cambridge University Press, 30. Hyphenation in the text.
[5] Baldung Grien, Hans (c. 1509-1510). *The Three Phases of Life and Death/Die drei Lebensalter und der Tod*. Oil on limewood. Kunsthistorisches Museum Wien. Web. 24 June 2020. <https://www.khm.at/objektdb/detail/96/>; *ibid*. (1541-1544). *The Ages of Woman and Death*. Oil on panel. Museo National del Prado Madrid. Web. 24 June 2020. <https://tinyurl.com/yxawn8w7>; and *ibid*. (1544). *The Seven Ages of Woman/Die sieben Lebensalter des Weibes*. Oil on oak wood. Museum der bildenden Künste Leipzig. Web. 24 June 2020. <https://tinyurl.com/y6yzco5e>.
[6] Cranach, Lucas (the Elder) (1546). *The Fountain of Youth*. Oil on canvas. Gemäldegalerie Berlin. *Cranach Digital Archive*. Web. 24 June 2020. <http://lucascranach.org/DE_smbGG_593>.

[7] Hogarth, William (1753). *A Rake's Progress*. Etching and engraving on paper. Tate Britain. Web. 15 June 2020. <https://www.tate.org.uk/art/artworks/hogarth-a-rakes-progress-plate-8-t01794>.
[8] Gilbert, Charles Allan (1902 [1892]). *All Is Vanity. Life* 40.1048, 459.
[9] See, for instance, the works of Claude Monet or Paul Cézanne.
[10] Hirst, Damien (2007). *For the Love of God*. Platinum, diamonds and human teeth. Web. 15 June 2020. <www.damienhirst.com/for-the-love-of-god>.
[11] Shakespeare, William (1975 [1609]). "Sonnet 60." *The Complete Works*. New York: Gramercy Books, 1201, lines 1-3.
[12] Turner, Bryan (1996). *The Body and Society*. 2nd ed. London: Sage, 65.
[13] Zigarovich (2013), 19.
[14] See Lewis, Matthew (2009 [1796]). *The Monk*. Ware: Wordsworth Editions. For a detailed analysis see Alexander Farber's contribution in this collection.
[15] See Shelley, Mary (1982 [1818]). *Frankenstein; or, The Modern Prometheus*. Chicago: University of Chicago Press. For a detailed analysis see Julia Schneider's contribution in this collection.
[16] Stevenson, Robert Louis (2003 [1886]). *The Strange Case of Dr. Jekyll and Mr. Hyde*. London: Norton Critical Editions, 49.
[17] See Wilde, Oscar (2001 [1891]). *The Picture of Dorian Gray*. Ware: Wordsworth Classics.
[18] Regelin, Briana (2015). *The Graceful Prince of a Trivial Comedy: Symbolism and Aesthetics in the Picture of Dorian Gray and "De Profundis"*. All Regis University Theses, 11. Web. 20 June 2020. <https://epublications.regis.edu/theses/650>.
[19] Wilde, Oscar (1962). "To the Editor of the Daily Chronicle." *The Letters of Oscar Wilde*. Eds. Rupert Hart-Davis and Vyvyan Holland. New York: Harcourt, Brace & World, 263-264, 263.
[20] Regelin (2015), 33.
[21] Fraser, Mariam, and Monica Greco (2005). "Introduction." *The Body: A Reader*. Eds. Fraser and Greco. New York: Routledge, 1-42, 4.
[22] Hillman, David, and Ulrika Maude (2015). "Introduction." *The Cambridge Companion to the Body in Literature*. Eds. Hillman and Maude. Cambridge: Cambridge University Press, 1-9, 1.
[23] Douglas, Mary (1996 [1970]). "The Two Bodies." *Natural Symbols: Explorations in Cosmology*. 3rd. ed. London and New York: Routledge. Rpt. in *The Body: A Reader*. Eds. Mariam Fraser and Monica Greco. New York: Routledge, 2005, 78-81, 79.
[24] Grosz, Elizabeth A. (1994). *Volatile Bodies: Toward a Corporeal Feminism*. Bloomington: Indiana University Press, 23. (Emphasis in the text.)
[25] Foucault, Michel (1995). *Discipline and Punish: The Birth of the Prison*. Trans. Alan Sheridan. New York: Random House, 25.

[26] Foucault (1995), 25.
[27] Schäfer-Althaus, Sarah (2016). *The Gendered Body: Female Sanctity, Gender Hybridity and the Body in Women's Hagiography*. Heidelberg: Universitätsverlag Winter, 77. For the performative aspect of the body and its relation to constructions of power and gender see also Butler, Judith (1990 [2007]). *Gender Trouble: Feminism and the Subversion of Identity*. New York and London: Routledge.
[28] Gilleard, Chris, and Paul Higgs (2013). *Ageing, Corporeality and Embodiment*. London: Anthem Press, 84.
[29] Gilleard and Higgs (2013), 21.
[30] See, for example, the contributions by Alessandra Boller, Elise Brault-Dreux and Christoph Singer in this volume.
[31] Hillman and Maude (2015), 1.
[32] *Ibid.*
[33] Fraser and Greco (2005), 3.
[34] Hillman and Maude (2015), 3.
[35] For recent studies of the human body and experiences of change and transience throughout the life phases and its representation in Anglophone literature and culture, see, for example, Boehm, Katharina, Anna Farkas and Anne-Julia Zwierlein (eds.) (2014). *Interdisciplinary Perspectives on Aging in Nineteenth-Century Culture*. New York and London: Routledge; Hartung, Heike (ed.) (2018). *Embodied Narration: Illness, Death and Dying in Modern Culture*. Bielefeld: transcript; Hillman, David, and Ulrika Maude (eds.) (2015). *The Cambridge Companion to the Body in Literature*. Cambridge: Cambridge University Press; Hofmann, Gert, and Snjezana Zoric (eds.) (2016). *Presence of the Body: Awareness in and beyond Experience*. Leiden: Brill/Rodopi; *Political Bodies*, a special issue of *Journal for the Study of British Cultures* 25.1 (2018, ed. by Cyprian Piskurek and Gerold Sedlmayr); Pankratz, Anette, Claus-Ulrich Viol and Ariane de Waal (eds.) (2012). *Birth and Death in British Culture: Liminality, Power, and Performance*. Newcastle: Cambridge Scholars Publishing; and Steinhoff, Heike (2015). *Transforming Bodies: Makeovers and Monstrosities in American Culture*. New York: Palgrave Macmillan.
[36] Gilleard, Chris, and Paul Higgs (2000). *Cultures of Ageing: Self, Citizen and the Body*. London: Prentice Hall. Rpt. in *The Body: A Reader*. Eds. Mariam Fraser and Monica Greco. New York: Routledge, 2005, 117-121, 117.
[37] *Ibid.*, 118.
[38] Hillman and Maude (2015), 2.
[39] Jonas, Hans (1996). *Mortality and Morality: A Search for the Good after Auschwitz* Evanston: Northwestern University Press. Rpt. in *The Body: A Reader*. Eds. Mariam Fraser and Monica Greco. New York: Routledge, 2005, 55-57, 57.

[40] Botting, Fred (2014). *Gothic*. 2nd ed. London: Routledge, 1.
[41] De Beauvoir, Simone (1970). *La Vieillesse*. Paris: Galimard, 349. Trans. Elise Brault-Dreux.
[42] Jonas, Hans (1996), 56.
[43] *Ibid.*, 56-57.
[44] *Ibid.*, 57.
[45] *Ibid.*
[46] Shakespeare, William (1975 [1609]). "Sonnet 73." *The Complete Works*. New York et al.: Gramercy Books, 1203, line 14.

Bibliography

Baldung Grien, Hans (c. 1509-1510). *The Three Ages of Man and Death*. Oil on limewood. Kunsthistorisches Museum Wien. Web. 24 June 2020. <https://www.khm.at/objektdb/detail/96/>.
--- (1541-1544). *The Ages of Woman and Death*. Oil on panel. Museo National del Prado Madrid. Web. 24 June 2020. < https://tinyurl.com/yxawn8w7>.
--- (1544). *The Seven Ages of Woman*. Oil on oak wood. Museum der bildenden Künste Leipzig. Web. 24 June 2020. <https://tinyurl.com/y6yzco5e>.
Blaikie, Andrew (1999). *Ageing and Popular Culture*. Cambridge: Cambridge University Press.
Boehm, Katharina, Anna Farkas and Anne-Julia Zwierlein (eds.) (2014). *Interdisciplinary Perspectives on Aging in Nineteenth-Century Culture*. New York and London: Routledge.
Botting, Fred (2014). *Gothic*. 2nd ed. London: Routledge.
Butler, Judith (1990 [2007]). *Gender Trouble: Feminism and the Subversion of Identity*. New York and London: Routledge.
Cranach, Lucas (the Elder) (1546). *The Fountain of Youth*. Oil on canvas. Gemäldegalerie Berlin. *Cranach Digital Archive*. Web. 24 June 2020. <http://lucascranach.org/DE_smbGG_593>.
De Beauvoir, Simone (1970). *La Vieillesse*. Paris: Galimard.
Douglas, Mary (1996 [1970]). "The Two Bodies." *Natural Symbols: Explorations in Cosmology*. 3rd. ed. London and New York: Routledge. Rpt. in *The Body: A Reader*. Eds. Mariam Fraser and Monica Greco. New York: Routledge, 2005, 78-81.
Foucault, Michel (1995). *Discipline and Punish: The Birth of the Prison*. Trans. Alan Sheridan. New York: Random House.
Fraser, Mariam, and Monica Greco (2005). "Introduction." *The Body: A Reader*. Eds. Fraser and Greco New York: Routledge, 1-42.

Gilbert, Charles Allan (1902 [1892]). *All Is Vanity*. *Life* 40.1048, 459.
Gilleard, Chris, and Paul Higgs (2000). *Cultures of Ageing: Self, Citizen and the Body*. London: Prentice Hall. Rpt. in *The Body: A Reader*. Eds. Mariam Fraser and Monica Greco. New York: Routledge, 2005, 117-121.
--- (2013). *Ageing, Corporeality and Embodiment*. London: Anthem Press.
Grosz, Elizabeth A. (1994). *Volatile Bodies: Toward a Corporeal Feminism*. Bloomington: Indiana University Press.
Hartung, Heike (ed.) (2018). *Embodied Narration: Illness, Death and Dying in Modern Culture*. Bielefeld: transcript.
Hillman, David, and Ulrika Maude (2015). "Introduction." *The Cambridge Companion to the Body in Literature*. Eds. Hillman and Maude. Cambridge: Cambridge University Press, 1-9.
Hirst, Damien (2007). *For the Love of God*. Platinum, diamonds and human teeth. Web. 15 June 2020. <www.damienhirst.com/for-the-love-of-god>.
Hofmann, Gert, and Snjezana Zoric (eds.) (2016). *Presence of the Body: Awareness in and beyond Experience*. Leiden: Brill/Rodopi.
Hogarth, William (1753). *A Rake's Progress*. Etching and engraving on paper. Tate Britain. Web. 15 June 2020. <https://www.tate.org.uk/art/artworks/hogarth-a-rakes-progress-plate-8-t01794>.
Jonas, Hans (1996). *Mortality and Morality: A Search for the Good after Auschwitz*. Evanston: Northwestern University Press. Rpt. in *The Body: A Reader*. Eds. Mariam Fraser and Monica Greco. New York: Routledge, 2005, 55-57.
Keats, John (1905 [1816]). "Sleep and Poetry." *The Poems of John Keats*. Ed. Ernest de Sélincourt. New York: Dodd, Mead and Company, 40-49.
Lewis, Matthew (2009 [1796]). *The Monk*. Ware: Wordsworth Editions Limited.
Pankratz, Anette, Claus-Ulrich Viol and Ariane de Waal (eds.) (2012). *Birth and Death in British Culture: Liminality, Power, and Performance*. Newcastle: Cambridge Scholars Publishing.
Piskurek, Cyprian, and Gerold Sedlmayr (eds.) (2018). *Political Bodies*. Special issue of *Journal for the Study of British Cultures* 25.1.
Regelin, Briana (2015). *The Graceful Prince of a Trivial Comedy: Symbolism and Aesthetics in the Picture of Dorian Gray and "De Profundis"*. All Regis University Theses. Web. 20 June 2020. <https://epublications.regis.edu/theses/650>.
Schäfer-Althaus, Sarah (2016). *The Gendered Body: Female Sanctity, Gender Hybridity and the Body in Women's Hagiography*. Heidelberg: Universitätsverlag Winter.
Shakespeare, William (1975 [1609]). "Sonnet 60." *The Complete Works*. New York et al.: Gramercy Books, 1201.

--- (1975 [1609]). "Sonnet 73." *The Complete Works*. New York et al.: Gramercy Books, 1203.

Shelley, Mary (1982 [1818]). *Frankenstein; or, The Modern Prometheus*. Chicago: University of Chicago Press.

Steinhoff, Heike (2015). *Transforming Bodies: Makeovers and Monstrosities in American Culture*. New York: Palgrave Macmillan.

Stevenson, Robert Louis (2003 [1886].) *The Strange Case of Dr. Jekyll and Mr. Hyde*. London: Norton Critical Editions.

"Transience." *Oxford English Dictionary*. Web. 1 April 2020. <www.oed.com /view/Entry/204787?redirectedFrom=transience#eid>.

Turner, Bryan (1996). *The Body and Society*. 2nd ed. London: Sage.

Wilde, Oscar (1962). "To the Editor of the Daily Chronicle." *The Letters of Oscar Wilde*. Ed. Rupert Hart-Davis and Vyvyan Holland. New York: Harcourt, Brace & World, 263-264.

--- (2001 [1891]). *The Picture of Dorian Gray*. Ware: Wordsworth Classics.

Zigarovich, Jolene (2013). "Introduction." *Sex and Death in Eighteenth-Century Literature*. Ed. Zigarovich. New York: Routledge, 1-29.

Sarah Schäfer-Althaus (Koblenz)

Dissecting Birth: Obstetrics, Bodily Transience and the Anatomist's Gaze in Eighteenth-Century Medical Atlases

> The body [...] evokes fear and loathing, serving as a constant reminder of the inevitability of death and decay – thus the excessive signification of the artistic representations of the body that led to early anatomical atlases explicitly serving as *memento mori*.
>
> Marcia D. Nichols

1. Introduction

In the eighteenth century, significant changes in thinking about men and women, sex and gender, and (reproductive) sexuality and bodily transience challenged the traditional understanding of the human body. "Those who lived during [the] eighteenth century", Regina Barreca remarks, "were obsessed by sex and death",[1] turning the century, according to Jolene Zigarovich, into a "unique period in terms of *eros* and *thanatos*".[2] This simultaneous fascination with sexuality as well as death and decay was paired with a growing medical and anatomical interest in the human body, resulting in a redefinition and terminological specification of the (gendered) body and its (reproductive) organs.[3] Hence, it is not surprising that the "period witnessed an explosion of printed works which dealt with matters of sex and reproduction, from midwifery and medical manuals to sex advice literature and erotica".[4] In fact, the high quantity of midwifery manuals and textbooks, ranging from Sarah Stone's *A Complete Practice of Midwifery* (1737) to William Smellie's influential *Treatise on the Theory and Practice of Midwifery* (1752), show that "birth and maternity increasingly came to be defined as matters that could only be fully managed and understood through detailed, objective, and professional learning".[5]

The controversial discourses surrounding pregnancy and childbirth in the eighteenth century reveal once more that the pregnant body – then and now – is not simply a body transitioning from one phase of life into another. Rather, they demonstrate that pregnancy is one of, if not *the* female body's most conceptualised, cultured and gendered rites of passage. At the end of nine months, the woman not only gives birth to both mother and baby, leading to the affirmation of another order and another hierarchy of the body in its post-pregnant state, but she also "[does] these things under the influence of centuries of imprinting".[6] "Her choices", as Adrienne Rich states, "are made, or outlawed, within the context of laws and professional codes".[7] In addition, as "the waste of female lives […] was high before the discovery of asepsis and the refinement of anatomical knowledge with dissection",[8] complicated births in the eighteenth century frequently ended tragically, turning the transient phase of pregnancy into the body's final stage of transience – death.

This essay seeks to explore the visual presentation of the transient gravid uterus in Smellie's *A Sett of Anatomical Tables with Explanations, and an Abridgment of the Practice of Midwifery* (1754) and William Hunter's *The Anatomy of the Human Gravid Uterus* (1774), both "benchmark publications in the history of midwifery […] setting new standards for description and visual instruction".[9] These atlases, in which "female reproductive anatomy is peeled away to reveal the secrets within",[10] are unique examples combining the century's fascination with female reproductive sexuality with its "preoccupation with mortality and the corpse, and the intense anxiety about bodily dissolution and disruption after death".[11] Both atlases, which feature Jan van Rymsdyk's life-sized, almost photorealistic illustrations of maternal anatomy and foetal development, document the transient pregnant body in order to produce and preserve obstetric knowledge, "provid[ing] a new layer to our understanding of the visual culture of eighteenth-century British midwifery".[12]

However, by "positioning […] women vis-à-vis the man of science",[13] these anatomical atlases and their medico-scientific illustrations, as I intend to show, mirror the gendered politics of pregnancy and childbirth at that time. They "exemplify the triumph of male science over the human body" and "epitomize men's desire to wrest from women their control over their bodies".[14] Furthermore, by presenting the transient female body as a morbid, sometimes eroticised spectacle – as an object of a male and medical gaze – it is in these images that scopophilic instincts are satisfied. As such, even more than the midwifery manual, these atlases arguably "[contribute] to the gradual objectification of the female body and its subjection to a controlling, professionalized gaze […] indicative of the gradual foray of male-connoted medical expertise into the delivery room".[15]

2. Challenging Authority: The Rise of Obstetrics in Eighteenth-Century Britain

The development of British midwifery and the rise of obstetrics, or "[h]ow the private world of the lying-in, which derived its authority from women's experiential knowledge of birth and reproduction",[16] was slowly turned into "the domain of the male physician is a complicated and yet often over-simplified story".[17] For centuries, pregnancy and childbirth were considered "secret, private affair[s], left to the management of women alone",[18] and medical documents "well into the seventeenth century described pregnancy and labour as mysterious events, veiled from men".[19] By "the turn of the eighteenth century", Lisa Forman Cody notes, women were still "treated […] as the natural authorities over birth",[20] as it was agreed that childbirth, this painful and arduous rite of passage, was "only fully understandable to women who had given birth".[21] Whereas the traditional midwife "not only gave prenatal care and advice, but came to the woman at the beginning of her labor and stayed with her till after delivery",[22] thereby providing women with physical assistance and psychological support, the "male birth-attendant was historically called in only to perform the functions […] which were forbidden to the midwife. He was a technician rather than a counsellor, guide, and source of morale; he worked 'on' rather than 'with' the mother".[23]

However, even though female midwives "retained authority in the birthing room, […] it was an authority ultimately managed by men".[24] It was through the rising number of medical treatises and public lectures in midwifery that men-midwives gained "access to the best gynaecological practices" offering "superior knowledge [to] the learned practitioner".[25] Unsurprisingly, most midwifery manuals dealing with childbirth and pregnancy in the seventeenth and eighteenth century, from Nicolas

Culpeper's *A Directory for Mid-Wives* (1651) to Smellie's *A Treatise on the Theory and Practice of Midwifery* (1752), are written by men. Female authors are exceedingly rare, with the exception of Jane Sharp's *The Midwives Book* (1671); Stone's *A Complete Practice of Midwifery* (1737), a passionate proto-feminist plea against the increasing number of men-midwives in London's birthing chambers; and Elizabeth Nihell's *A Treatise on the Art of Midwifery* (1769), in which Nihell famously criticises Smellie's obstetrical machines used for teaching.

Whether written by men or women, what these midwifery texts have in common is that they, as Pamela Lieske reminds us, "focus on women and all aim to educate readers on the practice of childbirth so that mothers have a safer and easier time during pregnancy, delivery and lying-in and their children are born alive and healthy".[26] However, even though these texts concentrate on the transient phase of pregnancy, the midwifery manuals of the time were more than just guidebooks. They document "the subjugation of women's bodies under the authoritative command of professional medical discourse"[27] as well as the growing conflict between female and male midwives. Moreover, in a century which saw the increasing interest in and availability of obstetric instruments, like the forceps, and a steadily rising number of accoucheurs living, teaching and being trained in London, these texts reveal that the "history of midwifery remains a contested one"[28] fuelled by "trade disputes between women and men midwives".[29] In 1737, Stone complained that

> almost every young Man, who hath served his Apprenticeship to a Barber-Surgeon, immediately sets up for a Man-Midwife; altho' as ignorant, and, indeed, much ignoranter, then the meanest Woman of the Profession. But these young Gentlemen-Professors put on a finish'd assurance, with pretence that their Knowledge exceeds any Woman's, because they have seen or gone thro', a Course of Anatomy […].[30]

But "dissecting the Dead, and being just and tender to the Living", she continues, "are vastly different; for it must be supposed that there is a tender regard one Woman bears to another, and a natural Sympathy in those that have gone thro' the Pangs of Childbearing".[31] Others, like Nihell, go even further, claiming "the intrusion of men into the profession [to be] a distortion of nature and a threat to familial and national stability".[32] Whereas Stone and Nihell passionately argue against the increasing male interference and usage of instruments in England's birthing chambers, practitioners like William Clark were of a different opinion. For him it was rather the female midwife's ignorance "to distinguish between Cases within their Abilities, and such Difficulties [...] for Want of necessary Assistance"[33] which caused the frequent death of mother and child during childbirth, and not the lack of education provided for men. As he claims in *The Province of Midwives in the Practice of Their Art* (1751),

> The Case of Child-bearing Women is very lamentable, in the Country especially, by Reason of the Ignorance and Unskilfulness of Midwives; for by their Negligence and perverse Management, many Mothers and Children are destroyed, to the great Misfortune of particular families.[34]

However, at the time Clark's manual was published, the gullibility and reputation of men-midwives was still recovering from the Mary Toft affair (1726),[35] which had publicly displayed the male examiners' "ignorance" of female reproduction. It was in "the wake of the Mary Toft debacle", Cody notes, that men-midwives had to "[develop] new strategies to assert their authority over the reproductive body and to win a regular clientele".[36] Therefore, new forms of medical training, such as public lectures, were introduced, subsequently having a long-lasting and lucrative impact on London's rising medical market.

Before the mid-eighteenth century, practical training for men-midwives in England was not only difficult to obtain but also frowned upon by medical authorities. Whereas in France and Scotland, (academic) programmes were established to train female and male-midwives, "the medical faculties at Oxford and Cambridge eschew[ed] midwifery", and "London's hospitals generally ignored pregnant women, leaving London's aspiring medical men no formal access to routine cases of pregnancy. Those who wished to learn were forced abroad".[37] Thus, many young scholars went to France or the Netherlands, where they were "either buying a quick degree in cities like Reims, or taking courses, viewing dissections, and shadowing masters in Leiden or Paris".[38] In 1740, William Smellie, the "father of British midwifery",[39] famous for his discovery of foetal rotation, moved from rural Lanark to buzzling London to open a medical practice. There he not only started to offer certified courses and lectures on obstetrics and midwifery, but also provided medical care to women from the lower classes, "deliver[ing] hundreds of poor women during a time when lying-in hospitals were virtually non-existent".[40] Professional assistance for pregnant women slowly improved in the next ten years, and by the time Smellie published the first volume of his midwifery manual, "philanthropic efforts to assist pregnant women and illegitimate children were well underway".[41] By the mid-eighteenth century, "the obstetric-training market was glutted",[42] and Smellie, who had educated around nine hundred students over a period of ten years,[43] handed his business over to William Hunter, his former student, who "continued to attract very large classes, with adoring male students".[44]

Consequently, next to the establishment of lying-in hospitals and maternity wards, the introduction of public lectures on midwifery "including presentations of the naked female body"[45] became popular and complemented the theoretical and often technical midwifery manuals with hands-on practice. "Lecturing men-midwives", as Cody summarises,

> revolutionized how a person became a midwife. Unlike female midwives teaching a deputy or a daughter the craft, these men advertised their courses in the press and on handbills. Instead of training their assistants privately only in mother's lying-in chambers (or possibly the parish workhouse), men-midwives taught large groups of pupils in rented rooms at coffee houses or in their own residences. Whereas midwives spent years training around the calendar, men-midwives offered short public courses in midwifery throughout the year.[46]

In these courses, lecturers such as Smellie taught the mechanisms and theories of (forceps-assisted) childbirth and demonstrated 'normal' and complicated births, supporting their lectures with charts, engravings, and three-dimensional, sometimes quite elaborate obstetric models and mannequins in "imitation of real women and children",[47] but also with privately owned foetal specimens and female uteruses and now and then with pregnant women from London's lower classes.[48] However, the public examination of women was criticised heavily. In 1748, William Douglas accused Smellie of indecent behaviour during his lectures: "Decency is a Thing that should be very particularly preserved in this Operation; that obscene Method you have brought into use, of exposing women *quite bare* to a whole Room full of Company, is sufficient to make every Woman abhor the Name or Sight of a *Man-midwife*".[49] In fact, the voyeuristic exposure of women and their most private parts to a room full of paying students and their unobstructed, "controlling and curious"[50] gaze turned the anatomy theatres of the time into arenas for an institutionalised and professionalised (sexual) objectification of women and their bodies. During these public examinations, the female reproductive body was constructed as a spectacle, passively enduring being gazed at, prodded, touched and presumably hurt by complete strangers who sometimes paid a little extra to try out certain manoeuvres or assist during childbirth without proper training. Enjoyed exclusively and actively by the male spectator, these examinations exemplify Laura Mulvey's claim that "[i]n a world ordered by sexual imbalance, pleasure in looking has been split between active/male and passive/female".[51]

Postmortem, however, "the female body was no longer bound by the strictures of modesty", and "male doctors were free to examine the corpse".[52] Thus, most of London's famous eighteenth-century obstetricians were also anatomists, who believed the study of female anatomy via close observation, experimentation and dissections to be absolutely necessary for understanding pregnancy and childbirth. Anatomy "informs the Head [and] guides the hand",[53] Hunter claimed in a lecture in the late eighteenth century, and Smellie argues in the first volume of his *Treatise*,

> Those who intend to practice midwifery, ought first of all to make themselves masters of anatomy, and acquire a competent knowledge in surgery and physic; because of their connexions with the obstetric art, if not always, at least in many cases. He ought to take the best opportunities he can find, of being well, instructed; and of practicing under a master, before he attempts to deliver by himself.[54]

However, female corpses of childbearing age, and particularly pregnant corpses, to present and dissect at public lectures were scarce. As Hunter notes in the preface to his atlas: "Few, or none of the anatomists, had met with a sufficient number of subjects, either for investigating, or for demonstrating the principal circumstances of uterogestation in the human species".[55] In fact, "opportunities of dissecting the human pregnant uterus at leisure, very rarely occur. Indeed, to most anatomists, if they have happened at all, it has been but once or twice in their whole lives" (par. 15).

3. Dissecting Birth: The Gravid Uterus and the Anatomist's Gaze

The anatomical atlases of the (female) body by Smellie and Hunter are thus rare cultural artefacts whose "visual presence" [56] alongside the traditional midwifery manuals of the time enriched the education of new generations of obstetricians, anatomists and midwives (both male and female) with hyperrealistic images of pregnancy and childbirth, while simultaneously linking sex, sexuality and reproduction with physical transience, death and decay. Smellie's *Sett of Anatomical Tables* and Hunter's *Anatomy of the Human Gravid Uterus* unfold the ambiguous and multilayered construction of the evanescent pregnant body. On the one hand, these images of mother and child – mostly "drawn from cadavers – or 'life' as it was described" [57] – meticulously uncover the processes of reproduction, pregnancy and childbirth. On the other hand, "[a]s more and more flesh gets shaved away and the processes of reproduction become clearer and clearer", Paul Youngquist argues, "the female body dies to science and motherless foetuses float in empty space". [58] Thus, with each image laid bare, the evanescent phase of pregnancy gives way to life's ultimate transience until nothing remains to identify the cadaver as either a mother's or a woman's. And yet through the visual preservation of life in death, these atlases create immortality within mortality and preserve both phases of bodily transience for eternity.

Like geographical maps, medical atlases are topographical depictions of the human body. They

> focus attention on a particular feature or on a particular set of spatial relationships. To fulfil their function they assume a point of view – they include some structures and exclude others; they strip away the plenum of sheer stuff that fills up the body – fat, connective tissue, and "insignificant variations" that are not dignified with names or individual identities. They situate the body in relation to death, or to this world, or to an identifiable face […]. [59]

Anatomical atlases display the human body as "'working objects' that form a 'collective empiricism'". [60] By selecting the image, posture and perspective of the object, these atlases "trained scientists on 'what is worth looking at, how it looks, and […] how it should be looked at'", [61] trying to "create a sense of the 'normal'". [62] "This normalizing function",

Nichols argues, "has implications for perceptions of the female body and female sexuality. Images in atlases were not merely an ideal, but the medico-scientific *norm* for how the female body should be".[63] Consequently, "[a]natomical illustrations", Laqueur adds, "are representations of historically specific understandings of the human body and its place in creation and not only of a particular state of knowledge about its structure".[64] Therefore, the anatomy displayed is

> not pure fact, unadulterated by thought or convention, but rather a richly complicated construction based not only on observation, and on a variety of social and cultural constraints on the practice of science, but on an aesthetics of representation as well.[65]

In general, both atlases are similar in their composition and arrangement of the transient female body. Smellie's *Sett of Anatomical Tables* consists of thirty-nine illustrations, the majority of which are anatomical drawings of pregnancy in various stages of gestation and childbirth, including images portraying the extraction of the foetus in difficult births with assistance of obstetric instruments such as the forceps or the crotchet (see tables XXXV and XXXVI).[66] Hunter's atlas, in comparison, includes thirty-four tables illustrating the developing foetus in utero, concluding with two plates featuring various forms of abortion (see table XXXIII) and images of conception (see table XXXIV). Interestingly, whereas the first ten plates in Hunter's work are drawn from the cadaver of a woman who passed away in the ninth month of her pregnancy, from the sixth "subject" onwards, the uterogestation presented decreases with each "subject" dissected – the thirteenth "subject" being only in the first trimester. Furthermore, the women anatomised in both works are "without history – existentially anonymous, interchangeable husks of flesh".[67] In fact, little is said about the cadavers' origins. Hunter mentions several times in the preface that the women dissected have been "procured" (see par. 4, 6, 7) – a euphemism for objects obtained by specific effort or simply stolen[68] – yet he is able to list the causes of death for at least two of the thirteen women anatomised for his atlas (see tables XI and XV). Smellie, in turn, notes in the preface to the *Tables* only "that the greatest part of the figures were taken from Subjects prepared on purpose, to shew [sic] every thing that might conduce to the improvement of the young Practitioner" (n. pag.).

"Whereas some images likely came from actual dissections" in Smellie's atlas,

> most of the images are compositions that Smellie and his artists arranged with prepared female body parts and preserved fetal corpses, which they posed to demonstrate the different techniques and positions Smellie taught in his lectures and writings. In these "experiments," the female corpse had become quite literally an obstetric phantom, giving birth strictly through the efforts of the male accoucheur. Further, the details of the women's bodies were added from "other preparations" indicating that whereas the foetuses were individuals, the "mother" depicted was a composite of several dissected bodies possessed by the anatomist.[69]

Moreover, in both works any signs of individuality have been removed – the bodies displayed are faceless torsos without breasts and extremities, reduced in death to their vaginal and abdominal cavities, skin, veins and intestines. "Anatomical knowledge of the female body", Youngquist asserts, "requires prior excision of individual womanhood to the point that what remains is a rudimentary mother flesh that all women – as women – have in common".[70]

It is doubtful whether the time-transcending fame of Smellie's and Hunter's obstetrical atlases would have been the same without the naturalistic, red-chalk drawings by Jan van Rymsdyk, which complement both works. However, Smellie mentions the artist's name only in passing and Hunter refrains from giving credit to van Rymsdyk at all, showing that in the eyes of the physicians, artistry was less significant than the "art" of anatomy and obstetrics.[71] In 1778, long after his engagement for Smellie and the Hunter brothers, Rymsdyk concludes in his *Museum Britannicum* that he "took a dislike to those Anatomical Studies etc. in which [he] was employed".[72]

Regardless of his lack of contemporary praise, his illustrations for Smellie's *Tables* were at that time "the most anatomically accurate depictions of the pregnant uterus ever yet created".[73] Full of detail, his images are close readings of the transient body, where, as van Rymsdyk notes, "every minute Part is discovered by being brought so near the Eye. *This Distance* I was obliged to make use of, for to represent Nature in its greatest Beauty"[74] – death. His images are "masterpieces of virtuosity, […] still lifes that fool one to seeing life in death".[75] As Deanna Petherbridge and Ludmilla Jordanova stress, they "are amazingly powerful, not only for their subject matter but also in the confidence and beauty of their treatment" of the dead.[76] Therefore, "[t]he relationship in these images between the real and the idealised, the whole and the fragment, and what is represented and what is repressed, […] invites complex readings".[77]

In the *Tables* two illustrations which display fragments of physical and reproductive transience are particularly noteworthy because of their artistic external and internal framing devices and their sexualised gaze at the female body, turning these images into erotic-death portrayals in which physical boundaries dissolve. In table VII, the viewer is exposed to a female torso with the remains of the extremities wrapped in light-coloured cloth. Comparable to many medico-scientific portrayals, the woman's viscera are opened and the skin tissue peeled back, breaking the barrier between interior and exterior body.[78] The transient body in this image is a "body without borders and containment"[79] and the exposure of the uterus is yet another means to claim scientific authority over the female (maternal and sexual) body and its most mysterious organ – the womb. Moreover, table VII is the only image in Smellie's atlas that features one well-rounded and uncovered breast in addition to an equally light-coloured vagina, slightly dilated and surrounded by precisely sketched pubic hair. This intactness of breast, vagina and pubic hair, these most visible and traditionally eroticised symbols of femininity, female sexuality and sexual maturity, are contrasted with the otherwise dark and abysmal abdominal cavity and humiliatingly expose the maternal body to the anatomist's gaze. As Nichols summarises, in this image it is "the woman's sex and her reproductive capacity – her sexuality in an inclusive sense that encompasses all her sexual functions (copulative, reproductive, and maternal)"[80] which is in focus and not the unborn infant. Thus, it is precisely the table's juxtaposition between interior and exterior, intact and damaged, veiled and exposed, erotic and necrotic which places the female transient body on "the verge of the obscene and deadly erotic".[81]

"In their traditional exhibitionist role, women", Mulvey claims, "are simultaneously looked at and displayed with their appearance coded for strong visual and erotic impact".[82] The erotic portrayal of bodily transience reaches its peak in table IV, which displays a horizontal image of the female pelvis. In it, the woman's legs are spread apart, and her abdomen as well as the stumps of her thighs are wrapped in bed-cloths, "provid[ing] an illusion of wholeness"[83] – the focal point being the vulva, clitoris and labia, once more surrounded by thick, carefully delineated pubic hair. The genitals' inherent vitality and the once again strangely intact depiction of the sexually mature woman – this portrayal of life-in-death – makes readers easily forget that they look at a truncated torso in an anatomical atlas and not at an illustration of the female body in eighteenth-century erotica. In table IV, the controlling gaze of the anatomist becomes that of a "spectator in direct scopophilic contact with the female form displayed for his enjoyment [...] set in an illusion of natural space, and through him gaining control and possession of the woman within the diegesis".[84] The image, with its morbidly erotic display of the genitals, mirrors the century's "concomitant eroticization of death"[85] and shows that the female womb was both "'fetishistically adored' and 'violently suppressed'".[86] The female transient body in table IV thus resembles "an act of desire" with "imagined female genitals waiting for a sexual embrace".[87] The carefully sketched pubic hair functions thereby as "an important element in this nexus of desire. As an indicator of a woman's humoral temperament, it provided invaluable information about her potential for fecundity and ardour".[88]

Moreover, both table IV and VII underline that particularly in death the "determining male gaze projects its (erotic) phantasy on to the female figure which is styled accordingly".[89] In death, the anatomist has the ultimate control over the female reproductive body, fragmenting it to suit his personal needs and pleasures. He becomes the director of the narrative, spectacle and gaze, which through its visual documentation can now be enjoyed repeatedly – in public and in private – by the dissector and, comparable to the examination of women in midwifery lectures, by everyone willing to pay for either the anatomical atlas or one specific engraving.

This attention placed on the sexual body is furthermore supported by the internal and external framing devices found in both engravings. Not only are both images framed by a black line "[a]s if to highlight [their] specialness",[90] but to use table IV as an example, the interior drapery of the body's posture, its wrapping and the interplay of lighter and darker crosshatched areas direct the viewer's gaze to the vulva. "These design elements focus the eye on the woman's sex, and the actual frame complicates claims of physical detachment of the image by bringing it into the realm of art",[91] which is especially striking at a time when men-midwives were still trying to prove their scientific objectivity and respectability.

By the time Hunter commissioned his atlas, the result of a twenty-year-long study, van Rymsdyk's skills had improved, his almost photographic images now strongly emphasizing the dichotomy between life and death, mother and child and the transitory phase of childbirth in juxtaposition with the body's transience and decay. Hunter dissected his first human gravid uterus in 1751, noting in his preface that

> a woman died suddenly, when very near the end of her pregnancy; the body was procured before any sensible putrefaction had begun; the season of the year was favourable to dissection; the injection of the blood-vessels proved successful; a very able painter, in this way, was found; every part was examined in the most public manner, and the truth was thereby well authenticated. (par. 4)

It was winter – the season of the year most "favourable to dissection", as the passage reveals – when the anonymous woman's body was meticulously examined by John Hunter in his brother's dissecting rooms near Covent Garden. The "procured" body was in perfect condition upon arrival, and van Rymsdyk, the "very able painter", skilfully captured each stage of its dissection, resulting in the first ten plates of Hunter's atlas.

Comparable to Smellie, Hunter's atlas also demonstrates that the boundary between artistry and objective documentation, which "carries the mark of truth" (Hunter, preface, par. 10), is in fact blurred. This is particularly present in Hunter's table XXVI, fig. iv, in which van Rymsdyk included a nine-paned window visible in the right side of the chorion. According to Wendy Moore, this may have been the window which shed light on the artist's work,[92] but even more than artistry, this window demonstrates that the artist's portraits of the cadavers are, as Hunter declared, "a faithful representation of what was actually seen" (preface, par. 11).

In contrast to Smellie, however, Hunter refrains from additional black frames to single out specific images, and yet, looking at the illustrations, Hunter's tables capture the transient female body in similar fashion. "At each stage", as Moore reminds us, they "evoke the awe at the simple beauty of the baby that would never draw breath and shock at the butchered body of its mother who had breathed her last".[93] In the first table the portrait of the transient pregnant body is still recognizably female. It shows the corpse's legs almost modestly covered with drapery, the abdominal cavity opened, the skin tissue unfolded in a triangular shape and resting on the upper thighs. The amniotic sac, with its fragile arteries shining through the lighter as well as darker areas, takes up the most room in the image. Comparable to Smellie's table VII, in this image the signs of female physicality are still visible – the vulva still intact, the labia slightly dilated with carefully sketched pubic hair – the symbol of sexual maturity – surrounding the vaginal opening. The female body is still "biologically distinct, sexually functional, but emphatically dead, anatomical testimony to a living process of which it is the occasion but not the cause".[94] Yet by table IV, the portrayal of the female reproductive body is dramatically altered: the stumps are no longer veiled with drapery, dreadfully revealing the hacked-away legs; labia and clitoris have also been cut away, leaving a ghastly black hole against which the still intact amnion is pushing; the skin above the *os pubis* is extremely stretched and "lengthened [...] that the contents might better be seen" (Hunter, exp. LL to table IV), rendering the remains of the transient body almost sexless. By table VII nothing is left to identify the corpse as either mother or woman. The dehumanised remains of the pregnant body are strikingly incomplete. Not only has the baby been removed, but the image itself is seemingly unfinished. Whereas the abdominal interior resembles the previous images of the series, the rest of the illustration, the thighs and vulva, are mere sketches, consisting of simple lines shifting the anatomist's gaze away from the woman's sex. As Youngquist argues,

> Hunter's engravings of the gravid uterus make the pregnant female body [...] a border where death crosses to life through a movement of abjection: not-life becoming life by shedding what's spent, not-I becoming I by extruding what's inert. Female bodies produce new bodies by dropping corpselike away, materializing the ambiguity of their own otherness to life.[95]

Moreover, with "its status as waste, its necrotic sexuality, [and] its morbid gestation [...] it becomes all but impossible to dissociate death from the reproductive capacity of the female body".[96]

The babies in Smellie's and Hunter's atlases, which fill the transient hollows of what once was life, are drawn in stark contrast to the lifeless, sometimes unidentifiable female reproductive cadavers – "[l]ife is all the child's while its mother's flesh incorporates death".[97] The babies are perfect aesthetic visualizations of life-in-death. Many images, particularly in Smellie's work, feature fully-formed, chubby and vital-looking babies, posed as if sleeping, some slightly smiling (see, for example, Smellie, tables X and XII), with curling fingers gently touching cheeks (see *ibid.*, table XIII) and with every wisp of hair carefully and tenderly sketched (see also Hunter, tables VI and XII). The baby's skin and sometimes even the umbilical cord is shining (see Smellie, table X; Hunter, tables XII and XIII), showing the artistic emphasis placed on the child and not the mother, whose transient body is reduced to a carcass holding the foetus. This particular focus on the unborn, "the only complete and lifelike people" in both works, as Cody argues,

> represent[s] an important shift in the transition from female to male midwives in eighteenth-century Britain. Whereas traditional female-authored treatises focusing on the subjective experience of pregnancy and several earlier midwifery texts included illustrations that showed the entire mother, smiling or sleeping, with arms and legs posed, and her abdomen opened up for display, eighteenth-century men-midwives projected a startling different body.[98]

Thus, apart from fragmenting and objectifying the female sexual and reproductive body, the images of the transient gravid uterus in Hunter's and Smellie's atlases also display the century's increasing emphasis on children and not on their mothers. "In the broader cultural context of an Enlightenment fascination with childhood and omnipresent calls for increasing the population," as Cody remarks, "these images of precious offspring suggested the man-midwife's contribution to both family and national ideals",[99] adding yet another facet to the atlases' complex visual attempts to demonstrate mastery over women, their bodies and their overall value in society.

4. Conclusion

In the eighteenth century, midwifery and childbirth underwent significant changes, from being a traditionally female trade to a profitable business in

London's rising medical market, managed by male obstetricians and leading to the commercialisation of midwifery by the end of the century. The pregnant body's natural yet fragile transition into the realms of motherhood became increasingly studied and debated, institutionalised and documented, and led to its exposure and display, whether "in life" or "in death", in the anatomy theatres of the time. It was examined, penetrated and cut open not only to understand reproduction and gestation but also to subordinate women to the gaze of an increasingly male-dominated medical discourse and clientele that claimed authority over a part of female anatomy which was "traditionally semanticized as dark, unchartered territory in the (male-)dominated cultural imagination".[100]

The analysis of Smellie's and Hunter's atlases and their preservation of the transient gravid uterus reveals that both are complex visual and cultural artefacts that "[invite] complex readings".[101] They mirror the century's transforming social, political and medical discourses on female (reproductive) sexuality and the gradual foray of men into the until-then all-female birthing chambers while at the same time depicting the century's fascination with sex and (the eroticization of) death. As such, the images show that in medical atlases like those produced by Smellie and Hunter, the "fragmentation of the female body"[102] to the point of dissolution of any human form not only helped to uncover "the 'secret' of female anatomy"[103] and to chronicle obstetric knowledge for future generations. They also demonstrate that by opening, displaying and visualizing the female reproductive body in its transient state, these images "remove ambivalence about the object of the female body by achieving mastery over it".[104] By preserving life-in-death, however, these images not only claim medical and male authority over the female body, thereby promoting the increasing medicalization of pregnancy and childbirth, but they also illustrate the fragility of human existence. As such, they are also aesthetic and powerful images, which, thanks to van Rymsdyk's artistic skills, manage to preserve the transient pregnant body for eternity.

Notes

[1] Barreca, Regina (2013). "Foreword." *Sex and Death in Eighteenth-Century Literature*. Ed. Jolene Zigarovich. New York: Routledge, ix-xii, ix.

[2] Zigarovich, Jolene (2013). "Introduction." *Sex and Death in Eighteenth-Century Literature*. Ed. Zigarovich. New York: Routledge, 1-29, 1.
[3] See Laqueur, Thomas (1992). *Making Sex: Body and Gender from the Greeks to Freud*. Cambridge: Harvard University Press, 149-192.
[4] Sommers, Sheena (2012). "Transcending the Sexed Body: Reason, Sympathy, and 'Thinking Machines' in the Debates over Male Midwifery." *The Female Body in Medicine and Literature*. Eds. Andrew Mangham and Greta Depledge. Liverpool: Liverpool University Press, 89-106, 92.
[5] *Ibid.*, 89.
[6] Rich, Adrienne (1995). *Of Woman Born: Motherhood as Experience and Institution*. New York: Norton, 128.
[7] *Ibid.*, 128.
[8] *Ibid.*, 141.
[9] Woods, Robert, and Chris Galley (2014). *Mrs Stone & Dr Smellie: Eighteenth-Century Midwives and their Patients*. Liverpool: Liverpool University Press, 11.
[10] Lieske, Pamela (ed.) (2016). *Eighteenth-Century British Midwifery*. 12 vols. Abingdon: Routledge, I: xxv.
[11] Zigarovich (2013), 1.
[12] Lieske (2016), I: xxviii.
[13] Mangham, Andrew, and Greta Depledge (2012). "Introduction." *The Female Body in Medicine and Literature*. Eds. Mangham and Depledge. Liverpool: Liverpool University Press, 1-15, 1.
[14] Cody, Lisa Forman (2005), *Birthing the Nation: Sex, Science, and the Conception of Eighteenth-Century Britons*. Oxford: Oxford University Press, 9.
[15] Schwanebeck, Wieland (2016). "The Womb as Battlefield: Debating Medical Authority in the Renaissance Midwife Manual." *Journal for the Study of British Cultures* 23.2, 101-114, 102.
[16] Sommers (2012), 89.
[17] *Ibid.*
[18] Cody (2005), 31.
[19] *Ibid.*
[20] *Ibid.*
[21] *Ibid.*
[22] Rich (1995), 150.
[23] *Ibid.*
[24] Lieske (2016), V: xv.
[25] *Ibid.*
[26] *Ibid.*, IV: vii.
[27] Schwanebeck (2016), 110.
[28] Woods and Galley (2014), 1.
[29] *Ibid.*

[30] Stone, Sarah (1737). *A Complete Practice of Midwifery*. London: T. Cooper, xi.
[31] *Ibid.*, xiv-xv.
[32] Lieske (2016), VI: ix.
[33] Clark, William (1751). *The Province of Midwives in the Practice of Their Art*. London: M. Cooper, 1.
[34] *Ibid.*
[35] Mary Toft was an English countrywoman from Godalming, Surrey, who claimed to have given birth to rabbits after craving for rabbit meat during pregnancy. She was examined by a number of leading specialists, including Nathaniel St. André, John Maubray, John Douglas and Sir Richard Manningham, until her "delivery of rabbits" was discovered to be a hoax and Toft imprisoned for fraud. The Mary Toft affair was a public sensation and resulted in long-lasting satire and ridicule for the practitioners involved. As S. A. Seligman notes, "Never can the Medical Profession have been made to appear so ridiculous in the eyes of the general public, and indeed of each other, than by the affair of Mary Toft in 1726". See Seligman, S. A. (1961). "Mary Toft – The Rabbit Breeder." *Medical History* 5.4, 349-360, 349. For St. André's extensive account of the case, see St. André, Nathaniel (1727). *A Short Narrative of an Extraordinary Delivery of Rabbets, Perform'd by Mr. John Howard, Surgeon at Guildford*, London: John Clarke.
[36] Cody (2005), 152.
[37] *Ibid.*, 157.
[38] *Ibid.*, 161.
[39] Lieske (2016), V: xvii.
[40] *Ibid.*
[41] *Ibid.*, IV: xi.
[42] Cody (2005), 163.
[43] See Lanark Museum & The Royal Burgh of Lanark Museum Trust. "Famous Lanarkians." *Lanark Museum & The Royal Burgh of Lanark Museum Trust*, n.d. Web. 25 October 2019.
[44] Cody (2005), 163. However, it is noteworthy that Smellie trained male as well as female students. See, for example, Lieske (2016), V: 262, and King, Helen (2007). *Midwifery Obstetrics and the Rise of Gynaecology: The Uses of a Sixteenth-Century Compendium*. Aldershot: Ashgate, 74.
[45] Cody (2005), 10.
[46] *Ibid.*, 162. In fact, most of Smellie's courses could be completed within two weeks; see Lieske (2016), V: 259.
[47] For a fascinating introduction to the world of obstetric machines, see Lieske, Pamela (2012). "'Made in Imitation of Real Women and Children': Obstetrical Machines in Eighteenth-Century Britain." *The Female Body in Medicine and*

Literature. Eds. Andrew Mangham and Greta Depledge. Liverpool: Liverpool University Press, 69-88. See also Cody (2005), 171-172.

[48] See Cody (2005), 166. That lecturers owned, collected and used anatomical specimen for teaching was not uncommon. See, for example, Schroeder Haslem, Lori (2012). "Monstrous Issues: The Uterus as Riddle in Early Modern Medical Texts." *The Female Body in Medicine and Literature*. Eds. Andrew Mangham and Greta Depledge. Liverpool: Liverpool University Press, 34-50, and Lieske (2012), 69. Upon Hunter's death in 1783, his large collection was moved to the University of Glasgow. It was reported that one room alone "contained 500 preparations and engravings of the gravid uterus, including a series of plaster casts of the pregnant uterus that correspond to illustrations of the gravid uterus found in Hunter's atlas" (*ibid.*).

[49] Douglas, William (1748). *A Letter to Dr. Smelle [sic]*. London: J. Roberts, 22. (Emphasis in the text).

[50] Mulvey, Laura (1975). "Visual Pleasure and Narrative Cinema." *Film Theory and Criticism*. Eds. Gerald Mast and Marshall Cohen. New York: Oxford University Press, 803-815, 806.

[51] *Ibid.*, 808.

[52] Staub, Susan C. (2012). "Surveilling the Secrets of the Female Body: The Contest for Reproductive Authority in the Popular Press of the Seventeenth Century." *The Female Body in Medicine and Literature*. Eds. Andrew Mangham and Greta Depledge. Liverpool: Liverpool University Press, 51-68, 60.

[53] Hunter, William (c. 1780). *Introductory Lecture to Students*. St. Thomas's Hospital Manuscripts 55:182, qtd. in Richardson, Ruth (2000 [1978]). *Death, Dissections and the Destitute*. Chicago: Chicago University Press, 30-31.

[54] Smellie, William (1752). *A Treatise on the Theory and Practice of Midwifery*. London: D. Wilson, 426.

[55] Hunter, William (1774). *The Anatomy of the Human Gravid Uterus Exhibited in Figures*. Birmingham: John Baskerville, preface, par. 4. Further references to this edition will be included in the text.

[56] Lieske (2016), I: xxviii.

[57] Cody (2005), 167.

[58] Youngquist, Paul (2003). *Monstrosities: Bodies and British Romanticism*. Minneapolis: University of Minnesota Press, 135.

[59] Laqueur (1992), 164.

[60] Datson, Lorraine, and Peter Galison (2007). *Objectivity*. New York: Zone Books, 19-26, qtd. in Nichols, Marcia D. (2013). "Venus Dissected: The Visual Blazon of Mid-Eighteenth-Century Medical Atlases." *Sex and Death in Eighteenth-Century Literature*. Ed. Jolene Zigarovich. New York: Routledge, 103-123, 104.

[61] *Ibid.*

[62] Nichols (2013), 104.
[63] *Ibid.* (Emphasis in the text).
[64] Laqueur (1992), 164.
[65] *Ibid.*, 163-164.
[66] Smellie, William (1754). *A Sett of Anatomical Tables.* London. Further references to this edition will be included in the text.
[67] Youngquist (2003), 135.
[68] The question how the Hunters and Smellie obtained their cadavers was and still is widely debated. Ruth Richardson argues, for example, that they were probably "neither from the legally sanctioned number or murderers, nor of those who had sold their own bodies. They were, quite simply, snatched". See Richardson (2000 [1978]), 53; see also *ibid.*, 30-72, and Moore, Wendy (2005). *The Knife Man: Blood, Body-Snatching and the Birth of Modern Surgery.* London: Bantam, 127. Don Shelton even accuses Smellie and Hunter of murdering several pregnant women for their dissections and experiments. See Shelton, Don (2010). "The Emperor's New Clothes." *Journal of the Royal Society of Medicine* 103.2, 46-50. Shelton's questionable article was widely and controversially discussed. For an overview of the controversy, see King, Helen (2011). "History without Historians? Medical History and the Internet." *Social History of Medicine*, 24.2, 212-221. For a recent study of Hunter's sources see McDonald, Stuart, and John Faithfull (2015). "William Hunter's Sources of Pathological and Anatomical Specimens, with Particular Reference to Obstetric Subject." *William Hunter's World: The Art and Science of Eighteenth-Century Collecting.* Eds. E. Geoffrey Hancock et. al. London: Routledge, 45-58.
[69] Nichols (2013), 114.
[70] Youngquist (2003), 135.
[71] Generally, it can be said that William Hunter's triumph would have been impossible without van Rymsdyk's drawings and his brother John's assistance. John Hunter, the famous surgeon, was probably the only operating dissector at work, yet, like the artist, he is barely mentioned in the preface and reduced to the status of assistant. See preface, par. 19; see also Moore (2005), 125-132.
[72] Van Rymsdyk, Jan, and Andreas van Rymsdyk (1778). *Museum Britannicum.* London: L. Moore, 83.
[73] Cody (2005), 167.
[74] Van Rymsdyk and Van Rymsdyk (1778), vii. (Emphasis in the text).
[75] Nichols (2013), 114.
[76] Petherbridge, Deanna, and Ludmila Jordanova (1997). *The Quick and the Dead: Artists and Anatomy.* Berkeley: University of California Press, 85.
[77] *Ibid.*
[78] See also Nichols (2013), 109.

[79] Nead, Lydia (1992). *The Female Nude*. London: Routledge, 2, qtd. in Nichols (2013), 110.
[80] Nichols (2013), 112.
[81] *Ibid.*, 110.
[82] Mulvey (1975), 808-809.
[83] Nichols (2013), 114.
[84] Mulvey (1975), 811.
[85] Zigarovich (2013), 1. People during the eighteenth century were generally fascinated by the sex-death paradigm, and numerous literary classics produced during the period include eroticised death scenes, most prominently Matthew Lewis's *The Monk* (1796) and Samuel Richardson's *Clarissa* (1748). For a critical assessment of the eroticisation of death in *The Monk*, see Alexander Farber's contribution to this volume.
[86] Sawday, Jonathan (1995). *The Body Emblazoned: Dissection and the Human Body in Renaissance Culture*. London: Routledge, 222-223, qtd. in Staub (2012), 43.
[87] Nichols (2013), 115. Nichols's fascinating article includes a convincing analysis of pubic hair in Smellie's atlas.
[88] *Ibid.*
[89] Mulvey (1975), 808.
[90] Nichols (2013), 115.
[91] *Ibid.*, 116.
[92] Moore (2005), 129.
[93] *Ibid.*, 128.
[94] Youngquist (2003), 135.
[95] *Ibid.*, 138-139.
[96] *Ibid.*, 137.
[97] *Ibid.*
[98] Cody (2005), 168-169.
[99] *Ibid.*, 169.
[100] Schwanebeck (2016), 105.
[101] Petherbridge, Deanna, and Ludmila Jordanova (1997), 85.
[102] Nichols (2013), 113.
[103] Schroeder Haslem (2012), 41.
[104] *Ibid.*

Bibliography

Barreca, Regina (2013). "Foreword." *Sex and Death in Eighteenth-Century Literature*. Ed. Jolene Zigarovich. New York: Routledge, ix-xii.

Clark, William (1751). *The Province of Midwives in the Practice of Their Art: Instructing Them in the Timely Knowledge of Such Difficulties as Require the Assistance of Men, for the Preservation of Mother and Child. Very Necessary for the Perusal of All the Sex Interested in the Subject, and Interspersed with Some New and Useful Observations*. London: M. Cooper.

Cody, Lisa Forman (2005). *Birthing the Nation: Sex, Science, and the Conception of Eighteenth-Century Britons*. Oxford: Oxford University Press.

Culpeper, Nicolas (1651). *A Directory for Midwives: or, A Guide for Women, in their Conception, Bearing, and Suckling their Children*. London: Peter Cole.

Datson, Lorraine, and Peter Galison (2007). *Objectivity*. New York: Zone Books.

Douglas, William (1748). *A Letter to Dr. Smelle* [sic]. *Shewing the Impropriety of his New-Invented Wooden Forceps; as also, the Absurdity of Teaching and Practicing Midwifery*. London: J. Roberts.

Hunter, William (1774). *Anatomia uteri humani gravidi tabulis illustrata / The Anatomy of the Human Gravid Uterus Exhibited in Figures*. Birmingham: John Baskerville.

--- (c. 1780). *Introductory Lecture to Students*. St. Thomas's Hospital Manuscripts. Mss. 55.

King, Helen (2007). *Midwifery Obstetrics and the Rise of Gynaecology: The Uses of a Sixteenth-Century Compendium*. Aldershot: Ashgate.

--- (2011). "History without Historians? Medical History and the Internet." *Social History of Medicine* 24.2. Oxford: Oxford University Press, 210-221.

Lanark Museum & The Royal Burgh of Lanark Museum Trust. "Famous Lanarkians." *Lanark Museum & The Royal Burgh of Lanark Museum Trust*, n.d. Web. 25 October 2019.

Laqueur, Thomas (1992*). Making Sex: Body and Gender from the Greeks to Freud*. Cambridge: Harvard University Press.

Lewis, Matthew (1999 [1796]). *The Monk*. London: Penguin.

Lieske, Pamela (2012). "'Made in Imitation of Real Women and Children': Obstetrical Machines in Eighteenth-Century Britain." *The Female Body in Medicine and Literature*. Eds. Andrew Mangham and Greta Depledge. Liverpool: Liverpool University Press, 69-88.

---, ed. (2016). *Eighteenth-Century British Midwifery*. 12 vols. Abingdon: Routledge.

Mangham, Andrew, and Greta Depledge (2012). "Introduction." *The Female Body in Medicine and Literature*. Eds. Mangham and Depledge Liverpool: Liverpool University Press, 1-15.

McDonald, Stuart, and John Faithfull (2015). "William Hunter's Sources of Pathological and Anatomical Specimens, with Particular Reference to

Obstetric Subject." *William Hunter's World: The Art and Science of Eighteenth-Century Collecting*. Eds. E. Geoffrey Hancock et. al. London: Routledge, 45-58.

Moore, Wendy (2005). *The Knife Man: Blood, Body-Snatching and the Birth of Modern Surgery*. London: Bantam.

Mulvey, Laura (1975). "Visual Pleasure and Narrative Cinema." *Film Theory and Criticism*. Eds. Gerald Mast and Marshall Cohen. New York: Oxford University Press, 803-815.

Nead, Lydia (1992). *The Female Nude*. London: Routledge.

Nichols, Marcia D. (2013). "Venus Dissected: The Visual Blazon of Mid-Eighteenth-Century Medical Atlases." *Sex and Death in Eighteenth-Century Literature*. Ed. Jolene Zigarovich. New York: Routledge, 103-123.

Nihell, Elizabeth (1769). *A Treatise on the Art of Midwifery. Setting forth Various Abuses therein, Especially as to the Practice with Instruments: The Whole Serving to Put all Rational Inquirers in a Fair Way of Very Safely Forming Their Own Judgement upon the Question; Which It Is Best to Employ, in Cases of Pregnancy and Lying-In, a Man-Midwife or a Midwife*. London: A. Morley.

Petherbridge, Deanna, and Ludmila Jordanova (1997). *The Quick and the Dead: Artists and Anatomy*. Berkeley: University of California Press.

Rich, Adrienne (1995). *Of Woman Born: Motherhood as Experience and Institution*. New York: Norton.

Richardson, Ruth (2000 [1978]). *Death, Dissections and the Destitute*. Chicago: Chicago University Press.

Richardson, Samuel (2004 [1748]). *Clarissa, or, the History of a Young Lady*. London: Penguin.

Sawday, Jonathan (1995). *The Body Emblazoned: Dissection and the Human Body in Renaissance Culture*. London: Routledge.

Schroeder Haslem, Lori (2012). "Monstrous Issues: The Uterus as Riddle in Early Modern Medical Texts." *The Female Body in Medicine and Literature*. Eds. Andrew Mangham and Greta Depledge. Liverpool: Liverpool University Press, 34-50.

Schwanebeck, Wieland (2016). "The Womb as Battlefield: Debating Medical Authority in the Renaissance Midwife Manual." *Journal for the Study of British Cultures* 23.2. Würzburg: Könighausen und Neumann, 101-114.

Seligman, S. A. (1961). "Mary Toft – The Rabbit Breeder." *Medical History* 5.4, 349-360.

Sharp, Jane (1671). *The Midwives Book: Or the Whole Art of Midwifery Discovered*. London: E. Thomas.

Shelton, Don (2010). "The Emperor's New Clothes." *Journal of the Royal Society of Medicine* 103.2, 46-50.

Smellie, William (1752). *A Treatise on the Theory and Practice of Midwifery*. London: D. Wilson.

--- (1754). *A Sett of Anatomical Tables, with Explanations and an Abridgment of the Practice of Midwifery, with a View to Illustrate a Treatise on That Subject, and Collection of Cases*. London.

Sommers, Sheena (2012). "Transcending the Sexed Body: Reason, Sympathy, and 'Thinking Machines' in the Debates over Male Midwifery." *The Female Body in Medicine and Literature*. Eds. Andrew Mangham and Greta Depledge. Liverpool: Liverpool University Press, 89-106.

St. André, Nathaniel (1727). *A Short Narrative of an Extraordinary Delivery of Rabbets, Perform'd by Mr. John Howard, Surgeon at Guildford*. London: John Clarke.

Staub, Susan C. (2012). "Surveilling the Secrets of the Female Body: The Contest for Reproductive Authority in the Popular Press of the Seventeenth Century." *The Female Body in Medicine and Literature*. Eds. Andrew Mangham and Greta Depledge. Liverpool: Liverpool University Press, 51-68.

Stone, Sarah (1737). *A Complete Practice of Midwifery. Consisting of Upwards of Forty Cases or Observations in That Valuable Art, Selected from Many Others, in the Course of a Very Extensive Practice. And Interspersed with Many Necessary Cautions and Useful Instructions ... Recommended to All Female Practitioners in an Art so Important to the Lives and Well-Being of the Sex*. London: T. Cooper.

Van Rymsdyk, Jan, and Andreas van Rymsdyk (1778). *Museum Britannicum, Being an Exhibition of a Great Variety of Antiquities and Natural Curiosities, Belonging to That Noble and Magnificent Cabinet, the British Museum. Illustrated with Curious Prints, Engraved after the Original Designs, from Nature, Other Objects; and with Distinct Explanations of Each Figure*. London: L. Moore.

Woods, Robert, and Chris Galley (2014). *Mrs Stone & Dr Smellie: Eighteenth-Century Midwives and their Patients*. Liverpool: University of Liverpool Press.

Youngquist, Paul (2003). *Monstrosities: Bodies and British Romanticism*. Minneapolis: University of Minnesota Press.

Zigarovich, Jolene (2013). "Introduction." *Sex and Death in Eighteenth-Century Literature*. Ed. Zigarovich. New York: Routledge, 1-29.

Julia Schneider (Paderborn)

Birth without a Woman: Mary Shelley's *Frankenstein* in the Context of Eighteenth-Century Ideas on Birth, Motherhood and Midwifery

1. Introduction

Mary Shelley's *Frankenstein; or, The Modern Prometheus* has become its own field of study. Apart from its influence on Gothic fiction, female authorship, the Romantic movement and science fiction, it is considered to be a landmark work in terms of its impact on popular culture. The story of the mad scientist who creates a monster is still frequently rewritten, retold and reinvented in a variety of contexts, such as in the latest instalment of the *Alien* prequel series, *Alien: Covenant* (2017). Yet the novel serves as material to examine not only Gothic literature and popular culture, but also medical methods. Critics such as H. Bruce Franklin are therefore convinced that no single book offers more meaningful interconnections between literature and medicine than *Frankenstein*.[1]

The novel presents the story of Victor Frankenstein, a scientist who – in his attempt to create human life on an artificial level – ends up 'giving birth' to a creature consisting of dead human body parts. As a result, the story engages with different bodies in transience, such as the decaying body and the body brought to life. Whereas many scholars examine Shelley's ideas in terms of the medical methods foreshadowed, such as genetic engineering, organ transplants and in vitro fertilization,[2] the following paper focuses on the way the novel deals with practices pertaining to medicine from a historical perspective. In my reading of the novel, Shelley not only anticipates medical practices but also critically engages with scientific ideas of the eighteenth century concerning birth, motherhood, midwifery and the transient body. Even though published in 1818, *Frankenstein* is arguably affected by the morals and principles of the eighteenth century, during which the field of obstetrics, formerly dominated by women, was invaded and eventually transformed by male practitioners. Shelley challenges this intrusion of 'male midwives' into the female field of birth by connecting Frankenstein's experiment with controversial methods of eighteenth-century obstetrics such as dissections and interventionist science.

The first part of this paper will discuss the representation of female characters in *Frankenstein*, since the criticism of eighteenth-century medical developments and male scientific power becomes visible through the depictions of women and their lack of agency. The portrayal of Elizabeth, Frankenstein's betrothed, who is killed by the creature, draws attention to the neglect of responsibility Victor Frankenstein makes himself guilty of as a scientist. The victimization of Justine, the Frankenstein family's housekeeper, who is falsely accused of murdering a child, will then be used to examine the novel's approach to the eighteenth-century infanticide trials and their connection to an encroachment of male physicians into the female-centred world of reproduction and childbirth.[3] Moreover, the main character's scientific approach will be addressed, since it is displayed as one that interferes with natural processes and tries to overcome the transience of life. Frankenstein's obsession with interventionist methods is thereby contrasted with a calm and idyllic nature representing rational behaviour. Furthermore, this essay intends to show that the production of Frankenstein's creature mirrors obstetrical methods of the eighteenth century. For this purpose, Sarah Stone's *A Complete Practice of Midwifery*, published in 1737, will be referred to, as it is one of the most famous publications attacking male midwives as well as being a treatise on the unique capacity of women in childbirth assistance. In this context, the transition of gender boundaries in the profession of the midwife will be analysed. Finally, the hypothesis of 'maternal imagination' will be set in relation to the concept of monstrosity and therefore to the question of the actual evil spirit of the story. The pseudoscientific theory of 'maternal imagination' was used to claim that monstrous births are caused by the female mind, which is portrayed as easily impressionable to such an extent that mothers can deform or kill the foetus in pregnancy.[4] With the idea of overcoming the transience of life by constructing a creature out of human body parts, it is, however, a male scientist who brings death to the living. Hence, this paper will show how Shelley's novel alludes to eighteenth-century ideas on midwifery, motherhood and birth and thereby undermines defamatory myths about female midwives and female bodies in England.

2. The Representation of Female Agency in *Frankenstein*

Set in the eighteenth century, the story of Victor Frankenstein is concerned with many scientific and social developments of its time. As the daughter of two political philosophers, Shelley grew up with free access to her father's library and to her parents' work.[5] According to Jay Clayton, Shelley was inspired by her mother, Mary Wollstonecraft, and shared her beliefs concerning intellectual progress, the virtue of education, and the rationality of women.[6] An influential issue already lamented by Wollstonecraft in her 1792 manifesto *A Vindication of the Rights of Woman* was the replacement of female midwives by men:

> Women might certainly study the art of healing, and be physicians as well as nurses. And midwifery, decency seems to allot to them, though I am afraid the word midwife, in our dictionaries, will soon give place to *accoucheur*, and one proof of the former delicacy of the sex be effaced from the language.[7]

Thus, it can be argued that Shelley was familiar with the growing exclusion of female midwives from birthing chambers and with the critique of it.

While men already controlled all other medical fields in the eighteenth century, male physicians tried to transform midwifery into a male monopoly as well. According to Franklin, "as males came to dominate the medical sphere in the thirteenth through seventeenth centuries, they viewed traditional midwives as threatening to their control of health care".[8] On that account, women were legally barred from surgery and only male midwives were allowed to use obstetrical instruments.[9] At first, this prohibition did not affect the good reputation of female midwives. The usage of tools like the crotchet was necessary only to pull out lifeless infants in obstructed births, so male practitioners were connected with difficult births and dead infants.[10] However, with the invention of the forceps, which became public between 1733 and 1735, the situation changed: "[O]nce it became known that a male practitioner could deliver a *living* child, the fear associated with the sight of a surgeon during lying-in was replaced with hope in cases of difficult births".[11] The forceps enabled male midwives to turn dangerous deliveries into successful ones, which was crucial to improve their reputation. The term 'male midwife' was often used as a derogatory term because of the profession's status as a female practice,[12] and "[a]s many eighteenth-century contemporaries were quick to remark, even the term 'man-midwife' was an oxymoron".[13] The skilled handling of the forceps, however, helped to justify the importance of male midwives for the medical sphere and institutionalised their superiority over their female colleagues. The female practitioners' handling of dangerous deliveries without the forceps was less successful and often fatal for mother or child, so the presence of female midwives in birthing chambers suddenly appeared to be insufficient and subsequently decreased.[14]

In *Frankenstein*, this development is mirrored in the lack of female agency throughout the narrative.

> Although written by a woman, *Frankenstein* consists almost entirely of male voices and seems to be all about the lives of male beings. The entire novel is narrated in letters from Robert Walton, the would-be grand global explorer. Inside his narrative is that of his creature. Women are thus presented as the objects of male perception, desires, and fears, and the main female character's primary role is that of victim.[15]

The limitation of women's agency is hence twofold: On the one hand, female characters are silenced throughout the narrative and are thus unable to voice their experiences of the story. On the other, all female characters are kept ignorant about the existence of the creature so that none of them is able to defend themselves against it.[16] Consequently, female powerlessness and victimhood is normalised.

In addition, as Peter Brooks argues, "*Frankenstein* is notable for the absence of living mothers".[17] The mother of the De Lacey family, whom the creature observes, and the mother of Safie, their son's love interest, are dead; Victor Frankenstein's mother dies from scarlet fever, and Frankenstein's creation, too, has no mother, only a 'father'. This is somewhat reminiscent of the replacement of female midwives by male practitioners in birthing chambers, because female midwives used to base their knowledge on their experience as childbearing women and mothers. Since the absence of women's influence and agency seems to be a crucial factor leading to the numerous murders of innocent people, the replacement of female experience with male science is presented as dangerous.

Furthermore, by assigning the role of the creature's victims almost exclusively to female characters, it can be claimed that women are the ones most threatened by Victor's science. With the deaths of Justine, the housekeeper of the Frankenstein family, and Elizabeth, Frankenstein's love interest, potential mothers are consistently eliminated one by one because of Frankenstein's creation. With the implication that women of childbearing age die as a result of male science, the novel alludes to the idea of the death-bringing male midwife, as described by Stone, a famous midwife of the eighteenth century:

> Tho' I have made it my Observation within these few years, That more Women and Children have died by the hands of Such Professors, than by the greatest imbecillity [sic] and ignorance of Some Women-Midwives, who never went thro', or so much as heard of, a Course of Anatomy.[18]

Even though it is the creature that kills the two female characters, it can be claimed that Victor bears responsibility for their deaths, since the creature is the result of his controversial experiment. Elizabeth and Justine die because of his careless handling of the situation, which mirrors the idea of the death-bringing work of male midwives as pointed out by Stone. Victor's success in creating life is followed by a dream foreshadowing Elizabeth's death, which exemplifies the interconnection between the two incidents:

> I thought I saw Elizabeth, in the bloom of health, walking in the streets of Ingolstadt. Delighted and surprised, I embraced her; but as I imprinted the first kiss on her lips, they became livid with the hue of death; her features appeared to change, and I thought that I held the corpse of my dead mother in my arms; a shroud enveloped her form, and I saw the grave-worms crawling in the folds of the flannel. (53)

Victor's dream plays with two different forms of bodies in transition. Both the creature's body and Elizabeth's body are located at the intersection of significant phases of life: its beginning and its end. Since the vision of the dead Elizabeth in Victor's vision resembles the corpse of Victor's mother, the nightmare underlines her potential maternity, which is endangered by Victor's scientific endeavour. Thus, the scientist's infusion of life into an inanimate body is equated with drawing life from the animate body of a woman.[19] This supports the notion that bodies in transition are at the mercy of scientists. They have the authority to decide life and death. This is underlined by the fact that it is Frankenstein's kiss that transforms Elizabeth into a corpse, which emphasises Frankenstein's responsibility for her fate. As a result, one can read the success of a birth without a woman not only as an attempt to exclude women from the procreative process, but also as a potentially life-threatening practice for mothers and mothers to be. The play with the two transient bodies of Elizabeth and the creature thereby draws attention to the grey zone between life and death, and to the power and the responsibility of the scientist to keep both apart.

Moreover, women are threatened not only by the effects of science, but also by the laws science has benefitted from. The victimization of Justine, the Frankenstein family's housekeeper, who is falsely accused of killing a child and is later convicted for murdering Victor's younger brother William, is reminiscent of the infanticide trials. The purpose of these trials was to investigate cases of stillborn children as well as children's sudden deaths in or shortly after childbirth. The infanticide law of 1624 was widely known as 'An Acte to Prevent the Destroying and Murthering of Bastard Children'.[20] Until the passing of this act, the death of a baby had been dealt with as a minor infraction. In the seventeenth century, however, infanticide was redefined as a crime and became "a unique type of homicide".[21] The trials were notorious, since they reversed the existing rules of evidence and "presumed the mother's guilt in the death of an infant unless she could prove otherwise".[22] The women were consequently sentenced to death. Since the corpses of the convicted mothers were often used as material for anatomy theatres, in which male surgeons were trained, the infanticide trials are frequently linked with the encroachment of male physicians into the female-centred world of reproduction and childbirth.[23] In *Frankenstein*, Justine has to prove her innocence in a process akin to the infanticide trials. Because of the murders Frankenstein's creature commits, she is accused of having killed Victor's younger brother, whom she has loved and nursed like a mother (see 88). The novel emphasises Justine's innocence, but despite Victor's and Elizabeth's passionate testimonies, the court condemns her to die on the scaffold. In the novel, Shelley explicitly underlines that "all judges had rather that ten innocent should suffer than that one guilty should escape" (81). This mirrors the overall impossibility of a mother's successful defence in the infanticide trials. What makes the case even more evocative of the infanticide law is Justine's portrayal as an unmarried and maternal figure of childbearing age, because the murdering of children was considered to be a crime "committed only by unmarried women".[24] Thus, even though readers do not learn that Justine's dead body is used by medical professionals, the conviction of her character relates to the infanticide trials and their benefits for the dissecting rooms. As Staub with reference to Jonathan Sawday notes, "if the scaffold afforded male bodies for the anatomists with some degree of regularity, female bodies were an altogether rarer commodity" that must have whet "the appetites of the anatomists", especially for the corpse of a woman of childbearing age.[25] It is therefore very likely that Justine's death on the scaffold points to the use of her body as anatomical material.

The injustice of the fate that female characters in the novel encounter is underlined in their depiction as innocent epitomisations of the angelic housewife and mother. Elizabeth, for example, is described as "docile and good tempered" (29) with an "uncommonly affectionate" disposition (30). This contrasts with the egocentric and irresponsible character of Frankenstein, whose only interest lies in his science. In addition, this juxtaposition between the scientist and the women in the novel alludes to the images often associated with male and female midwives in the eighteenth century. Characteristics like sympathy and compassion were regarded as exclusively female attributes, which were believed to stem from shared experience and intuitive understanding.[26] The depiction of Justine and Elizabeth as gentle and caring reinforces the naturalness of this connection. Frankenstein, by contrast, is portrayed as a careless practitioner of black magic, which not only contrasts with the tender nature of women but also deconstructs the notion that women healers are the ones making use of witchcraft:

> The raising of ghosts or devils was a promise liberally accorded by my favourite authors, the fulfilment of which I most eagerly sought; and if my incantations were always unsuccessful, I attributed the failure rather to my own inexperience and mistake, than to a want of skill or fidelity in my instructors. (34)

In his childhood, books offering ideas on life and death, the supernatural and the undead fascinate Frankenstein. By transferring the obsession with supernatural ideas to a male scientist, the novel frees women from their standing as witches and depicts male science as closer to black magic in its endeavour to overcome the transience of life. Furthermore, Frankenstein concentrates on his task alone and ignores the worries of his family:

> I knew well therefore what would be my father's feelings; but I could not tear my thoughts from my employment, loathsome in itself, but which had taken an irresistible hold of my imagination. I wished, as it were, to procrastinate all that related to my feelings of affection until the great object, which swallowed up every habit of my nature, should be completed. (50)

According to Stuart Sim, "Frankenstein's vision is restricted to the demands of the project and he never looks beyond those".[27] Hence, he lacks compassion and does not care for moral values, which mirrors the idea of distanced and unsympathetic deliveries as favoured by physicians in the eighteenth century. According to Sheena Sommers, male practitioners quite successfully presented themselves as possessing the necessary distance and objectivity for true reproductive knowledge.[28] Because his scientific endeavour ends in a catastrophe, "Frankenstein stands as a warning [...] about the dangers of scientific enquiry conducted for its own sake without regard to social consequences or moral codes"[29] – a warning that might have been directed at male readers against the transgression of life's boundaries.

However, since the addressee of the narrator's letters is a woman, it can be claimed that the critique is directed, first and foremost, at the female readership of the novel. Margaret Saville, as the implied listener to the story, witnesses the deconstruction of male superiority in the medical field. While Frankenstein overcomes death and thereby justifies male scientific dominance, his experiment results in the deaths of people he loves, so that the initial empowerment of male science is undermined in the end. As a 'cautionary tale', which presents its readers with a moral, the story warns women about the devastating effects of male science gone too far.[30] As a result, even though the female characters in *Frankenstein* lack agency, Shelley seems to encourage her readers to become active themselves regarding decisions about medical assistance.

3. Challenging Transience through Interventionist Science

Victor Frankenstein's attempt to overcome bodily transience is related to his ignorance of nature, which becomes especially explicit in the process of creating the being, during which Victor turns away from nature:

> The summer months passed while I was thus engaged, heart and soul, in one pursuit. It was a most beautiful season; never did the fields bestow a more plentiful harvest, or the vines yield a more luxuriant vintage: but my eyes were insensible to the charms of nature. (50)

Interestingly, Shelley depicts Victor as frantic in his pursuit, which contrasts with rational behaviour. Since, as Sommers notes, male midwives in their writings widely stressed their own superior rationality in the field of obstetrics, the irrationality of Victor's passionate work portrays nature as the truly rational concept and thereby ridicules this claim.[31]

Furthermore, as Anne K. Mellor argues, Shelley depicts nature as feminine and motherly, hence alluding to the idea of 'Mother Nature': "A reader of Wordsworth, Shelley understood nature in his terms, as a sacred all-creating mother, a living organism or ecological community with which human beings interact in mutual dependence".[32] In the novel, Victor chooses to specialise in those branches of natural philosophy which relate to physiology, a field defined by Humphrey Davy's *A Discourse, Introductory to a Course of Lectures on Chemistry*, which was published in 1802.[33] In this pamphlet, Davy defines nature as female and points out two scientific ways of dealing with "her": "One could practice what we might call 'descriptive' science, an effort to understand the workings of Mother Nature. Or one could practice an 'interventionist' science, an effort to change the ways of nature".[34] Since Frankenstein tries to "penetrate into the recesses of nature, and shew [sic] how she works in her hiding places" (42), he practices interventionist science. He tries to overcome mortality by changing the way of nature – something he perceives as feminine – hence, it can be claimed that Victor sees death and transience as emanating from the maternal: "The maternal creation is superseded on two scores – the maternal body is no longer necessary as site for creation and the 'flaw' inscribed in each human of woman born, the mother's given mark of mortality, the navel, would be overcome".[35]

Thus, the interventionist discipline can be compared to the dissections of female bodies, since it tries to manipulate the life-giving and nourishing elements of nature in order to transcend biological boundaries. In the sixteenth and seventeenth centuries, medical professors started to reveal the uteruses of actual women publicly in so-called 'anatomy theatres' in order to demystify them.[36] Up to this period, the uterus was perceived as 'monstrous' because of the inexplicability of the processes connected with it. Comparable to these scientists, Frankenstein uses the interventionist approach to understand the process of creating new life, which, according to Mellor, is an attempt to appropriate female biological reproduction.[37]

In the novel's title, *Frankenstein; or, The Modern Prometheus*, Shelley even accuses Frankenstein of having disrupted the natural cycle of life just as Prometheus, a hero of Greek mythology, did. By stealing the fire from the gods to give it to man to permit progress, Prometheus overthrew the established order of heaven and earth.[38] Frankenstein, as the modern Prometheus, tries to conquer the natural system of female childbearing to bring enlightenment to the field of reproduction.

> Life and death appeared to me ideal bounds, which I should first break through, and pour a torrent of light into our dark world. A new species would bless me as its creator and source; many happy and excellent natures would owe their being to me. (49)

He tries to overcome transience and to transgress natural boundaries. But ultimately, Frankenstein is punished in a way similar to the immortal Prometheus. While the latter is bound to a rock to have his perpetually regenerating liver eaten by an eagle, Frankenstein is tortured by infinite pangs of remorse (see 186). As a result, the novel endorses natural methods and discourages its readers from supporting scientific endeavours that violate natural processes.

4. The Creation of Frankenstein's Monster in the Context of Eighteenth-Century Midwifery

Apart from the effects the appearance of male physicians in the birthing chambers brought about, like the muting of female influence and the turning away from nature, *Frankenstein* also attacks the actual work of male midwives. The process of giving life to a dead body and thus overcoming the transience of life recalls many methods and approaches used by male physicians in the eighteenth century. First, like eighteenth-century male midwives who favoured tools like forceps to deliver babies, Frankenstein makes use of diverse apparatuses to bring his project to life: "With an anxiety that almost amounted to agony, I collected the instruments of life around me, that I might infuse a spark of being into the lifeless thing that lay at my feet" (52). The fatal consequences of Frankenstein's methods thereby mirror the negative attitude towards obstetrical equipment expressed in Stone's *A Complete Practice of Midwifery*. Stone criticises men's attempt to take over the business of childbirth from female midwives by stating that the work done by women, uninfluenced by anatomy classes, causes fewer deaths during deliveries: "Infants have been born alive, with their Brains working out of their Heads: occasion'd by the too common use of Instruments: which I never found but very little use to be made of, in all my practice".[39] Similar to Stone's claim that the equipment causes the births of dead babies with living organs, Shelley describes the appearance of Frankenstein's creation in terms of a living conglomeration of dead body parts and organs. Since Victor gathered the components for his creation from graveyards, dissecting rooms and butcheries, Shelley alludes to the practice of body snatching. According to Ruth Richardson, Shelley was familiar with this business because her husband's personal physician, John William Polidori, with whom the Shelleys spent many evenings, had dissected bodies supplied by grave-robbers himself.[40] In addition, Shelley lived in the vicinity of St. Pancras churchyard, where her mother was buried and which had a local reputation as a favoured place for body snatchers: "[Shelley] may indeed have lived for years with the fear that despite the willows her father had planted there, her mother's body might have been stolen and dismembered".[41] Grave-robbery was highly successful in the eighteenth century, since the need for anatomical subjects had grown immensely. Dissections had become a regular practice in medical schools, which resulted in an increased demand for dissecting material, for which the supply of convicted murderers was insufficient. According to English law, the theft of corpses was not considered to be a crime because people did not own their dead bodies. Consequently, grave-robbing became a common medical practice paid for by anatomists.[42]

According to Monette Vacquin, Shelley condemns the idea of viewing human beings as mere objects that must reveal truths in cold laboratories.[43] Hence, Frankenstein, who perceives life and death as "ideal bounds, which [he] should first break through" (49), is depicted as an evil force in Shelley's novel. She thereby expresses the "need to preserve the difference between living and dead, to draw a non-transgressible boundary between the animate and the inanimate".[44] Rather than drawing inspiration from dead bodies to overcome the transience of life, Shelley seems to advise humbleness when confronted with death and mortality in order to genuinely appreciate life in its transience.

The tragedy of Frankenstein and his lack of sympathy for his creation implies that scientific knowledge gained from dead bodies affects the treatment of the living negatively – an attitude shared by Stone, who claims that

> [...] dissecting the Dead, and being just and tender to the Living, are vastly different; for it must be supposed that there is a tender regard one Woman bears to another, and a natural Sympathy in those that have gone thro' the Pangs of Child-bearing; which, doubtless, occasion a compassion for those that labour under those circumstances, which no man can be a judge of.[45]

Stone argues that attending dissections does not equip male practitioners with the character traits necessary to take care of processes as important as birth. Stone thereby refers to the different reputations male and female midwives had in the eighteenth century. Whereas women were criticised for their lack of professional learning, men were told to minimise compassion and sympathy.[46] Male practitioners opposed criticism of this practice by asserting that their distance from the suffering of childbirth allowed them the objectivity needed to arrive at reproductive truths.[47] Shelley seems to disagree with these arguments by showing that Frankenstein's emotional distance is the main reason his creature acts monstrously. After Victor has 'given birth', he abandons all 'paternal' responsibility for 'his child'; hence, he lacks a human conscience: "[H]is desire to simply have the problem disappear, as if he had never been involved in it, does not speak well of his character or sense of social responsibility".[48] The fact that Frankenstein uses instruments in artificial reproduction does not relieve him from his moral duty.

Consequently, with *Frankenstein* Shelley argues in favour of female compassion and motherly bonding and against the emotional distance of purely scientific methods. By reinforcing the negative aspects associated with male midwives, she draws connections between their scientific approach and apparently monstrous tendencies. According to Ludmilla Jordanova, the theme of monstrosity was indeed taken up quite explicitly in 'man-midwifery'.[49] Evidence can be found in the caption underneath the popular frontispiece of Samuel William Fores's *Man-Midwifery Dissected*, which shows a figure made up of one half of a female midwife and one half of a male midwife.[50] In the caption, this figure is referred to as "a monster lately discovered". As Jordanova notes, the monstrosity alluded to rests on the idea that joining man and woman together in one person was seen as against nature, so that the profession of a male midwife was perceived as transgressing morality.[51] This also relates to the idea of bodies in transition, since gender boundaries are transgressed by the male midwife, who works in a field shaped by an allegedly female tradition. The story of the fatal attempt to replace women with science seems to naturalise the concept of gender-specific traits and to support the notion of male midwifery as immoral in its gender transition. As is typical for nineteenth-century Gothic fiction, *Frankenstein* points out that monstrosity does not manifest itself in hideous physical features but in the harmful behaviour of individuals.[52] As a result, the distance of Frankenstein towards his creature portrays him as the true monster of the story.

5. Undermining 'Maternal Imagination' as a Cause for Mortality and Monstrosity

What is closely related to the idea of monstrosity is the concept of 'maternal imagination' which claimed that mothers possess the ability to influence the condition of babies. This claim was made especially when a baby happened to be deformed or 'monstrous' in appearance.[53] The hypothesis evolved in the early eighteenth century and tried to attribute malformations and deaths of infants to an easily impressionable female mind, which possessed the corporeal power to deform a foetus because of confused impulses:

> Enlightenment commentators had inherited a centuries-old explanation for why monsters were born: it had been long and widely maintained that 'maternal imagination' could alter the plastic form of a child in utero when a mother's desires or fears overwhelmed her and her foetus.[54]

Frankenstein, however, attacks this notion, since the deformed creation of the scientist has not been shaped in utero. Victor decides the outward appearance of his creature by selecting the different body parts. Therefore, the creature's ugliness can be interpreted as the outcome of male overconfidence, which deconstructs the belief in the superiority of male rationality.[55] Shelley thus undermines the stereotype of the mental inferiority of women and portrays maternal intuition as preferable to the hubris of male scientists.

With her depiction of a misshapen creation, Shelley also alludes to Erasmus Darwin, whose theories have significant bearing on *Frankenstein*. While at first he, too, claimed that deformities result from either excessive or insufficient nourishment in the egg cell or uterus and therefore blamed women for the appearance of deformed foetuses, he altered his approach in 1801:

> Interestingly, while Darwin no longer attributed monstrous births to uterine deficiencies or excesses, he continued to hold the male imagination at the moment of conception responsible for determining both the sex of the child and its outstanding traits.[56]

By placing the responsibility for the monstrous appearance of the creation on Frankenstein alone, Shelley ascribes men with the power to influence a child's condition, too. However, Victor is too focused on the prospect of fame to really grasp the responsibility he bears: "A new species would bless me as its creator and source; many happy and excellent natures would owe their being to me. No father could claim the gratitude of his child so completely as I should deserve their's [sic]" (49).

Shelley furthermore illustrates that the tragedy of the story could have been prevented, since Frankenstein's being "suggests the capacity to develop the finer feelings of humanity, but is given no opportunity to do so".[57] In contrast to its creator, the creature yearns for companionship and a family life:

> [Y]ou had endowed me with perceptions and passions, and then cast me abroad an object for the scorn and horror of mankind. But on you only had I any claim for pity and redress, and from you I determined to seek that justice which I vainly attempted to gain from any other being that wore the human form. (136)

The vengeful spirit of the creature thus emerges from the rejection it experiences: "I was benevolent and good; misery made me a fiend. Make me happy, and I shall again be virtuous" (95). Victor's creation even offers a solution to its misery, but it is Frankenstein himself who throws away the chance of pacifying his 'son' by destroying the female companion he promised to bring to life. Therefore, he is depicted as "a character of monstrous intentions and practices".[58]

According to Fred Botting, monsters as figures of vice serve their stories as examples of what people should not do. They are typical of the Gothic and often serve to strengthen norms and values by representing the danger of deviant behaviour.[59] It is in fact Frankenstein's distanced behaviour that turns into the catalyst for his creation to become the ultimate symbol of transience by bringing death to the living, demonstrating that the novel discourages the pursuit of irresponsible scientific endeavour.

6. Conclusion

All in all, Mary Shelley's *Frankenstein* is not only a narrative foreshadowing future phenomena in science, but also a story about "the monstrous and fatal consequences of masculine creation"[60] and hence, a critique of male physicians' attempt to overcome transience and their intrusion into the female realm of birth. While men tried to exclude women from the medical field in the eighteenth century, Shelley implies that this attempt put human survival significantly at risk. In her novel, Frankenstein succeeds in creating immortal life that is able to survive without women, but he is not able to assume responsibility for this being. He is depicted as lacking rationality and empathy; therefore, he causes his creature to act as monstrously as the appearance Frankenstein has provided him with. The creature's turn into a death-bringing living corpse thereby underlines the idea of male hubris and the inevitability of transience. In his experiment Frankenstein tries to ban fatal diseases from life, which he sees as emanating from female bodies. By being constructed from dead body parts, his creature, however, epitomises the transience of life. As such, Victor Frankenstein's downfall can be understood as Shelley's attempt to discredit male midwifery and the interventionist scientific methods connected with it.

In addition, in being the product of a well-educated scientist, the creature arguably deconstructs the notion of male superiority in medical knowledge. With *Frankenstein*, Shelley criticises scientific approaches of the eighteenth century, such as grave-robbery and the public exposure of female uteruses and their dissections, and marks them as insufficient to understand the process of giving birth. According to the novel, these practices do not provide their practitioners with the compassion and sympathy necessary for this task. The choice of a female addressee could furthermore be read as an attempt to approach potential mothers with this cautionary tale, so that they reject the exclusion of female midwives from the birthing chamber. After all, with William, Elizabeth and Justine, the main victims of the story are children or possible mothers, so Victor Frankenstein can be interpreted as an example of the death-bringing male midwife who endangers women and their infants with his work. His failed attempt to overcome the transience of life by replacing the female body with interventionist science hence possesses the potential to undermine defamatory myths about female midwives and the power of reproductive female bodies.

Notes

[1] See Franklin, H. Bruce (2011). "*Frankenstein* Comments on the Male Construction of Medical Science." *Bioethics in Mary Shelley's Frankenstein*. Ed. Gary Wiener. Detroit: Greenhaven Press, 71-78, 71.

[2] See Nagy, Peter, et al. (2018). "The Enduring Influence of a Dangerous Narrative: How Scientists Can Mitigate the Frankenstein Myth." *Journal of Bioethical Inquiry* 10 March, 279-292.

[3] See Staub, Susan C. (2011). "Surveilling the Secrets of the Female Body: The Contest for Reproductive Authority in the Popular Press of the Seventeenth

Century." *The Female Body in Medicine and Literature*. Eds. Andrew Mangham and Greta Depledge. Liverpool: Liverpool University Press, 51-68, 53.
[4] See Braidotti, Rosi (1999). "Signs of Wonder and Traces of Doubt: On Teratology and Embodied Differences." *Feminist Theory and the Body: A Reader*. Eds. Janet Price and Margrit Shildrick. Edinburgh: Edinburgh University Press, 290-301, 296.
[5] See Richardson, Ruth (2014). "Frankenstein: Graveyards, Scientific Experiments and Body Snatchers." *British Library*. n. pag. Web. 10 May 2019. <http://www.bl.uk/romantics-and-victorians/articles/frankenstein-graveyards-scientific-experiments-and-bodysnatchers>.
[6] See Clayton, Jay (2011). "Artificial Creatures of Modern Films Renew Sympathy for Frankenstein's Creation." *Bioethics in Mary Shelley's Frankenstein*. Ed. Gary Wiener. Detroit: Greenhaven Press, 97-104, 102.
[7] Wollstonecraft, Mary (1792). *Mary Wollstonecraft: A Vindication of the Rights of Men and a Vindication of the Rights of Woman and Hints*. Ed. Sylvana Tomaselli. 1995. Cambridge: Cambridge University Press, 238.
[8] Franklin (2011), 71.
[9] See *ibid.*, 75.
[10] See Sommers, Sheena (2011). "Transcending the Sexed Body: Reason, Sympathy, and 'Thinking Machines' in the Debates over Male Midwifery." *The Female Body in Medicine and Literature*. Eds. Andrew Mangham and Greta Depledge. Liverpool: Liverpool University Press, 89-106, 90.
[11] *Ibid.*, 90-91. (Emphasis in the text).
[12] See *ibid.*, 91.
[13] *Ibid.*, 93.
[14] See *ibid.*, 90.
[15] Franklin (2011), 73.
[16] See Shelley, Mary (1818). *Frankenstein; or, The Modern Prometheus*. Chicago: University of Chicago Press, 131. Further references to this edition will be included in the text.
[17] Brooks, Peter (1995). "What Is a Monster?" *Frankenstein: Mary Shelley*. Ed. Fred Botting. Basingstoke: Macmillian, 81-106, 90.
[18] Stone, Sarah (1737). *A Complete Practice of Midwifery*. London: T. Cooper, xii.
[19] See Bronfen, Elisabeth (1992). *Over Her Dead Body: Death, Femininity and the Aesthetic*. Manchester: Manchester University Press, 134.
[20] Staub (2011), 53.
[21] *Ibid.*, 54.
[22] *Ibid.*
[23] See *ibid.*, 53.
[24] *Ibid.*, 54.

[25] Sawday, Jonathan (1995). "The Body Emblazoned: Dissection and the Human Body in Renaissance Culture." 220-221, qtd. in Susan C. Staub (2011). "Surveilling the Secrets of the Female Body: The Contest for Reproductive Authority in the Popular Press of the Seventeenth Century." *The Female Body in Medicine and Literature*. Eds. Andrew Mangham and Greta Depledge. Liverpool: Liverpool University Press, 51-68, 55.

[26] See Sommers (2011), 92.

[27] Sim, Stuart (2008). *The Eighteenth-Century Novel and Contemporary Social Issues: An Introduction*. Edinburgh: Edinburgh University Press, 151.

[28] See Sommers (2011), 92.

[29] Sim (2008), 157.

[30] See Botting, Fred (1991). *Making Monstrous: Frankenstein, Criticism, Theory*. Manchester: Manchester University Press, 167.

[31] See Sommers (2011), 95.

[32] Mellor, Anne K. (1991). "A Feminist Critique of Science." *Frankenstein: Mary Shelley*. Ed. Fred Botting. Basingstoke: Macmillian, 107-139, 130.

[33] See Mellor, Anne K. (2011). "Frankenstein Is a Mad Scientist Who Attempts to Revise Nature." *Bioethics in Mary Shelley's Frankenstein*. Ed. Gary Wiener. Detroit: Greenhaven Press, 79-85, 80.

[34] *Ibid.*

[35] Bronfen (1992), 132.

[36] See Haslem, Lori Schroeder (2011). "Monstrous Issues: The Uterus as Riddle in Early Modern Medical Texts." *The Female Body in Medicine and Literature*. Eds. Andrew Mangham and Greta Depledge. Liverpool: Liverpool University Press, 34-50, 39.

[37] See Mellor (2011), 83.

[38] See Mellor (1991), 121.

[39] Stone (1737), xiii.

[40] See Richardson (2014).

[41] *Ibid.*

[42] See Frank, Julia B. (1976). "Body Snatching: A Grave Medical Problem." *The Yale Journal of Biology and Medicine* 49, 399-410, 400.

[43] See Vacquin, Monette (1991). *Die Geburt ohne Frau: Frankensteins Kinder und die Gen-Technik*. Bad Münstereifel: Edition Tramontane, 145.

[44] Bronfen (1992), 138.

[45] Stone (1737), 12-13.

[46] See Sommers (2011), 92.

[47] See *ibid.*, 92, 95.

[48] Sim (2008), 152.

[49] See Jordanova, Ludmilla (1994). "Melancholy Reflection: Constructing Identity for Unveilers of Nature." *Frankenstein, Creation and Monstrosity.* Ed. Stephen Bann. London: Reaktion Books, 60-76, 73.

[50] See Cruikshank, Isaac (1793). "A Man-Mid-Wife." Frontispiece to *Man-Midwifery Dissected; or, the Obstetric Family-Instructor* by Samuel William Fores. London: S. W. Fores for the author.

[51] See Jordanova (1994), 74.

[52] See Buzwell, Greg (2014). "Gothic Fiction in the Victorian Fin de Siècle: Mutating Bodies and Disturbed Minds." *British Library.* n. pag. Web. 10 May 2019. <https://www.bl.uk/romantics-and-victorians/articles/gothic-fiction-in-the-victorian-fin-de-siecle>.

[53] See Braidotti (1999), 296.

[54] Rousseau, G. S. (1971). "Pineapples, Pregnancy, Pica, and *Peregrine Pickle.*" Tobias Smollett. Eds. Rousseau and P.-G. Boucé, New York: Oxford University Press, 79-109, qtd. in Lisa Forman Cody (2005). *Birthing the Nation: Sex, Science, and the Conception of Eighteenth-Century Britons*. Oxford: Oxford University Press, 120.

[55] See Vacquin (1991), 146.

[56] Mellor (1991), 117.

[57] Sim (2008), 155.

[58] Bishop, M. G. H. (2011). "Victor Frankenstein Is Shelley's True Immortal Monster." *Bioethics in Mary Shelley's Frankenstein.* Ed. Gary Wiener. Detroit: Greenhaven Press, 63-70, 63.

[59] See Botting, Fred (1995). "Introduction." *Frankenstein: Mary Shelley.* Ed. Botting. Basingstoke: Macmillian, 1-20, 6.

[60] Bronfen (1992), 130.

Bibliography

Bishop, M. G. H. (2011). "Victor Frankenstein Is Shelley's True Immortal Monster." *Bioethics in Mary Shelley's Frankenstein.* Ed. Gary Wiener. Detroit: Greenhaven Press, 63-70.

Botting, Fred (1991). *Making Monstrous: Frankenstein, Criticism, Theory*. Manchester: Manchester University Press.

--- (1995). "Introduction." *Frankenstein: Mary Shelley.* Ed. Botting. Basingstoke: Macmillian, 1-20.

Braidotti, Rosi (1999). "Signs of Wonder and Traces of Doubt: On Teratology and Embodied Differences." *Feminist Theory and the Body: A Reader.* Eds.

Janet Price and Margrit Shildrick. Edinburgh: Edinburgh University Press, 290-301.
Bronfen, Elisabeth (1992). *Over Her Dead Body: Death, Femininity and the Aesthetic.* Manchester: Manchester University Press.
Brooks, Peter (1995). "What Is a Monster?" *Frankenstein: Mary Shelley.* Ed. Fred Botting. Basingstoke: Macmillian, 81-106.
Buzwell, Greg (2014). "Gothic Fiction in the Victorian Fin de Siècle: Mutating Bodies and Disturbed Minds." *British Library.* n. pag. Web. 10 May 2019. <https://www.bl.uk/romantics-and-victorians/articles/gothic-fiction-in-the-victorian-fin-de-siecle>.
Clayton, Jay (2011). "Artificial Creatures of Modern Films Renew Sympathy for Frankenstein's Creation." *Bioethics in Mary Shelley's Frankenstein.* Ed. Gary Wiener. Detroit: Greenhaven Press, 97-104.
Cody, Lisa Forman (2005). *Birthing the Nation: Sex, Science, and the Conception of Eighteenth-Century Britons.* Oxford: Oxford University Press.
Cruikshank, Isaac (1793). "A Man-Mid-Wife." Frontispiece to *Man-Midwifery Dissected; or, the Obstetric Family-Instructor* by Samuel William Fores. London: S.W. Fores for the author.
Frank, Julia B. (1976). "Body Snatching: A Grave Medical Problem." *The Yale Journal of Biology and Medicine* 49, 399-410.
Franklin, H. Bruce (2011). "*Frankenstein* Comments on the Male Construction of Medical Science." *Bioethics in Mary Shelley's Frankenstein.* Ed. Gary Wiener. Detroit: Greenhaven Press, 71-78.
Haslem, Lori Schroeder (2011). "Monstrous Issues: The Uterus as Riddle in Early Modern Medical Texts." *The Female Body in Medicine and Literature.* Eds. Andrew Mangham and Greta Depledge. Liverpool: Liverpool University Press, 34-50.
Jordanova, Ludmilla (1994). "Melancholy Reflection: Constructing Identity for Unveilers of Nature." *Frankenstein, Creation and Monstrosity.* Ed. Stephen Bann. London: Reaktion Books, 60-76.
Mellor, Anne K. (1991). "A Feminist Critique of Science." *Frankenstein: Mary Shelley.* Ed. Fred Botting. Basingstoke: Macmillian, 107-139.
--- (2011). "Frankenstein Is a Mad Scientist Who Attempts to Revise Nature." *Bioethics in Mary Shelley's Frankenstein.* Ed. Gary Wiener. Detroit: Greenhaven Press, 79-85.
Nagy, Peter, et al. (2018). "The Enduring Influence of a Dangerous Narrative: How Scientists Can Mitigate the Frankenstein Myth." *Journal of Bioethical Inquiry* 10 March, 279-292.
Richardson, Ruth (2014). "Frankenstein: Graveyards, Scientific Experiments and Body Snatchers." *British Library.* n. pag. Web. 10 May 2019.

<http://www.bl.uk/romantics-and-victorians/articles/frankenstein-graveyards-scientific-experiments-and-bodysnatchers>.

Shelley, Mary (1818). *Frankenstein; or, The Modern Prometheus*. Reprint 1982. Chicago: University of Chicago Press.

Sim, Stuart (2008). *The Eighteenth-Century Novel and Contemporary Social Issues: An Introduction*. Edinburgh: Edinburgh University Press.

Sommers, Sheena (2011). "Transcending the Sexed Body: Reason, Sympathy, and 'Thinking Machines' in the Debates over Male Midwifery." *The Female Body in Medicine and Literature*. Eds. Andrew Mangham and Greta Depledge. Liverpool: Liverpool University Press, 89-106.

Staub, Susan C. (2011). "Surveilling the Secrets of the Female Body: The Contest for Reproductive Authority in the Popular Press of the Seventeenth Century." *The Female Body in Medicine and Literature*. Eds. Andrew Mangham and Greta Depledge. Liverpool: Liverpool University Press, 51-68.

Stone, Sarah (1737). *A Complete Practice of Midwifery*. London: T. Cooper.

Vacquin, Monette (1991). *Die Geburt ohne Frau: Frankensteins Kinder und die Gen-Technik*. Bad Münstereifel: Edition Tramontane.

Wollstonecraft, Mary (1995 [1792]). *Mary Wollstonecraft: A Vindication of the Rights of Men and a Vindication of the Rights of Woman and Hints*. Ed. Sylvana Tomaselli. Cambridge: Cambridge University Press.

Sandra Dinter (Erlangen)

Child Bodies in the British Novel of the 1980s

1. Introduction

Childhood is one of the most popular themes in the contemporary British novel. The child characters and narrators in Nick Hornby's *About a Boy* (1998), Ian McEwan's *Atonement* (2001), Ali Smith's *The Accidental* (2006), A. S. Byatt's *The Children's Book* (2009), Stephen Kelman's *Pigeon English* (2011), and countless other works have proved a recipe for critical and commercial success. Childhood was rediscovered as an object of literary inquiry in the early 1980s. It had, of course, been a central theme in previous literary epochs, particularly in the Romantic and Victorian periods, but from the 1980s onwards novels began to examine childhood from a new perspective. They were not so much concerned with their protagonists' development towards adulthood anymore; they began to pay attention to the phase of childhood itself. Even if the Bildungsroman remained a popular genre, many works began to focus on young characters who remain children for the duration of the plot, or adult characters who remember a specific period in their childhood. This new attentiveness allowed narrative fiction to assume a metaperspective. Many novels departed from an essentialist concept of childhood and approached it as a contingent discursive construct instead. They explored and questioned the institutions, interests and conflicts involved in the cultural construction of childhood. I propose that the constructivist paradigm shift which radically transformed the academic study of childhood following the publication of Philippe Ariès's influential study *Centuries of Childhood* (1960) and the subsequent formation of the so-called 'new' sociology of childhood in the 1980s and 1990s has been equally discernible in contemporary literature.[1]

This essay illustrates how this relatively recent critical perspective on childhood has shaped literary depictions of the child's body. In what follows, I will reconstruct how contemporary British fiction includes the child's body in its constructivist agenda. Like poststructuralist approaches to the body that, as David Hillman and Ulrika Maude put it, regard the body "as a discursively organized product of institutionalized knowledge and control",[2] many contemporary novels from the UK direct attention to the ways in which the child's body is constructed. The child's body in such works does not develop neutrally in accordance with nature. Instead, it is shown to arise from a complex web of discursive practices and institutional frameworks. This does not mean that these works disregard the materiality of the child's body. Rather, they insist on the idea that it can be perceived only according to a discursive framework of childhood that is always already in place, so that the child's body cannot be separated from or exists outside of dominant perspectives. Moreover, many authors uncover how children's bodies are normalised and disciplined, and in doing so, they deconstruct hegemonic discourses of the child's body, particularly the assumption that it is vulnerable and innocent.

After a brief consideration of the hegemonic notion of the child's body as a transient body, this paper will analyse how exactly narrative fiction implements its constructivist standpoint. For this purpose, I will dissect the representation of the child's body in three literary examples from the early phase of contemporary fiction: Iain Banks's *The Wasp Factory* (1984), Ian McEwan's *The Child in Time* (1987) and Doris Lessing's *The Fifth Child* (1988).

2. Transience of the Child's Body

Two modes of transience apply to the child's body. One is historical, and one is social. The child's body is transient in the sense that different historical understandings of it have arisen and superseded each other. In society, in turn, childhood is regarded as a specific phase of the human body that follows after infancy and finally merges into adulthood. The first mode of transience relates to one of the most profound turns in the academic study of the human body, that is, the shift from positivism to constructivism. As Bryan S. Turner suggests, most scholars in the humanities and social sciences are now "exponents of the idea that the body is socially constructed and they have deployed this constructivist epistemology to criticize taken-for-granted notions of the body in the public realm".[3] According to Darin Weinberg, "[o]ne preliminary point that social constructionists have going for them is that the human body had been conceptionalized, engaged and, indeed, experienced in a multitude of different ways throughout history and across cultures".[4] The body of the child is a case in point: although the young, small bodies of those members of society habitually referred to as 'children' have always existed, the manners in which they have been perceived, represented and treated in Western cultures has varied significantly. Renaissance culture, for instance, did not link the child's physical smallness to the ideas of innocence and vulnerability, as has been the case in Europe since the eighteenth century. As Ariès famously argued in *Centuries of Childhood*, in the Middle Ages and the early modern period, infancy was not followed by another distinct and extensive phase of childhood: "as soon as the child could live without the constant solicitude of his mother, his nanny or his cradle-rocker, he belonged to adult society".[5] Since childhood was not regarded as a significant or distinct phase of life, differences between the child and adult body were of only marginal interest. That is why the modern spectator often spots 'miniature adults' in visual depictions of childhood prior to the eighteenth century or may be surprised that children participated in the same activities as adults and wore similar clothes whilst doing so. If the child's smallness and its limited fine-motor skills were regarded at all, they were most likely seen as disadvantages that had to be overcome.

In modernity, childhood is understood as a distinct and formative phase in the life cycle between infancy and adulthood, and more recently also adolescence. The modern Western child has been entitled and legally sanctioned to remain unproductive and to devote its body to play, exploration and education. Parents and the state, in turn, protect and nurture this particular concept of the child's body; clothing and toys further emphasise the distinctness of this corporeality. From a historical perspective, concepts and representations of the child body have thus always been transient. Different discursive constructions of the child's body develop over time, which indicates that there is not one stable and natural body that every child inhabits. Although this may be an obvious point for cultural historians and literary critics, it is crucial for the present paper because it is a view that contemporary narrative fiction itself often adopts and articulates. As we will see, many contemporary novels are aware of their own historical entanglement and draw attention to how conceptions of children and their bodies have changed over time. This ultimately also implies that these novels do not assume that their particular perspectives on the child body constitute universal truths.

Within the historically transient construct of modern childhood, transience also functions as a central social paradigm to demarcate childhood from adulthood and to regulate it in an institutional setting. As Nick Lee explains, "[g]rowing up [...] is often taken to be a process in which something (a child) turns into its opposite (an adult), a process in which the boundary between becoming and being is crossed".[6] The implicit aim of modern childhood is therefore always its end. Childhood is understood as a temporary state that prepares a person for the allegedly permanent state of adulthood. According to this logic, children are "becomings" and adults are "beings".[7] For scholars in childhood studies it is important to note that this hegemonic discursive framework establishes difference and, with that, hierarchies, privileges and power structures. As Lee argues further,

> [t]he human being is, or should be, stable, complete, self-possessed and self-controlling. The human being, is, or should be, capable of independent thought and action, an independence that merits respect. The human becoming, on the other hand, is changeable and incomplete and lacks the self-possession and self-control that would allow it the independence of thought and action that merits respect. The division between beings and becomings is that between the complete and independent and the incomplete and dependent.[8]

This hierarchy holds so much authority precisely because the materiality of the child's small body legitimises it so plausibly, even if it has already been established that this is not the only way to interpret it. As Alan Prout demonstrates, the child's body is a crucial resource for the conception of childhood as a transient phase because, by reason of its rapidly changing height and weight, it emerges as unfinished and particularly unstable.[9] The assumption that children are innocent and therefore require more protection than adults is tied to an understanding of its body as not yet sexual, not yet self-sufficient and not yet productive. Accordingly, Allison James maintains that "bodily change becomes a marker of child identity".[10] Even though the human body ages and thus changes constantly from birth to death, Western culture has subdivided this process into neat, coherent and separate phases.

Although the adult body is similarly always in flux, this aspect is not central to the dominant notion of adulthood. The body of a twenty-year-old woman remains 'adult', even sixty years later when it looks and feels very different. While the adult body 'ages', the child body 'grows'. In fact, it must 'grow' before it can subsequently 'age'.

The notion of the child as 'becoming' also implies that it cannot be left as it is. As Claudia Castañeda explains, "[s]hould a given child either fail to possess or to realize its potential (as in the notion of 'stunted growth'), he or she remains a flawed child and an incomplete adult".[11] Hence, the child and its body need to be normalised and disciplined. The child's body transforms into an adult body in a complex institutional setting that includes paediatrics, schools, the media, family members and peers. As will become clear, this view provides another cue for literature. Various works show how the child's transient body is produced and acted upon by parents as well as various medical and social authorities.

3. Body Experiments in Iain Banks's *The Wasp Factory* (1984)

The first literary example I will discuss with reference to the denaturalisation of the child's body is Banks's *The Wasp Factory*. Because of its cynical and graphic depiction of violence, Banks's debut novel is often mentioned in the same breath with other scandalous novels of the twentieth century, such as Anthony Burgess's *A Clockwork Orange* (1962) or Bret Easton Ellis's *American Psycho* (1991). At the centre of *The Wasp Factory* stands the ultraviolent and misogynist first-person narrator, Frank Cauldhame. Together with his father, Angus, Frank lives on a secluded Scottish island where he spends most of his time torturing and killing animals. Frank hates his mother and his brother Eric, who have both left the island. Sixteen-year-old Frank proudly declares to have completed the transient phase of childhood. He tells us, "I'm not a child anymore".[12] Nevertheless, most of the novel consists of a retrospective account of this phase. Frank confesses that between the ages of five and eight, he murdered two cousins and his brother Paul. His casual remark that "[i]t was just a stage I was going through" (49) indicates that he feels no remorse. Killing is a mere necessity for Frank because "[t]here just aren't enough natural deaths" (9).

The Wasp Factory highlights and explores the constructedness of the child's body through its astonishing plot revolving around Frank's gender identity. This plot begins with detailed and often discomforting descriptions of his personal hygiene, his clothing and his body shape. Frank informs his readers how after going to the toilet, he "clean[s] [his] arse quickly" (15) or how he collects "precious substances such as toenail cheese or belly button fluff" (51) and shaves off "the downy brown growth of the previous day and night with dexterity and precision" (52). We observe how Frank usually dresses himself in militaristic style, wearing boots, army jumpers, or combat jackets and knives (52). Through such descriptions the novel encourages its readers to assume that Frank has a male body. Frank's clichéd clothing, body language and bluntness further underline his stereotypical masculinity.

Nevertheless, Frank indicates that he is not entirely satisfied with his body because it does not reflect his violent nature as straightforwardly as he desires. Feeling "too fat. [...] Strong and fit, but still too plump" (19), Frank wishes to be appear "dark and menacing [...] the way I should look, the way I might have looked if I hadn't had my little accident" (19-20). Further vague references to his "disability" (10, 14) suggest that something may be 'wrong' with Frank's genitalia. However, his proud declaration "I consider myself an honorary man [...]. I can feel it in my bones, in my uncastrated genes" (154) clarifies that Frank perceives and experiences his body to be male.

The novel ends with a notorious epiphany: Frank finds out that the body he has lived in for over sixteen years and that he has described to his readers in vivid detail as masculine was in fact once female. Frank realises that "what I've always thought was the stump of a penis is really an enlarged clitoris" (240). We learn that Frank's violent masculinity is the product of an experiment that his father undertook after Frank's female genitals had been disfigured in a dog attack when he was three years old. Angus used this opportunity to dose his daughter with male hormones and to dress her as a boy, calling her Francis instead of Frances. In the novel, these measures are successful: even though he cannot remember the accident nor his early childhood, Frank is convinced that he lost his penis in the accident and that he is biologically male.

To some extent *The Wasp Factory* therefore exploits what Hillman and Maude refer to as

> [t]he fact is that there are no bodies in literature. Not only there is [sic] no obvious way for the concrete materiality of the body to be fully present in or on the written page; even more profoundly, there would seem on the face of it to be an apparent mutual exclusivity of the body and language – the one all brute facticity, the other presupposing precisely the absence of matter.[13]

This would mean that because as readers we are not confronted with Frank's material body and receive only a verbal description of it, we can be easily fooled into believing that it is in fact male. While *The Wasp Factory* relies on this specific mode of representation, I would argue that the novel similarly employs it as a possibility to investigate *how* Frank's body is constructed. As Hillman and Maude suggest further, because of its inability to represent the material body, literature as a medium acknowledges that the body is "always already mediated through representation".[14] Frank's body never exists outside of his narrative and as such is presented to us as a textual construct, and I propose that this principle applies as much to his gender as it does to his identity as a child.

In *The Wasp Factory*, the depiction of gender offers one way to examine how the child's body and its identity are constructed. As Emily Garside and Katherine Cox note, *The Wasp Factory* can be read as a complex literary treatise of antiessentialism.[15] Frank's childhood is not a phase in which masculinity unfolds naturally and gradually as the causal outcome of male genes, but it is acquired, internalised and practiced by him according to a narrative and norm that the patriarchal authority sets up for him. This discursive framework is so powerful that not only does it let readers fall into the essentialist trap, but Frank himself buys and embodies the truth Angus constructs for him. Accordingly, Berthold Schoene-Harwood convincingly argues that Banks anticipates Judith Butler's concept of gender performativity:

> In *The Wasp Factory*, patriarchal masculinity, traditionally the bedrock of all communal and individual identification, undergoes an elaborate process of ironic unwrapping. Banks employs gender parody to reveal the imitative artifice of normative standards that compel individuals to

fashion themselves in compliance with an imperative ideal that does not originate in biological nature but is in itself a derivative of social conditioning.[16]

Butler argues that the strict distinction between a biological sex and a social and cultural gender cannot be maintained because "[a]s both *discursive* and *perceptual*, 'sex' denotes a historically contingent epistemic regime, a language that forms perception by forcibly shaping the interrelationships through which physical bodies are perceived".[17] *The Wasp Factory* similarly shows that Frank's genitalia are not self-evident body parts that are somehow exempted from the totality of discourse. From beginning to end, they appear in the novel as discursive objects.

With its antiessentialist approach to gender, *The Wasp Factory* also paves the way for an understanding of childhood as a performative identity. In fact, Frank himself notes that as a young child he does not feel the 'natural' innocence that Western societies have attributed to the child and its body. After the murder of his younger brother, the hegemonic assumption that children are innocent helps him to conceal his guilt. It functions as a strategic device "to convince the adults around me that I was totally innocent. I even carried out a double-bluff of appearing slightly guilty *for the wrong reasons*, so that adults told me I shouldn't blame myself [...]. I was brilliant" (112, emphasis in the text). His image as "an obviously happy, and well-adjusted child, responsible and well-spoken" (112) eliminates the very possibility that he is his brother's murderer, which again illustrates the power of dominant discourses. *The Wasp Factory* suggests that the equation of a small infantile body with innocence is ultimately an arbitrary one, just as this is the case with sex and gender. What appears to be more important than essence in this novel is perception, or the way adults look at children and interpret and produce their innocent bodies in this very process.

The Wasp Factory challenges the concept of the naturally good child further by ridiculing one of the seminal texts that developed and disseminated this very idea, Jean-Jacques Rousseau's famous *Émile, or On Education* (1762). In his treatise, Rousseau appears as a benevolent tutor who educates his fictional pupil Émile. Even if Banks's novel does not contain any explicit intertextual references to *Émile*, its peripheral setting, the constellation between child and adult, and its focus on a male child ironically invoke Rousseau's pedagogical principles. Like Frank, Émile grows up in the countryside, far away from the bad influence of human civilisation. "[S]olitary education would be preferable",[18] writes Rousseau. Furthermore, he proposes that "[n]ature, not man, is his schoolmaster, and he learns all the quicker because he is not aware that he has any lesson to learn".[19] As Roger Cox puts it, Rousseau believed that "childhood must be seen in its own terms as a natural state with its own natural development, not to be contradicted or interfered with by the adult".[20] Accordingly, the adult does not have to guide the child's physical and mental development because this happens 'naturally'. By presenting a parent-child relationship that is first and foremost defined by violence and power, Banks's novel radically breaks with Rousseau's naturalised conception of childhood.

4. Absent Child Bodies in Ian McEwan's *A Child in Time* (1987)

My second example of a literary work that deconstructs the child body is McEwan's *The Child in Time*. Set in the mid-1990s in London, McEwan's novel envisions a bleak future in which the radical policies of a Conservative government have led to licensed beggary, a private health system and accelerated global warming. The government's primary concern is childcare; the Official Commission on Childcare is supposed to compile a guide, *The Authorised Childcare Handbook*. McEwan's protagonist and internal focaliser, Stephen Lewis, is an author of children's books and acts as an expert on a subcommittee of this commission. The detailed accounts of the commission's meetings from his point of view are one of the overt means through which this novel approaches childhood as a discursive construct that is enforced through an ensemble of social, political and institutional sites. While different adult authorities argue about the 'true' nature of childhood, no children ever participate in these discussions or appear as central characters. As Katherina Dodou explains, McEwan "explores 'the child' as an entity removed from children",[21] as he displays how children are "relentlessly debated, interpreted and represented, defined, shaped and instrumentalised".[22] Stephen also experiences this marked physical absence of children on a personal level. He and his wife, Julie, have to cope with the loss of their daughter, Kate, who was kidnapped at the age of three. Having to face "the difficult truth that Kate was no longer a living presence",[23] Stephen can only remember but never hold Kate's "little body [that] smelled of bed warmth and milk" (8). In line with *The Wasp Factory*, McEwan's novel suggests from the start that adults construct and define children and their bodies.

As Gerd Stratmann rightly suggests, "McEwan's novel, written in 1986, shared or even anticipated important developments in the field of social sciences",[24] by which he means the formation of the so-called 'new sociology of childhood' that conceived childhood as a cultural construct. *The Child in Time* signals its awareness of this academic paradigm in an important paratext: its acknowledgements. Here McEwan credits Christina Hardyment's monograph *Dream Babies: Child Care from Locke to Spock* (1983), which examines historical shifts in childcare in the spirit of Ariès. Numerous passages in the novel are indicative of Hardyment's notion of childcare as a variable discursive practice. During one of the committee's meetings, for instance, Stephen contemplates the idea that

> [f]or three centuries, generations of experts, priests, moralists, social scientists, doctors – mostly men – had been pouring out instructions and ever-mutating facts for the benefit of mothers. No one doubted the absolute truth of his judgements, and each generation knew itself to stand on the pinnacle of common sense and scientific insight which its predecessors had merely aspired. (85)

This passage reflects the idea of childcare as a contingent discursive regime that involves competing patriarchal discourses, including religion, sociology and medicine. It also questions and relativises the principle of an absolute truth, positing that truths change from generation to generation. Stephen also considers the consequences these shifting discourses have had on the understanding and treatment of children's bodies. Having read relevant background material, Stephen is familiar with past practices such as "the necessity of binding the newborn baby's limbs to a board to prevent movement and self-inflicted damage" or

> the importance of purges and enemas, severe physical punishment, cold baths and, earlier in this century, of constant fresh air, however

inconvenient; the desirability scientifically controlled intervals between feeds, and, conversely of feeding the baby whenever it is hungry. (85)

References to such absurd and often contradictory childcare practices illustrate that McEwan's novel questions the idea of a universal self-evident body of the child and suggests that conceptions of the body of the child are indeed transient.

Even the excerpts of the ultraconservative and reactionary *Authorised Childcare Handbook* that precede each chapter and mock the fictional Thatcherite government articulate this point. One of the excerpts claims that

> [i]t was not always the case that a large minority comprising the weakest members of society wore special clothes, were freed from the routines of work [...]. It should be remembered that childhood is not a natural occurrence. There was a time when children were treated like small adults. Childhood is an invention, a social construct [...]. Above all, childhood is a privilege. No child as it grows older should be allowed to forget that its parents, as embodiments of society, are the ones who grant this privilege, and do so at their own expense. (99)

The *Handbook* attempts to instrumentalise the historical transience of childhood for its own interests, as it advocates an authoritative and punitive childcare to parents that does not shy away from corporeal punishment. Like *The Wasp Factory*, *The Child in Time* repeatedly alludes to the imbalance of power between children and adults that underlies the child body.

This also happens in another episode in the novel when Stephen enters a school where he observes a group of pupils who stand in a queue to jump over a wooden horse. Stephen sees how

> each child sprang to attention, military style, after stumbling across the mat. At no time did the teacher, who was a kind of circus ringmaster, offer encouragement or instruction. His 'hup' never varied in tone. [...] The children ran straight from the mat to the end of the queue without talking or touching. It was difficult to imagine the process being brought to a halt. (157)

In the distinctly Foucauldian setting of the gymnasium, Stephen witnesses a scene in which schoolchildren are supposed to adapt their bodies and movements to a norm that the teacher – here tellingly described as a ringmaster – sets up and monitors. In this monotonous cycle, the children and their bodies lose their individuality. To Stephen they merely appear as uniform automata fulfilling the adult's order, not unlike soldiers, as the term "military style" indicates. Once again, this novel shows how child bodies are formed by the means of disciplinary power, rather than evolving naturally.

The Child in Time also employs its subplot about Charles Darke as another occasion to denaturalise the child's body. Stephen's friend Charles is a former Conservative MP who resigns and moves to Suffolk, where he wants to live out his fantasy of being a young boy again. As his wife, Thelma, elucidates, Charles yearns for "the security of childhood, the powerlessness, the obedience, and also the freedom that goes with it, freedom from money, decisions, plans, demands" (222). Shortly after his resignation, Stephen notices that Charles looks "suppler, younger" and "much smaller" (40, 41), an observation that foreshadows the peculiar physical transformation Charles undergoes during his regression into childhood. He dresses like a boy and adapts his body language as well as his speech to that of a child. Stephen eventually sees Charles in the woods, where he appears as "the kind of boy who used to fascinate and terrify him at school" (115). Instead of a suit, Charles now wears a "grey flannel shirt with rolled-up sleeves and loosened tails, baggy shorts supported by a striped, elastic belt with a silver snake clasp, [and] bulging pockets from which a handle protruded, and scabby, blood-streaked knees" (115). Stephen is "impressed by what appeared to be very thorough research. It was as if his friend had combed libraries, diligently consulted the appropriate authorities to discover just what it was a certain kind of boy was likely to have in his pockets" (122-123). And indeed, Stephen eventually finds the sources that inspired Charles's performance of childhood. In Charles's tree house, he spots several boys' adventure stories, Stephen's own novel *Lemonade*, and some editions of Richmal Crompton's *Just William* book series.

As various critics have shown, it is revealed that Charles copies the outfit of Crompton's fictional character William Brown.[25] Regarding conceptions of the child body, this is a significant moment in the novel because it implies that Charles can only ever access the child's body through discourse, in this case children's books written by adult authors.

Charles's performance of childhood echoes Butler's concept of drag, which exposes the performative quality of gender. Just as drag "is subversive to the extent that it reflects on the imitative structure by which hegemonic gender is itself produced and disputes heterosexuality's claim on naturalness and originality",[26] Darke's embodiment of boyhood reminds us that the same principle applies to childhood. Charles's performance is obviously based on textual sources, and as such it undermines yet again the idea that childhood is a natural identity.

5. The Deviant Child Body in Doris Lessing's *The Fifth Child* (1988)

My third example of a literary work that denaturalises the child's body is Lessing's novella *The Fifth Child*. It is about the conservative couple Harriet and David Lovatt, whose idyllic family life falls apart when their fifth child, Ben, is born. Their first four children, Luke, Helen, Jane and Paul, all conform to their parents' ideal of carefree and innocent childhood, both in terms of their looks and behaviour. Helen and Luke, for instance, appear as "little creatures […], all wispy fair hair and blue eyes and pink cheeks"[27] and Harriet admires Paul's "comical soft little face, with soft blue eyes – like bluebells […] and his soft little limbs" (66). Their physical delicacy is reminiscent of the angelic children of Romantic poetry. Furthermore, they always obey their parents and never challenge their authority as 'beings'. In other words, these children respect their inferior position as 'becomings'. This is not the case with Ben. His coarse corporeality, unusual development and violent behaviour contrast with his seemingly perfect siblings. Ben remains an outsider in his own family. However, while Harriet is obsessed with Ben's 'condition', the novella itself never provides any clear-cut answers or diagnoses to her question "'*What* is he?'" (66, emphasis in the text). Ben's position in the narrative remains ambiguous from beginning to end, and as such, I propose, it allows Lessing to examine from a critical distance how different discourses and authorities construct, categorise and control children and their transient bodies.

An important formal prerequisite for this metaconstructivist agenda is the narrative situation. An anonymous heterodiegetic narrator tells the story almost entirely from Harriet's point of view. Often, she serves as an internal focaliser, which gives readers an insight into her emotional state, such as when she experiences an extremely painful pregnancy with Ben and imagines "that she took the big kitchen knife, cut open her own stomach, lifted out the child" (59). While this point of view invites readers to sympathise with Harriet as a mother, I argue that her dominance as focaliser similarly draws attention to the power structures involved in the discursive construction of children and their bodies. As Ruth Robbins points out, "the child Ben is afforded no interiority, and a vocabulary that would render any subjective self severely limited".[28] Even Ben's rare instances of direct speech are always filtered through Harriet's perception. The marginality and silence of Ben and his siblings are even more marked than in *The Child in Time* because the children are always present. In contrast to Stephen, Harriet frequently interacts with the young characters. This internal focalisation thus implements the imbalance of power between children and adults we have already encountered in *The Wasp Factory* and *The Child in Time* on a narrative level. Moreover, Harriet's dominance as internal focaliser provides one of the overt ways through which Lessing demonstrates that the discursive construction of childhood is never neutral or innocent. Ben's body is always a construct of his mother's perspective. In this way, the novella articulates the idea that the child and its body cannot be perceived from any neutral or prediscursive vantage point. It is available and accessible only through discourse, and Harriet assesses her children according to the historically and culturally specific knowledge that is available to her.

From the moment Ben is conceived and grows in Harriet's womb, his mother perceives him in terms of difference. Looking at him after the birth in the hospital, she thinks that

> [h]e was not a pretty baby. He did not look like a baby at all. He had a heavy-shouldered hunched look, as if he were crouching there as he lay. His forehead sloped from his eyes to his crown. His hair grew in an unusual pattern from the double crown where started a wedge or triangle that came low on his forehead, the hair lying forward in a thick yellowish stubble, while the side and back hair grew downwards. His hands were thick and heavy, with pads of muscle in the palms. (61)

Here as well as in numerous other passages, Ben's physique harbours violent potential. Because Ben does not conform to Harriet's notion of what a baby should look like, she excludes him from this category altogether. His head is described with a vocabulary that recalls the nineteenth-century discourses of phrenology and craniometry, which adds to his otherness. From Harriet's point of view, Ben's body is presented as evolutionarily less advanced. She even calls him a "Neanderthal baby" (65) and "an angry, hostile little troll" (69) and compares him to a fish or leech, a rhetoric that even calls his humanity into question. Racist language is discernible in references to Ben as a "savage thing" or as a "yellowish", "poor little beast" (60, 61). Ben's body appears – in deliberate contrast to his 'normal' and distinctly fair-skinned siblings – as an uncivilised and primitive other.

Ben's bodily growth also contests the order and duration of the sequences of 'normal' successive child development. The narrator notes that

> [h]e outgrew his barred cot at nine months: [...] He walked easily, holding on to the walls, or a chair. He had never crawled, had pulled himself straight up on his feet. There were toys all over the floor – or, rather, the fragments of them. He did not play with them: he banged them on the floor or the walls until they broke. The day he stood alone, by himself, without holding on, he roared out his triumph. All the other children had laughed, chuckled, and wanted to be loved, admired, praised, on reaching this moment of achievement. This one did not. It was a cold triumph, and he staggered about, eyes gleaming with hard pleasure, while he ignored his mother. (73)

Ben is once again positioned in relation to the other child characters who embody the ideal against which Harriet measures him. Harriet perceives him to deviate from crucial markers of infantile growth: the process and sequence of finding one's feet, the attachment to her as a mother, and his play behaviour. As Castañeda notes, children's growth is commonly understood as an inherently positive teleological process,[29] and we can infer that as a literary character Ben violates precisely this hegemonic notion of development.

Because she fails to normalise Ben's development, Harriet sets out on a journey to find a label for what she perceives as his deviance. Throughout the novel, she sees doctors, pedagogues, social workers and the police and asks them to provide a diagnosis for Ben. For a short time, David and Harriet even admit Ben to a dubious psychiatric institution. The novel thus dismantles the institutional apparatus that manages supposedly deviant children and their bodies. Amy, the daughter of Harriet's sister, has received a clear and irrevocable diagnosis of Down's syndrome from medical experts. Because of this diagnosis, Harriet ruthlessly regards her as a "defective child" (34) and is appalled by what she refers to as her "squashed little face and her slitty eyes" (29). Because of Amy's medical diagnosis, Harriet can be certain of what she is. However, for the doctors, Ben is within "the range of normality" (125). In contrast to Ben, Amy is an unambiguously 'abnormal' child, and as such she gains the affection of her family members. Ben's ambiguous deviance, in turn, remains problematic for his mother.

Interestingly, *The Fifth Child* is one of the few works about childhood in British literature that also regards biology and medicine as discourses, that is, as modes of speaking about and constructing Ben's body. Eventually Harriet realises that all she needs to be relived from the burden of her fifth child is a verbal diagnosis from a discursive authority. She demands, "'I want it said. I want it recognized. I just can't stand it never being said'" (127). When David wants to send Ben to an institution, she similarly observes, "'Then we have to find a doctor who says he's abnormal'" (87). In stressing the crucial role of language, *The Fifth Child* conceives of medicine as just another mode of discourse, the only way that the child's body can be made sense of. Lessing's novel therefore reveals the mechanisms through which society routinely constructs and regulates children's 'normal' and 'abnormal' bodies without, however, ever granting one discourse absolute authority over Ben, not even biology or medicine. All *The Fifth Child* consequently confronts its readers with are competing modes of speaking about his body.

6. Conclusion

It is evident that *The Wasp Factory*, *The Child in Time* and *The Fifth Child* all regard the notion of a natural body with scepticism and dispense with the concept of a prediscursive body of the child. They take into account how the body of the child is produced by discourse and institutions. The three novels employ different thematic and narrative means to do this. While *The Wasp Factory* deconstructs the child's body first and foremost through its performative conception of gender, *The Child in Time* uncovers the institutional authorities and discourses involved in the construction of childhood and deliberately leaves child characters out of the picture. *The Fifth Child* presents us with a 'deviant' child character who fails to be normalised and thereby exposes the discourses involved in the construction of children. There are certainly more works that approach infantile bodies from such a constructivist perspective. I would therefore propose that the constructivist approach to the child's body constitutes a distinct trend in contemporary British fiction. This tendency is remarkable, particularly if we consider that childhood usually serves, even more strongly than gender, as an irrevocable universal point of reference in our culture because it is a transient phase that we have all gone through.

Notes

[1] I examine and illustrate this claim in greater detail in my recent monograph *Childhood in the Contemporary English Novel* (2019). My following readings of the child bodies in Ian McEwan's *The Child in Time* (1987) and Doris Lessing's *The Fifth Child* in this essay draw significantly on chapters 4 and 5 of my book.
[2] Hillman, David, and Ulrika Maude (2015). "Introduction." *The Cambridge Companion to the Body in Literature*. Eds. Hillman and Maude. Cambridge: Cambridge University Press, 1-9, 2.
[3] Turner, Bryan S. (2012). "Introduction: The Turn of the Body." *Routledge Handbook of Body Studies*. Ed. Turner. London and New York: Routledge, 1-18, 9.
[4] Weinberg, Darin (2012). "Social Constructionism and the Body." *Routledge Handbook of Body Studies*. Ed. Bryan S. Turner. London and New York: Routledge, 144-156, 144.
[5] Ariès, Philippe (1962 [1960]). *Centuries of Childhood: A Social History of Family Life*. Trans. Robert Baldick. New York: Vintage, 125.
[6] Lee, Nick (2005). *Childhood and Society: Growing Up in an Age of Uncertainty*. Maidenhead: Open University Press, 8.
[7] *Ibid.*, 5.
[8] *Ibid.*
[9] Prout, Alan (2000). "Childhood Bodies: Construction, Agency and Hybridity." *The Body, Childhood and Society*. Ed. Prout. Basingstoke: Macmillan, 1-18, 8.

[10] James, Allison (2000). "Embodied Being(s): Understanding the Self and Body in Childhood." *The Body, Childhood and Society*. Ed. Alan Prout. Basingstoke: Macmillan, 19-37, 20.

[11] Castañeda, Claudia (2002). *Figurations: Child, Bodies, Worlds*. Durham, NC: Duke University Press, 4.

[12] Banks, Iain (1998 [1984]). *The Wasp Factory*. New York: Simon & Schuster, 13. Further references to this edition will be included in the text.

[13] Hillman and Maude (2015), 3.

[14] *Ibid.*

[15] See Garside, Emily, and Katherine Cox (2013). "Teaching Banks: *The Wasp Factory* and *Frankenstein*." *The Transgressive Iain Banks: Essays on a Writer beyond Borders*. Eds. Martyn Colebrook and Katherine Cox. Jefferson, NC, and London: McFarland & Company, 113-122, 115.

[16] Schoene-Harwood, Berthold (1999). "Dams Burst: Devolving Gender in Iain Banks's *The Wasp Factory*." *ARIEL: A Review of International English Literature* 31.1, 131-148, 132.

[17] Butler, Judith (2007 [1990]). *Gender Trouble: Feminism and the Subversion of Identity*. New York and London: Routledge, 155. (Emphasis in the text).

[18] Rousseau, Jean-Jacques (1997 [1762]). *Émile, or On Education*. Trans. Barbara Foxley. London: Everyman, 82.

[19] *Ibid.*, 99.

[20] Cox, Roger (1996). *Shaping Childhood: Themes of Uncertainty in the History of Parent-Child Relationships*. London and New York: Routledge, 66.

[21] Dodou, Katherina (2009). *Childhood without Children: Ian McEwan and the Critical Study of the Child*. Diss. Uppsala Universitet, 103.

[22] *Ibid.*, 122.

[23] McEwan, Ian (1992 [1987]). *The Child in Time*. London: Vintage, 168. Further references to this edition will be included in the text.

[24] Stratmann, Gerd (1992). "Constructions of Childhood and the Thing Itself: Ian McEwan's *The Child in Time*." *A Decade of Discontent: British Fiction of the Eighties*. Eds. Wolfgang Riedel and Thomas M. Stein. Heidelberg: Winter, 79-87, 83.

[25] See, for instance, Ryan, Kiernan (1994). *Ian McEwan*. Plymouth: Northcote House, 51.

[26] Butler, Judith (2011 [1993]). *Bodies That Matter: On the Discursive Limits of Sex*. London and New York: Routledge, 85.

[27] Lessing, Doris (2007 [1988]). *The Fifth Child*. London: Harper Perennial, 27. Further references to this edition will be included in the text.

[28] Robbins, Ruth (2011). "(Not Such) Great Expectations: Unmaking Maternal Ideals in *The Fifth Child* and *We Need to Talk about Kevin*." *Doris Lessing:*

Border Crossings. Eds. Alice Ridout and Susan Watkins. London: Bloomsbury, 92-106, 99.

[29] See Castañeda (2002), 4.

Bibliography

Ariès, Philippe (1962 [1960]). *Centuries of Childhood: A Social History of Family Life.* Trans. Robert Baldick. New York: Vintage.

Banks, Iain (1998 [1984]). *The Wasp Factory.* New York: Simon & Schuster.

Butler, Judith (2007 [1990]). *Gender Trouble: Feminism and the Subversion of Identity.* New York and London: Routledge.

--- (2011 [1993]). *Bodies That Matter: On the Discursive Limits of Sex.* London and New York: Routledge.

Castañeda, Claudia (2002). *Figurations: Child, Bodies, Worlds.* Durham, NC: Duke University Press.

Cox, Roger (1996). *Shaping Childhood: Themes of Uncertainty in the History of Parent-Child Relationships.* London and New York: Routledge.

Dinter, Sandra (2019). *Childhood in the Contemporary English Novel.* New York and London: Routledge.

Dodou, Katherina (2009). *Childhood without Children: Ian McEwan and the Critical Study of the Child.* Diss. Uppsala Universitet.

Garside, Emily, and Katherine Cox (2013). "Teaching Banks: *The Wasp Factory* and *Frankenstein.*" *The Transgressive Iain Banks: Essays on a Writer beyond Borders.* Eds. Martyn Colebrook and Katherine Cox. Jefferson, NC, and London: McFarland & Company, 113-122.

Hardyment, Christina (1983). *Dream Babies: Child Care from Locke to Spock.* London: Jonathan Cape.

Hillman, David, and Ulrika Maude (2015). "Introduction." *The Cambridge Companion to the Body in Literature.* Eds. Hillman and Maude. Cambridge: Cambridge University Press, 1-9.

James, Allison (2000). "Embodied Being(s): Understanding the Self and Body in Childhood." *The Body, Childhood and Society.* Ed. Alan Prout. Basingstoke: Macmillan, 19-37.

Lee, Nick (2005). *Childhood and Society: Growing Up in an Age of Uncertainty.* Maidenhead: Open University Press.

Lessing, Doris (2007 [1988]). *The Fifth Child.* London: Harper Perennial.

McEwan, Ian (1992 [1987]). *The Child in Time.* London: Vintage.

Prout, Alan (2000). "Childhood Bodies: Construction, Agency and Hybridity." *The Body, Childhood and Society.* Ed. Prout. Basingstoke: Macmillan, 1-18.

Robbins, Ruth (2011). "(Not Such) Great Expectations: Unmaking Maternal Ideals in *The Fifth Child* and *We Need to Talk about Kevin*." *Doris Lessing: Border Crossings*. Eds. Alice Ridout and Susan Watkins. London: Bloomsbury, 92-106.

Rousseau, Jean-Jacques (1997 [1762]). *Émile, or On Education*. Trans. Barbara Foxley. London: Everyman.

Ryan, Kiernan (1994). *Ian McEwan*. Plymouth: Northcote House.

Schoene-Harwood, Berthold (1999). "Dams Burst: Devolving Gender in Iain Banks's *The Wasp Factory*." *ARIEL: A Review of International English Literature* 31.1, 131-148.

Stratmann, Gerd (1992). "Constructions of Childhood and the Thing Itself: Ian McEwan's *The Child in Time*." *A Decade of Discontent: British Fiction of the Eighties*. Eds. Wolfgang Riedel and Thomas M. Stein. Heidelberg: Winter, 79-87.

Turner, Bryan S. (2012). "Introduction: The Turn of the Body." *Routledge Handbook of Body Studies*. Ed. Turner. London and New York: Routledge, 1-18.

Weinberg, Darin (2012). "Social Constructionism and the Body." *Routledge Handbook of Body Studies*. Ed. Bryan S. Turner. London and New York: Routledge, 144-156.

Lena Schneider (Trier)

"It Was Her Own Body She Remembered": Female Bodily Experience in *Sunset Song*

1. Introduction

While some female bodily experiences such as menstruation and mastectomy remain a taboo even today and are rarely represented accordingly, pregnancy seems to have lost its association with secrecy in most Anglophone cultures.[1] It is probably Demi Moore who first broke with the tradition by posing pregnant and nude for the cover of *Vanity Fair* in 1991.[2] And it is most certainly Beyoncé who, by exposing and artistically framing her pregnant belly on her Instagram account in 2017, has once and for all dispelled the cultural taboo concerning the representation of pregnant women.[3] While the *Vanity Fair* cover featuring Moore was deemed improper in some stores in the US and Europe, even being placed alongside pornographic publications,[4] one of Beyoncé's pregnancy photos received the most likes on Instagram in 2017 – incidentally, even more than a later staged photograph with her one-month-old twins. Even though these and similar images play a part in the breaking of a taboo, the way they are framed and the context in which they usually appear – most commonly celebrity magazines or, more recently, social media profiles – contribute to an idealisation of pregnancy.[5] According to these (admittedly staged) representations, pregnant women seem to inhabit a world of eternal beauty, quiet contentment and never-ending bliss.[6]

Such representations frame the experience of pregnancy as straightforward and unequivocal, contributing to its naturalisation. In contrast to these recent examples, we can find more complex and differentiated manifestations of female embodiment in earlier texts such as *Sunset Song* by Lewis Grassic Gibbon (James Leslie Mitchell's nom de plume). The novel, which was published in 1932 and which constitutes the first part of the trilogy *A Scots Quair*, remains one of Scottish literature's classics and Scottish readers' favourites to this day.[7] This modernist and early feminist text is relevant for a discussion of female embodiment as it offers a unique insight into the sexual awakening of a young woman, her pregnancy, and the pain of labour. At the same time, it portrays these rites of passage with surprising ambivalence for such an early text. Similar to feminist phenomenology, the novel conceives of female experience as inherently transient and embodied. By depicting the main protagonist's lived body, it provides a comment on the transformation of body images during the formative stages of sexual maturing, pregnancy and childbirth.

The narrative of *Sunset Song* revolves around the main protagonist, Chris Guthrie, and her rites of passage in rural Scotland at the beginning of the twentieth century, an era of considerable technological and cultural change. Apart from providing a metaphorical comment on the transitoriness of agricultural life, the four main sections of the 'song' – Ploughing, Drilling, Seed-Time and Harvest – parallel the (bodily) transformations Chris experiences. The novel spans Chris's development from being a gifted and intelligent young girl within a farming family, torn between two Chrisses – the English, educated Chris and the Scottish, down-to-earth Chris[8] – to widowed life with her son, Ewan, after the First World War. In the meantime, Chris not only watches her own family disintegrate but lives as an independent young woman, marries, has a child, and loses her husband and many other people dear to her to the war.

Many authors have discerned a "'feminist' dimension"[9] in Grassic Gibbon's work, be it through its implicit critique of the traditional role of women as portrayed in Kailyard literature[10] or, as Deidre Burton puts it, through depicting "a recognizably female 'reality' for and through Chris".[11] Most certainly, the feminist dimension owes much to, as Dixon calls it, its "'obscene' celebration of female sexuality and sexual desire".[12] Other critics, however, voice reservations concerning the feminist potential of the trilogy. Alison Lumsden points out that most feminist readings of *A Scots Quair* are based on Anglo-American models of feminist criticism, so that its analyses of positive images of women in the novel lead to an "impasse which renders the trilogy problematic for the feminist reader".[13] Instead, she suggests approaching the trilogy from continental European feminist thought and provides such a reading based on Julia Kristeva's 'radical writing', which "allows the feminine to erupt into the text, thus continually disrupting patriarchal, totalizing impulses within it".[14] I consider feminist phenomenology another constructive alternative to Anglo-American models because of its inclusion of philosophers such as

Merleau-Ponty, Spinoza and Bergson, who provide a much more nuanced and holistic approach to bodily experience.[15] In fact, this essay argues that by means of its emphasis on the transient female body, *Sunset Song* already anticipates the major concerns that embodiment theory later engages with and is thus much more progressive in terms of its feminism than is generally assumed. It is above all the rites of passage of sexual awakening, pregnancy, and childbirth and the resulting plurality of body images that establish the ineffaceable connection between (female) embodiment and transience and provide the link to both past and current feminist concerns.

2. Feminist Phenomenology: From the Body to Lived Experience

Embodiment theory has instigated a turn away from the 'body' (in the singular) as a mere object [16] or means of representation to an acknowledgement of living and experiencing bodies (in the plural). As Richardson and Locks contend,

> We experience life through our bodies and our senses of touch, smell, sight, sound and taste allow us to interpret the world around us. Humans are always located in some particular place, and at some particular time, and our awareness is profoundly influenced by the fact that we have a body.[17]

Since thought, reason and consciousness are dependent on the body, they are also determined by factors such as sex, gender, race, age and class. Corporeal feminism and feminist phenomenology in particular scrutinise female embodiment and the impact a sexualised and gendered body has on subjectivity and one's standing in society. Moreover, they put emphasis on the inherent transience and volatility, that is, the changeability of bodies.

In feminist phenomenology, the change in one's body is most commonly expressed via the concept of the 'body image'.[18] 'Body image' refers to a "conscious awareness" of one's body.[19] This does not mean that a body image provides us with a mental map of our body that is disconnected from the body. To be precise, body images should be thought of as an unconscious awareness of our capabilities and bodily functions. As Kathleen Lennon explains, body images are "modes of experiencing our body, enabling or inhibiting our operation in the world".[20] Body images, then, rather than simply being formed through a cognitive representation of a body, are formed via the experience of but also the emotional investment in one's body. Thus, body images are necessarily dynamic because they change based on factors such as race, ethnicity, age and (dis)ability and because they are contingent on situation, time and place. However, because of the body's transience and the transformations it undergoes as a result of ageing, deliberate or unintended situations (such as pregnancy or cancer), and social, cultural or psychical alterations, there is a multiplicity of body images each subject can incorporate.[21] Gail Weiss emphasises in this respect that each human being has "an almost unlimited number of body-images".[22] All in all, what the concept of the body image bears witness to is that (human) bodies are inherently transient. Yet a body's transitoriness does not merely constitute a physical or biological fact but, instead, affects the whole subject, that is, the mind, emotions, consciousness and thought. Therefore, the concept of the body image undoes a clearly defined division between mind and body.

As part of its wide-ranging critique of a dichotomy between the mind and the body and nature and culture, feminist phenomenology scrutinises particular 'female' conditions such as pregnancy and labour in other than strictly biological or 'natural' terms and instead suggests conceiving of these transitory states less as a process of producing a baby and rather "as a way of being-in-the-world with uniquely interesting characteristics".[23] Even though pregnancy constitutes an "embodied temporal experience",[24] feminist phenomenology calls into question the supposition that pregnancy is "a deviant condition, a temporary inconvenience instrumental to the social value of babies".[25] Accordingly, a feminist phenomenological reading of the portrayal of the experience of sexual maturing, pregnancy and childbirth in *Sunset Song* challenges well-established notions of a mind-body and nature-culture dualism and provides more complex, albeit less comforting, accounts of subjectivity.

3. Sexual Awakening

The portrayal of the female protagonist's sexual awakening in *Sunset Song* foregrounds female sexuality and thus renders an aspect of human subjectivity that has been and remains concealed in Scottish culture. The novel's idiosyncratic depiction envisions Chris's sexuality as active and self-determined. The young woman takes pleasure in her body from early on in the novel, as made manifest in the scenes in which she is shown looking at herself in a mirror.[26] The first of these scenes is particularly striking: Chris is alone in her room, stands at the window and enjoys the smells that enter through the window. All of a sudden, she undergoes a physical transformation:

> And without beginning or reason a strange ache came in her, in her breasts, so that they tingled, and in her throat, and below her heart, and she heard her heart beating, and for a minute the sound of the blood beating through her own head. And she thought of the tink lying there in the barn and how easy it would be to steal down the stairs and across the close, dense black in its shadows, to the barn. (70)

Chris's corporeal response is the result of an encounter with a "tink" who offers to sleep with her.[27] Even though she declined his proposition previously, while standing at the open window the young woman nevertheless thinks about the possibility. The 'open' window parallels the range of possibilities she has and further alludes to the sexual self-awareness she is beginning to develop. The strange ache, the tingling in her breasts and her quickened pulse are all indicators of her awakened sexual desire. The tink's offer is sufficient for Chris to experience a sexual urge. She proceeds by inspecting her body, takes off her clothes and looks at herself in the mirror, and she enjoys what she sees: her "wild, wonderful" auburn hair (70), and "her skin was like satin, it tickled her touching herself" (71). Chris is not ashamed of looking at and touching herself, and she continues examining her body:

> Below the tilt of her left breast was a dimple, she saw it and bent to look at it and the moonlight ran down her back, so queer the moonlight she felt the running of that beam along her back. And she straightened as the moonlight grew and looked at the rest of herself, and thought herself sweet and cool and fit for that lover who would some day come and kiss her and hold her, so. (71)

Here, the dimple below her left breast is first established as a symbol of the positive relationship with her body. In the course of the novel and the whole trilogy Chris will return to the dimple and thereby trace bodily transformations and changes in the experience of her body, including the experience of sexuality.[28] At this point, sexuality is not simply constituted as a given fact but as part of Chris's lived body. The protagonist is naked and *feels* the moonbeam run along her back at this moment; it is framed in terms of a cutaneous feeling, skin becoming the dominant sensory organ. Sarah Ahmed and Jackie Stacey note, "Skin opens our bodies to other bodies: through touch, the separation of self and other is undermined in the very intimacy or proximity of the encounter".[29] Even though Chris has not had sex yet, her body is depicted as opening up to herself as she explores her budding sexuality, but she also knows that sooner or later she will meet and touch her lover, for she is eager to explore her sexuality further.

In the course of Chris's relationship with her husband, Ewan (whom their son is named after), the way she sees and perceives her own body changes. Although most scholars agree that Chris's subjectivity is split,[30] most prevalently expressed by means of the "two Chrisses" (32), they fail to fully acknowledge that the different subject positions Chris takes up are not exclusively tied to social or psychological positions. In fact, they are, for the most part, linked to her body. The night before Chris and Ewan's marriage we can see that change is already starting to affect her lived body:

> [S]trange to think that to-morrow and all the to-morrows Ewan would share her room and her bed with her.
> She thought that cool and unwarmed, still in the grip of the strange white dreaming that had been hers, looking down at herself naked as though she looked at some other than herself [...]. And still impersonally she bent to see if that dimple still hid there under her left breast, it did, it was deep as ever. [...] [S]omehow it seemed that never again would she be herself, have this body that was hers and her own, those fine lines that curved from thigh to knee hers, that dimple she'd loved when a child – oh, years before! (147)

Once more the dimple is conjured as a marker of bodily change, transience and transition. Even though it is still there, it does not have the same meaning now as it did when Chris was younger. In addition, once more the young woman is naked, exposed. Yet she examines her body 'impersonally', as if it were not hers. Here the text exposes what many feminist phenomenologists have pointed out: Other people's reactions to one's body have an impact and transform one's body image. Gail Weiss argues that "[t]o describe embodiment as intercorporeality is to emphasize that the experience of being embodied is never a private affair, but is always already mediated by our continual interactions with other human and nonhuman bodies".[31] Because of her relationship with Ewan, Chris's awareness of and feeling toward her own body have changed. This is why she feels that her body will never be the same again, for the meaning of her body within a new interpersonal constellation is altered and consequently so is her relationship to her body. Nevertheless, here and elsewhere, the young woman is presented as 'actively' experiencing sexual desire – she is the one feeling and thinking – and in that sense can be considered an agent rather than a passive recipient of desire.[32] While this is very much in line with Anglo-American feminist readings of the novel, which are concerned with positive images of female characters, by exposing Chris in these situations of intense bodily sensations Grassic Gibbon further demonstrates that his female protagonist has agency, not in spite of, but because of her body.

4. Pregnant Embodiment

Even though pregnancy is often understood in terms of a transitory physical change, the text reveals that pregnancy does not merely represent a physical transformation but also a transformation of subjectivity.[33] Chris does not tell Ewan that she is with child but instead

> watch[es] her own body with a secret care and fluttering eyes for the marks and stigmata of this thing that had come to her. And she saw her breast nipples change and harden and grow soft again, the breasts that Ewan had kissed and thought the wonder of God, a maid's breasts a maid's no longer, changing in slow rhythm of purpose with the sway and measure of each note in the rhythm, her belly rounding to plumpness below the navel, she looked in the glass and saw also her eyes changed, deeper and most strange, with red lights and veinings set in them. (176)

Chris watches her own body transform. Yet this is not simply an external, physical transformation. The emotional investment the protagonist has in these body parts changes. Her breasts are not the same as they used to be; she perceives them to be different from the breasts she had before she met

Ewan. The young woman's investment in her breasts has altered because their function has changed: They are not merely a source of pleasure but will also serve a new function, namely nourish a child. Accordingly, Chris watches her own body and also her mind evolve, conveyed via the change of her 'eyes': they are "deeper", "almost strange", and with "red lights" in them, carrying significant connotations of the more intense and unknown psychological state she finds herself in. Attention is drawn to how transient physical and emotional states mutually influence each other. Physical changes are never merely physical, disengaged from the mind, but invariably have an impact on a subject's consciousness.[34] In *Sunset Song*, the mind and the body are intricately and inevitably linked.

Furthermore, the protagonist feels estranged from her body during her pregnancy.[35] She refers to her pregnancy in a distant way as "[t]he thing that had come to her" and "the thing she had met" (176) and seems disengaged from what is happening to her: she "felt neither gladness nor pain, only dazed" (176). In the passage quoted above, "marks and stigmata" further hint at the potential sinfulness of pregnancy. This distance is related to cultural, and in Chris's case, familial connotations of pregnancy; it is partly connected to her mother's harrowing experience of pregnancy and childbearing and her father's troubled relationship with sex. Having had four children already due to her husband's strong sexual urges, Chris's mother, Jean, commits suicide and infanticide when she learns of another unwanted pregnancy shortly after the painful delivery of twins. The birth of the twins is deeply troubling for Chris because she is a witness to her mother's pain – both physical *and* mental. Moreover, because of his fervent Calvinist beliefs, Chris's father, John Guthrie, justifies his need for sexual gratification on the grounds of religious duty:[36]

> Dod came, then Alec came, and mother's fine face grew harder then. One night they heard her cry to John Guthrie *Four of a family's fine; there'll be no more*. And father thundered at her, that way he had *Fine? We'll have what God in His mercy may send to us, woman. See you to that*. (28, emphasis in the text)

After Chris's mother dies, John Guthrie's sexual urges even push him at one point almost to commit incest (see 72). Owing to her father, then, the protagonist is made aware that sex and pregnancy can be the result of sexual exploitation. This is why she does not tell Ewan initially that she is pregnant, instead at one point actually resenting and even hating him for having caused the state she is in (see 178-179).

Chris's feeling of estrangement also derives from the culturally imposed idea that pregnancy is "a time of quiet [...] uneventful waiting".[37] Grassic Gibbon deliberately raises the reader's awareness of this cultural imposition by means of his protagonist's reflections. Chris does not wait quietly for birth to happen, but instead lies wondering and worrying in her bed in the early hours. She describes the unease she feels concerning her pregnancy as "this terror-daze in the night" (177) and mentions "a crying in the night for things that were lost and foregone and ended" (177). Because of her family history, Chris fears that she might share her mother's fate, for the "things that were lost and forgone and ended" refer to her mother's death and the changes it brought about. Consequently, the young woman's rite of passage is marked by a heightened awareness of both ephemerality and the subordination of women:

> They went sleepless in the long, dark hours for the fruitage of love that the sower slept all unaware, they were the plants that stood dark and quiet in the night, unmoving, immobile, the bee hummed home and away, drowsy with treasure, and another to-morrow for the hunting his.
> So was the way of things, there was the wall and the prison that you couldn't break down, there was nothing to be done – nothing [...]. (177)[38]

The imagery of nature, at first glance, appears to promote a traditional argument of pregnancy as a natural process. But the criticism of a lack of agency is quite explicit: Women are constructed as passive; they 'stand' inactively, are "unmoving, immobile". Women are granted merely limited space and are confined within the home and the hearth. By contrast, men are allowed to move freely and return to their home when the day's work is done. Chris's comment that this "was the way of things" and "there was nothing to be done" would sound like surrender if it were not for the lines that follow: "[B]abble of a world that still marched and cried beyond the prison walls, fair and unutterable its loveliness still outside the doors of Blawearie house" (177). There is a world outside the prison, "beyond the prison walls", a world that is even "fair" and "lovely". Yet this world is not accessible to Chris anymore now that she is pregnant. As the novel implies, then, the burden is not pregnancy itself, but rather women's isolation, an isolation enforced by a patriarchal society that expects women to be static and unchanging.

For the same reason, during the later stages of her pregnancy, Chris struggles increasingly with being 'herself': "And then it seemed to Chris that her world up Blawearie brae began to draw in, in and about her and the life she carried, [...]. In, nearer and nearer round herself and the house the days seemed to creep" (185). It is to be expected that the young woman has to make adjustments in the later stages of her pregnancy, owing to her changed physique. As Young asserts, "pregnancy is most paradigmatic of [the] experience of being thrown into awareness of one's body".[39] Chris feels the new life growing inside her own body and is surprised by the impact it has: "[T]he life she carried, that moved now often and often, turning slow under her heart in the early days, but jerking with suddenness, a moment at a stretch now, sometimes, so that she would sit and gasp with closed eyes" (185). Nevertheless, the problem here is not her body, but rather constraints of time. The "world [begins] to draw in" because time becomes a burden – it is 'days' that creep, 'moments' that cause her pain.[40] Here pregnancy is connected to a feeling of spatial and temporal limits, even claustrophobia, a feeling of being locked in – the opposite of uneventful, quiet waiting. In addition, the young woman is filled with fear: "[F]ear that all sounds would go, fear of the night when it might be so nearly still" (185). Needless to say, the fear of the absence of sound is the fear of death. Hence, the representation of Chris's lived pregnancy suggests that even though pregnancy constitutes an ostensibly biological transient state, it is, in fact, a rite of passage imbued with cultural values.[41]

5. Signs of Labour

Many of Grassic Gibbon's contemporary readers and reviewers reacted somewhat adversely to the graphic depiction of sex and childbearing in *Sunset Song*.[42] In the novel, the onset of Chris's labour is indeed drawn in negative, if not disturbing, terms:

> [I]t was torment: the beast moved away from her breasts, scrabbled and tore and returned again, it wasn't a beast, red-hot pincers were riving her apart. Riven and riven she bit at her lips, the blood on her tongue, she couldn't bite more, she heard herself scream then, twice. And then there

> were feet on the stairs, the room rose and fell, hands on her everywhere, holding her, tormenting her, she cried out again, ringingly, deep, a cry that ebbed to a sigh, the cry and the sigh with which young Ewan Tavendale came into the world in the farm-house of Blawearie. (190)

The metaphorical figure of the beast is not enough to convey the pain the protagonist is in. Instead, Chris's physical agony is compared to a "sword" driving through her, "iron hooks" tearing her body (187) and burning pincers tearing her apart. The extreme pain of Chris's contractions is expressed in extreme metaphors; all of her wounds are inflicted with metal.[43] The young woman is in so much pain that she actually bites her lips and draws blood, adding another recognisably shocking element to the scene. I would like to suggest that the graphic and sensationalist depiction of Chris's rite of passage serves an empathic and affective function: The experience of the particular pain is made more accessible to the reader, who is made witness to the protagonist's pain. Thus, the text intends to make the reader feel one with the penetrated, agonised body. The disturbing portrayal of labour is therefore also meant to draw attention to its dangers for women in rural communities at the time.[44] When Chris knows that "her time ha[s] come" (189), this, ostensibly, refers to giving birth. Nevertheless, this phrase also connotes life's transience, for there is a realistic chance that the young woman might 'pass' while giving birth.

The lived quality of this passage is conveyed via its quick pace, a speeding up of story time, the almost staccato rhythm, and the short enumerations. Moreover, there is an emphasis on the senses: Chris's body is touched and held, taste features by means of the blood on the tongue and sound is prominent because of Chris's screams. Hence, the novel puts an emphasis on the lived body and in particular the lived experience of pain. In pain, Chris remembers her own body (189). At this point, then, she is most aware of 'being her body'.[45] Yet it is not simply a heightened awareness of her body that the text carves out. Instead, it implies that the physical sensation of pain has an influence on Chris's mental processes, including consciousness and thought.[46] In a situation such as this, external markers become incoherent and events become blurred, such as the 'rising' and 'falling' room. Other perceptive impulses are ignored, blanked out, as for instance whose feet are on the stairs and whose hands are touching. Consequently, during labour, pain and an awareness of transience become an integral part of Chris's body image.

6. Conclusion

This paper illustrates that *Sunset Song* can be regarded as an important precursor to feminist phenomenological ideas as it helps to shed light on some of the concepts that have evolved since the 1990s within this field of study, in particular the concept of the body image. By means of the various body images the main protagonist Chris incorporates during her rites of passage, the novel firmly links female agency to the transient, lived body. First, in representing Chris's budding sexuality the novel does not merely break with a taboo, but it also establishes the body as a source of pleasure instead of an instrument of constraint. Second, Chris's pregnancy poses a radical challenge to dominant nature and culture discourses. The novel establishes ambivalence in regard to pregnancy by showing a character struggling with pregnancy because of the values it entails for her and for society in general.[47] *Sunset Song* thus clarifies how profoundly culture shapes the 'biological' condition of pregnancy, making it impossible to differentiate between what constitutes nature and what constitutes culture. Third, the painful ordeal of labour is established as one of the means through which subjectivity is firmly linked to the body. Chris's pain is not merely a physical sensation but has an impact on how she engages with her surroundings and herself, becoming representative of the body's influence on the mind, or rather their inherent inseparability. Even though labour constitutes a markedly female and transient situation, by means of the empathy and identification readers are made to feel with Chris, her feeling of pain becomes representative of all bodily experience. In presenting markedly female rites of passage such as sexual awakening, pregnancy and childbirth as both pleasurable *and* painful, the novel undermines some of the present-day constructions of pregnancy and motherhood as uncomplicated and unequivocal. Thus, *Sunset Song* constitutes a prime example of the representation of transient female embodiment.

Notes

[1] Arguably, this is also related to medical and technological advances, in particular sonogram technology.

[2] Imogen Tyler, who provides an excellent analysis of the magazine cover featuring Demi Moore, contends, "Given the general invisibility of pregnant bodies in popular media this photograph was highly unusual when it was first published". Thus, according to the author, the photograph has contributed to breaking the taboo surrounding the representation of pregnancy. Tyler, Imogen (2001). "Skin-Tight: Celebrity, Pregnancy and Subjectivity." *Thinking through the Skin*. Eds. Sarah Ahmed and Jackie Stacey. London: Routledge, 69-83, 75.

[3] Bruner, Raisa (2017). "This Beyoncé Picture Is the Most-Liked Instagram Photo of 2017." *Time*. 29 November 2017. n. pag. Web. 3 January 2018.

[4] See Tyler (2001), 82.

[5] Even celebrity magazines that usually enjoy picking on women when they are not at their best seem to be surprisingly generous when it comes to pictures of pregnant women.

[6] In contrast to the idealised depiction of pregnancy, labour is often portrayed as extremely complicated, with many women (or children, or both) on the verge of death if we are to trust series such as *Call the Midwife*. A sociological study in 2010 analysed representations of pregnancy and childbirth in reality television programs in the United States and found that in these shows "[w]omen's bodies were typically displayed as incapable of birthing a baby without medical intervention. The shows also lacked diversity in the representations of birthing women and, in particular, overrepresented married women and heterosexual women". Morris, Theresa, and Katherine McInerney (2010). "Media Representations of Pregnancy and Childbirth: An Analysis of Reality Television Programs in the United States." *Birth: Issues in Perinatal Care* 37.2, 134–140, 134. Depictions of labour seem to be rather exaggerated as well. Another study suggests, "([R]eality) television […] often portrays birth as risky, dramatic and painful". Luce, Ann, et al. (2016). "'Is It Realistic?' The Portrayal of Pregnancy and Childbirth in the Media." *BMC Pregnancy and Childbirth* 16.40, 1-10, 1. In addition, issues such as 'postpartum mood disorder', better known as postnatal depression, or the issue of regrets in regard to motherhood are only slowly finding their way into public discourse and are rarely an issue in celebrity representations of pregnancy. In 2016, the Israeli scholar Orna Donath published the study *Regretting Motherhood*, in which some women spoke up about ambivalent feelings and regrets they felt as mothers. This study led to an outcry in Germany. The author of the study comments that "in Israel, it [the debate] was settled in a week. In Germany, it has lasted for months". Febvre, Coralie (2016). "After Israeli Study, 'Regretting Motherhood' Debate Rages in Germany." *The Times of Israel*. 27 June 2016. n. pag. Web. 30 May 2017. These are but two examples that suggest some taboos revolving around pregnancy and motherhood are slowly finding their way into public debates.

[7] See Flood, Alison (2016). "Lewis Grassic Gibbon's Sunset Song Voted Scotland's Favourite Novel." *The Guardian.* 18 October 2016. n. pag. Web. 27 October 2016.

[8] See Grassic Gibbon, Lewis (2006). *Sunset Song.* Edinburgh: Canongate, 32. Further references to this edition will be included in the text.

[9] Dixon, Keith (1990). "Rough Edges: The Feminist Representation of Women in the Writing of Lewis Grassic Gibbon." *Studies in Scottish Fiction: Twentieth Century.* Eds. Joachim Schwend and Horst W. Drescher. Frankfurt am Main: Peter Lang, 289-301, 291.

[10] Dixon, for instance, maintains that "Grassic Gibbon's representation of women in his fictional writing is undoubtedly subversive, in that it breaks radically with dominant literary stereotypes, revealing not only the realities of women's oppression but also insisting on the positive dimensions of their reactions to their condition. He develops neither a paternalistic nor a miserabilist vision of women and femininity". Dixon (1990), 298.

[11] Burton, Deirdre (1984). "A Feminist Reading of Lewis Grassic Gibbon's *A Scots Quair.*" *The British Working-Class Novel in the Twentieth Century.* Ed. Jeremy Hawthorn. London: Edward Arnold, 35-46, 35.

[12] Dixon (1990), 291.

[13] Lumsden, Alison (2003). "'Women's Time': Reading the *Quair* as a Feminist Text." *A Flame in the Mearns: Lewis Grassic Gibbon: A Centenary Celebration.* Eds. Margery Palmer and Sarah M. Dunnigan. Glasgow: Association for Scottish Literary Studies, 41-53, 42.

[14] *Ibid.*, 43.

[15] Furthermore, feminist phenomenology is concerned with what Lumsden considers "analysing the inherent problematics of femininity in relation to an essentially patriarchal social order". *Ibid.*, 42.

[16] Object here also refers to the body as a biological entity to be studied, neatly separated from the cultural body. Body studies and embodiment theory challenge this view.

[17] Richardson, Niall, and Adam Locks (2014). *Body Studies: The Basics.* London: Routledge, ix. Embodiment theorists all make a similar point. George Lakoff and Mark Johnson, for instance, emphasise, "Reason is not disembodied, as the tradition has largely held it, but arises from the nature of our brains, bodies, and bodily experience. This is not just the innocuous and obvious claim that we need a body to reason; rather, it is the striking claim that the very structure of reason itself comes from the details of our embodiment" (4). Nick Crossley stresses that embodiment forms "the corporeal basis of agency, communication and thought". Crossley, Nick (2001). *The Social Body: Habit, Identity and Desire.* London: Sage, 3.

[18] Body image can refer to two separate ideas. It can either refer to what phenomenologists call body schema, *Körperschema*, the position of one's body

in time, space and culture, or as Merleau-Ponty puts it, "a manner of expressing that my body is in and toward the world" (103); or body image can refer to representations of bodies as used in the context of the media. In line with phenomenology, I will adhere to the first usage of the term.

[19] Gallagher, Shaun (1986). "Body Image and Body Schema: A Conceptual Clarification." *The Journal of Mind and Behavior* 7.4, 541-554, 544.

[20] Lennon, Kathleen (2014). "Feminist Perspectives on the Body." *The Stanford Encyclopedia of Philosophy.* Ed. Edward N. Zalta. n. pag. Web. 14 February 2016.

[21] Weiss, Gail (1999). *Body Images: Embodiment as Intercorporeality*. New York: Routledge, 167.

[22] *Ibid.*, 9.

[23] Young, Iris Marion (2005). *On Female Body Experience: "Throwing Like a Girl" and Other Essays*. Oxford: Oxford University Press, 10. Further references to this edition will be abbreviated.

[24] Fisher, Linda (2011). "Gendering Embodied Memory." *Time in Feminist Phenomenology*. Eds. Christina Schües, Dorothea E. Olkowski and Helen A. Fielding. Bloomington: Indiana University Press, 91-110, 105.

[25] Young (2005), 10.

[26] Isobel Murray claims that this writing is "a kind of voyeurism" (62) and that the "sexual desirability of the female Chris is regularly seized on by her (male) creator and displayed to the male gaze" (59). However, Murray fails to acknowledge that the representation of Chris's pleasure in her body establishes the body as a means of agency and feminist potential. Murray, Isobel (2003). "Gibbon's Chris: A Celebration with Some Reservations." *A Flame in the Mearns: Lewis Grassic Gibbon: A Centenary Celebration*. Eds. Margery Palmer and Sarah M. Dunnigan. Glasgow: Association for Scottish Literary Studies, 54-63.

[27] In the novel 'tink' primarily refers to an "itinerant labourer", gypsy or traveller. Grassic Gibbon, Lewis (2006). *A Scots Quair*. Edinburgh: Polygon, 696.

[28] Throughout the trilogy, *Sunset Song*, *Cloud Howe* and *Grey Granite*, Chris's dimple is closely tied to her sexuality. In *Sunset Song*, Chris contemplates the dimple the night before she marries Ewan (a passage I quote in the third part of this paper) and thus at the beginning of her exploration of sexuality. In *Cloud Howe*, she is reminded of the dimple, which she had forgotten, probably because her second husband, Robert, reveals a "passionless coldness" (Grassic Gibbon, *A Scots Quair*, 554). This suggests that during her relationship with Robert she cannot live her sexuality fully. The dimple resurfaces in *Grey Granite* when she has grown older but all the same feels sexual desire: "She had had her time, and now it was ended, she'd to follow the road that others took, into long wrinkles and greying hair and sourness and seats by the chimney-corner and a drowsy mumble as she heard the rain going by on its business in a closing dark.

Finished: when her heart could still move to that singing, when at night in her bed she would turn in unease, wakeful, sweet as she knew herself, men had liked her well long ago, still the same body and still the same skin, that dimple still holding its secret place—Och, Ma would say that she wanted a man" (Grassic Gibbon, *A Scots Quair*, 554). Chris defies the assumption that she, as an elderly woman, is 'finished'. Instead, she remains sexually active and marries Ake Ogilvie in the third part of the trilogy.

[29] Ahmed, Sarah, and Jackie Stacey (eds.) (2001). "Introduction: Dermographies." *Thinking through the Skin*. London: Routledge, 1-17, 6.

[30] Lumsden highlights the "divided nature of [Chris's] own subjectivity" (43). Burton, who also offers a feminist reading of the text, refers to this as "Chris's awareness of her own split subjectivity and contradictory social and psychological positions" (36). Unlike the author of this paper, Burton relies on Lacanian theory in her analysis.

[31] Weiss (1999), 5.

[32] Later on in the narrative, Chris is also the one initiating a sexual encounter with her neighbour Long Rob of the Mill.

[33] Interestingly, current research suggests that pregnancy causes long-lasting changes in brain structure. Davis, Nicola (2016). "Pregnancy Causes Long-Term Changes to Brain Structure, Says Study." *The Guardian*. 19 December 2016. n. pag. Web. 19 December 2016.

[34] This is also why Chris pictures her change in the following way: "No night would she ever be her own again, in her body the seed of that pleasure she had sown with Ewan burgeoning and growing, dark, in the warmth below her heart. And Chris Guthrie crept out from the place below the beech trees where Chris Tavendale lay and went wandering off into the waiting quiet of the afternoon, Chris Tavendale heard her go, and she came back to Blawearie never again" (176). Here, one of Chris's body images is replaced by another.

[35] Grassic Gibbon's contemporary Olive Moore also addresses pregnancy and motherhood in her novel *Spleen* (1930). For its protagonist, Ruth, pregnancy is yet more alienating than it is for Chris. In addition, Ruth does not feel as loving towards her child as other mothers do, which she believes to have caused his disability.

[36] According to Douglas Young, Gibbon considers Calvinism to have a "distorting effect […] on Scottish attitudes towards sex". Young, Douglas (1986). *Lewis Grassic Gibbon's Sunset Song*. Glasgow: Association for Scottish Literary Studies, 14.

[37] Young (2005), 54.

[38] Unfortunately, I cannot go into detail here concerning the idiosyncratic second-person narration in the novel. Suffice it to say that it is used to create intensity and that it is a device of changing focalisation that leads to ambiguity in the text.

[39] Young (2005), 51.
[40] This is in line with Lumsden's reading of time in the novel. Based on Kristeva's distinction between 'eternal time' and 'linear time', she claims that the trilogy, by means of Chris and her son, Ewan, exemplifies "a tension between essentially masculine and feminine value systems" (48).
[41] Lumsden accurately maintains that "the novel repeatedly explores a tension between the horrors, and the often unspoken joys, of a woman's biological condition" (46).
[42] See Crawford, Tom (2006). "Introduction." *Sunset Song.* Ed. Crawford. Edinburgh: Canongate, vii.
[43] Moreover, the use of said imagery represents a foreshadowing and parallel to WWI, which is going to cost Ewan his life.
[44] This resonates eerily with current issues because, to this day, childbirth remains a potential threat to women's lives. Even though maternal mortality rates have decreased on average, at least in the 'developed West', the US, to give one example, has the "highest maternal mortality rate of all the world's wealthy democracies". Ehrenreich, Barbara, and Alissa Quart (2018). "Let's Call the Pro/Lifers What They Are: Pro/Death." *The Guardian.* 22 January 2018. n. pag. Web. 26 January 2018. The trilogy also traces improvements for women, however, because it depicts the introduction of birth control into Scottish society. In *Cloud Howe*, Chris supports a lecturer on birth control (Grassic Gibbon, *A Scots Quair*, 455-456), and in *Grey Granite*, Ellen Johns reads a book about birth control (Grassic Gibbon, *A Scots Quair*, 551).
[45] Incidentally, Merleau-Ponty claims, "I am my body". Merleau-Ponty, Maurice (2012) [1974]. *Phenomenology of Perception.* Trans. Donald A. Landes. London: Routledge, 250.
[46] Even though I refer to pain as a physical sensation or feeling, it cannot be easily classified as such. As Peter Fifield suggests, pain can "take in both bodily suffering associated with harm, but also certain experiences less clearly attached to the body such as grief or guilt. Pain appears to share qualities with fundamental sensations like hearing and sight, but also with emotions such as happiness". And he further explains that "[m]edical research has been unable to identify a dedicated afferent network or brain area, and pain instead appears to emerge from the interplay of different bodily events". Fifield, Peter (2015). "The Body, Pain and Violence." *The Cambridge Companion to the Body in Literature.* Eds. David Hillman and Ulrika Maude. Cambridge: Cambridge University Press, 116-131, 117.
[47] *Sunset Song* can be characterised as a novel that is ambivalent in its messages, not least as regards politics (for more details see Burton).

Bibliography

Ahmed, Sarah, and Jackie Stacey (eds.) (2001). "Introduction: Dermographies." *Thinking through the Skin*. London: Routledge, 1-17.

Bruner, Raisa (2017). "This Beyoncé Picture Is the Most-Liked Instagram Photo of 2017." *Time*. 29 November 2017. n. pag. Web. 3 January 2018.

Burton, Deirdre (1984). "A Feminist Reading of Lewis Grassic Gibbon's *A Scots Quair*." *The British Working-Class Novel in the Twentieth Century*. Ed. Jeremy Hawthorn. London: Edward Arnold, 35-46.

Call the Midwife. Dir. Philippa Lowthorpe and Jamie Payne. 2012. DVD. Universal Pictures Germany, 2013.

Crawford, Tom (2006). "Introduction." *Sunset Song*. Ed. Crawford. Edinburgh: Canongate, vii-xii.

Crossley, Nick (2001). *The Social Body: Habit, Identity and Desire*. London: Sage.

Davis, Nicola (2016). "Pregnancy Causes Long-Term Changes to Brain Structure, Says Study." *The Guardian*. 19 December 2016. n. pag. Web. 19 December 2016.

Dixon, Keith (1990). "Rough Edges: The Feminist Representation of Women in the Writing of Lewis Grassic Gibbon." *Studies in Scottish Fiction: Twentieth Century*. Eds. Joachim Schwend and Horst W. Drescher. Frankfurt am Main: Peter Lang, 289-301.

Donath, Orna (2016). *Regretting Motherhood: Wenn Mütter Bereuen*. München: Albrecht Knaus Verlag.

Ehrenreich, Barbara, and Alissa Quart (2018). "Let's Call the Pro/Lifers What They Are: Pro/Death." *The Guardian*. 22 January 2018. n. pag. Web. 26 January 2018.

Febvre, Coralie (2016). "After Israeli Study, 'Regretting Motherhood' Debate Rages in Germany." *The Times of Israel*. 27 June 2016. n. pag. Web. 30 May 2017.

Fifield, Peter (2015). "The Body, Pain and Violence." *The Cambridge Companion to the Body in Literature*. Eds. David Hillman and Ulrika Maude. Cambridge: Cambridge University Press, 116-131.

Fisher, Linda (2011). "Gendering Embodied Memory." *Time in Feminist Phenomenology*. Eds. Christina Schües, Dorothea E. Olkowski and Helen A. Fielding. Bloomington: Indiana University Press, 91-110.

Flood, Alison (2016). "Lewis Grassic Gibbon's Sunset Song Voted Scotland's Favourite Novel." *The Guardian*. 18 October 2016. n. pag. Web. 27 October 2016.

Gallagher, Shaun (1986). "Body Image and Body Schema: A Conceptual Clarification." *The Journal of Mind and Behavior* 7.4, 541-554.

Grassic Gibbon, Lewis (2006). *A Scots Quair*. Edinburgh: Polygon.

--- (2006). *Sunset Song*. Edinburgh: Canongate.

Lakoff, George, and Mark Johnson (2014) [1999]. *Philosophy in the Flesh: The Embodied Mind and Its Challenge to Western Thought*. New York: Basic Books.

Lennon, Kathleen (2014). "Feminist Perspectives on the Body." *The Stanford Encyclopedia of Philosophy*. Ed. Edward N. Zalta. n. pag. Web. 14 February 2016.

Luce, Ann, et al. (2016). "'Is It Realistic?' The Portrayal of Pregnancy and Childbirth in the Media." *BMC Pregnancy and Childbirth* 16.40, 1-10.

Lumsden, Alison (2003). "'Women's Time': Reading the *Quair* as a Feminist Text." *A Flame in the Mearns: Lewis Grassic Gibbon: A Centenary Celebration*. Eds. Margery Palmer and Sarah M. Dunnigan. Glasgow: Association for Scottish Literary Studies, 41-53.

Merleau-Ponty, Maurice (2012) [1974]. *Phenomenology of Perception*. Trans. Donald A. Landes. London: Routledge. Trans. of *Phénoménologie de la perception*. Paris: Éditions Gallimard.

Moore, Olive (1996) [1930]. *Spleen*. Normal, IL: Dalkey Archive Press.

Morris, Theresa, and Katherine McInerney (2010). "Media Representations of Pregnancy and Childbirth: An Analysis of Reality Television Programs in the United States." *Birth: Issues in Perinatal Care* 37.2, 134-140.

Murray, Isobel (2003). "Gibbon's Chris: A Celebration with Some Reservations." *A Flame in the Mearns: Lewis Grassic Gibbon: A Centenary Celebration*. Eds. Margery Palmer and Sarah M. Dunnigan. Glasgow: Association for Scottish Literary Studies, 54-63.

Richardson, Niall, and Adam Locks (2014). *Body Studies: The Basics*. London: Routledge.

Tyler, Imogen (2001). "Skin-Tight: Celebrity, Pregnancy and Subjectivity." *Thinking through the Skin*. Eds. Sarah Ahmed and Jackie Stacey. London: Routledge, 69-83.

Weiss, Gail (1999). *Body Images: Embodiment as Intercorporeality*. New York: Routledge.

Young, Douglas (1986). *Lewis Grassic Gibbon's Sunset Song*. Glasgow: Association for Scottish Literary Studies.

Young, Iris Marion (2005). *On Female Body Experience: "Throwing Like a Girl" and Other Essays*. Oxford: Oxford University Press.

Alexander Farber (Koblenz)

Love beyond Life's Boundaries: Transient Bodies in Matthew Lewis's *The Monk*

1. Introduction

In the second half of the eighteenth century, with the rise of the Gothic, taboos such as "extreme and excessive desire, violent sexuality, victimization, and erotic submission"[1] became often-employed motifs in British literature. Hence, the literature of this period frequently contains topics that combine love, desire and bodily transience, sometimes leaning towards necrophilia, as Samuel Richardson's *Clarissa* and Horace Walpole's *The Castle of Otranto* show. In addition to necrophilia, the literature of the period also explored structures of power that defined the roles between the persecutor and victim. The body in transience becomes an object of desire, an object that needs to be possessed and is abused to satisfy sexual urges. Another novel that depicts features of necrophilia is Matthew Lewis's *The Monk*, in which the passive (female) body in its deathlike state evokes desire and lust. Yet as the analysis of Lewis's novel will show, love for the transient as well as deceased body can also appear in nonsexualised forms in which the relation between the living and the dead is not bound to erotic superiority.

The following paper explores the interconnection of power, bodily transience and divergent affection as depicted in Lewis's novel and argues that loving a transient body may be realised in both repellent and sympathetic forms. In order to illustrate the connection between these concepts, it will first set the scene by defining transience in general and with regard to Gothic literature and show its relationship to necrophilia, power and motherhood. Subsequently, the link between forbidden desire and supremacy of the transient body in Lewis's novel will be analysed. In addition, the depiction of nonsexualised forms of love for the transient body will be addressed. In this variation, a maternal love towards her infant's death connects to power differently, displaying either an indirect influence or even a lack of power.

2. Setting the Scene

'Transience' can be defined as "passing especially quickly into and out of existence".[2] It is hence an omnipresent concept that manifests itself inside and outside of a subject. Sigmund Freud elaborates on this by posing that "[t]ransience value is scarcity value in time. Limitation in the possibility of an enjoyment raises the value of the enjoyment".[3] Consequently, the brevity of life enables us to see the meaning and worth of objects as well as of life itself. Transience in all facets can therefore also be connected to enjoyment, taking on even grotesque forms in the Gothic.

The appreciation of life inspired by transient bodies' impermanence exemplifies the Gothic's use of "negative aesthetics"[4] and the juxtaposition of light and dark, which define this literary style prevalent in the mid-eighteenth century. This contrast is established, on the one hand, by the Enlightenment, which refers to a period of "light associated with sense, security and knowledge"[5] also influencing the social order. On the other hand, during the Romantic period the Gothic novel uses a "carefully constructed antithesis, the obscurity of figures of feudal darkness and barbarism providing the negative against which it can assume possible value".[6] This "dyad",[7] as Brian Baker calls this oppositional relation, even becomes sexualised in the Gothic by representing often extreme forms of carnal desire, such as incest or rape,[8] portraying passion as superior to reason. As such, Gothic novels frequently symbolise "perversion and obsession" that result in "disgust and terror",[9] thereby reflecting the political context of the time. The terror evoked by Gothic motifs can especially be related to the French Revolution and the revolution in Britain, signalling drastic changes and destructiveness to then-current orders.[10] Through this, the Gothic raises awareness of the boundaries of vice and virtue, going beyond what seemed natural and transgressing the limits of rules, entering the taboo.[11] These aspects become explicit in Lewis's novel, which features "extreme and excessive desire, violent sexuality, victimization, and erotic submission"[12] as well as love for transient bodies, both in natural and forced transitory states.

One drastic example of combining transience and Gothic motifs in *The Monk* is necrophilia. According to the etymology, the word can be split into two morphemes; 'necro-', meaning "death" but also "disappearing", and '-philia', resembling the "fondness [or] loving"[13] of something. Therefore, it denotes the affection and devotion to someone who has ceased or is ceasing to exist. Downing further defines necrophilia "as a desirous and idealizing relation to death, manifest[ed] in actual perversion or in representation [with] blurring boundaries between necrophilia and neighbouring phenomena",[14] stressing that sexual intercourse is not necessarily its only indicator. By comparing both definitions, it becomes visible that the degrees of sexualised desire vary. In addition to referring to sexual arousal or intercourse, the term can also be applied to the fondness of someone who has disappeared.[15] Furthermore, Jonathan P. Rosman and Phillip J. Resnick distinguish three different forms of necrophilia: 'necrophilic homicide', referring to the act of killing a person for pleasure; 'regular necrophilia', indicating sexual arousal utilizing a corpse for satisfaction; and 'necrophilic fantasy', defining imagined sexual actions that are not bound to actual contact with a dead body.[16] This arousal caused by a dead body originates from the perpetrator's power over a (deceased) person and the resulting motive to "possess an unresisting and unrejecting partner".[17] Referring to forms of necrophilia that entail actual intercourse, such as 'regular necrophilia' and possibly also 'necrophilic homicide', the perpetrator forces the physical act of satisfaction on a passive, transient body unable to give or withhold consent.[18]

With regard to this, Michel Foucault focuses on the importance of hierarchy in power relations, for it enables the dominator to influence others.[19] Due to their higher position in society, the superior person is able to set his or her own norms. This also represents characteristics of the Gothic villain, who is "beyond law, reason, or social restraint".[20] The dominant individual is not obliged to follow rules but decides what is considered vice or virtue and can punish whoever acts against the order imposed.[21] Foucault himself emphasises the arbitrary source of norms in this concept of 'normalization' because

> [i]t is opposed, therefore, term by term, to a judicial penalty whose essential function is to refer [...] to a corpus of laws and texts that must be remembered; that operates not by differentiating individuals, but by specifying acts according to a number of general categories.[22]

This suggests that these norms are not bound to common codes but rather entail personal doctrine of the one deciding on the norms. Consequently, vice and virtue could be reversed. Even before Foucault's influential work, Max Weber had already emphasised that the helplessness and dependence of the subject make justification of power superfluous.[23] Released of all normative restrictions, the holder of power is able to use particular techniques to gain knowledge about the submissive other. One way of acquiring knowledge is the surveillance of the body for the purpose of controlling it. The observer should be at a "seat of a power that must be all the stronger, but also all the more discreet, all the more effective and on the alert".[24] The people monitoring, therefore, find themselves in a superior position because they can surveil everything but cannot be seen by others.

Foucault defines the submissive individual as a "docile [body] that may be subjected, used, transformed and improved".[25] In this regard he uses the term 'discipline', which can be performed, for instance, by segregating the subject from others,[26] hindering the establishment of a collective counterpower. As such, discipline can especially be applied to socially unaccepted sexual practices, such as necrophilia, in which power "reflects the oppressive and exploitative effects of relations of domination".[27] The transient or deceased body is used for the satisfaction of (sexual) pleasure, its flesh being literally exploited for carnal desires. Thereby, necrophilia connects to the terrifying displays of antipathetic Gothic concepts of transgressing the boundaries of reason and the interplay of excessive sexual desire. Hence, these sexual deviances are an extreme form of exerting power over someone, for "sexuality itself becomes a mode of social knowledge and control",[28] which portrays intercourse as an interplay of domination and submission.[29]

However, as the following analysis will show, the emotional affection for a transient body is not always linked to sexual or physical desire and the (ab)use of power relations. When looking at Lewis's implementation of a mother's love for her deceased child, it is rather a lack of power that is applicable. In general, mothers in the eighteenth century were not considered to have power in the first place. Marilyn Francus describes being a mother as a role "without any privileges or rewards",[30] stressing her lack of agency and control. Particularly as "society judged mothers by their children",[31] mothers were under constant surveillance. According to

Foucault, mothers would hence be considered inferior, observed by society from various angles. Society here represents the dominant party, observing from various angles, "each gaze [forming] a part of the overall functioning of power".[32] Consequently, motherhood becomes subjected to public opinion and mothers adjust their behaviour to stay in favour with the public.

In contrast to the attention paid to the mother in order to judge her, when it came to raising a child, mothers were usually left alone, without any support from the community.[33] According to Francus, "motherhood was being silenced; it was a performance in plain sight that was not supposed to express, much less comment upon, itself".[34] As such, this treatment of mothers resembles Foucault's isolation of the individual.[35] Moreover, this expected 'performance' can be seen as a result of power which "must trigger off the required behaviour".[36] Society is the executor of this power over motherhood, expressing expectations and urging mothers to fit into a picture designed by society. Thus, "motherhood in itself does not grant women status or social authority"[37] and therefore does not embody power per se. Instead, motherhood is connected to the opposite: powerlessness.

These complex interconnections between love and desire, transience and power are depicted in *The Monk* by the protagonists' behaviour towards their loved ones. For one, the monk Ambrosio feels drawn to Antonia and approaches her in a sexual manner while deliberately disregarding her lack of consent and even placing his victim in a transient, deathlike state. He expresses necrophilic tendencies by the irresistible force of abusing his power to fulfil his sexual desire. In addition, the novel depicts Agnes in a way whereby she, held captive and a victim of power herself, expresses love for her transient infant in a culturally accepted way that lacks characteristics of necrophilia altogether.

3. Love and the Deathbed in *The Monk*

In *The Monk*, the desire and love for the transient body is a central and multilayered concept. In novels like this "where there are signs of decay and death, there are frequently signs of aestheticized eroticism and pleasure. Deathbed scenes become favoured loci of libidinal expression".[38] As such, these often sexualised deathbed scenes also entail a disequilibrium of power when the dead or transient "body becomes an element that may be placed [and] moved"[39] by the one in power, a construct frequently found in Gothic literature, in which terror and pleasure appear as interconnected motifs.[40]

Lewis's main character, Ambrosio, a highly praised monk who has lived his entire life in the convent of the Capuchins,[41] is initially depicted as a virtuous and pious clergyman, but he develops necrophilic fantasies that he increasingly executes throughout the novel's development. Ambrosio's affinity for death ignites when Rosario, a novice of the convent, reveals 'his' true sex to Ambrosio and threatens to kill herself by rupturing her garment and pointing a knife to her breast (see 50). Hence, Ambrosio's first exposure to a woman's naked skin is connected to the "possibility of death".[42] An additional instance occurs with Antonia, a young girl coming to Madrid with her mother. When she appeals to Ambrosio for her mother's intercession, Antonia herself appears "less physically composed and healthy, like a faded copy of her mother".[43] Her physical frailty triggers Ambrosio's affection, as "[h]er very tears became her, and her affliction seemed to add new lustre to her charms" (178).

Apart from Ambrosio's increasing passion and desire for transient female bodies, *The Monk* also features Agnes, a victim of the prioress's abuse of power, who gives birth to a child but who loves it despite it being stillborn (see 301). Unable to detach herself physically as well as emotionally from her dead infant, she keeps it in her arms until she is rescued from the catacombs in which she is incarcerated. Consequently, both characters, Ambrosio and Agnes, find themselves in deathbed scenes, desiring a transient body. Yet while Ambrosio "facilitates the necrophilic parts of the novel"[44] and becomes more actively involved in satisfying his longings, Agnes's maternal love for her deceased infant, as this paper argues, works as a counterbalance to the taboo and perverse subject matter.

3.1 Perverting the Deathbed

Ambrosio's necrophilic desire is initially executed in the convent's hospital. Here, the monk breaks his vows with Rosario/Matilda at her deathbed, which signifies the beginning of his sexual deviance. When a venomous snake bites Ambrosio, Matilda sucks out the venom and poisons herself, resulting in her getting lethally sick. She thereby evokes Ambrosio's lust at the deathbed, for "[h]e thought upon Matilda's beauty and affection; upon the pleasures which he might have shared with her, had he not been restraint by monastic fetters" (66). His inner struggle between reason versus passion becomes apparent when he declares, "Wretched woman, what can I say to you? I cannot…I must not" (68, ellipses in the text). Yet when Matilda claims that "[f]olded in your [Ambrosio's] arms, I shall sink to sleep; your hand shall close my eyes for ever, and your lips receive my dying breath" (68), Ambrosio gives in and lets his passion control his actions. According to Laura Miller, Matilda "models the potential erotic qualities implied by the deathbed's intimate space",[45] which increases Ambrosio's physical desire for her. As such, the scene combines elements of bodily transience and physical decay with those of lovers' intimacy, which trigger and ultimately reveal Ambrosio's suppressed (sexual) desires. Even though the scene lacks sexual intimacy with a dead body, Matilda's deathlike state confirms Downing's definition of necrophilia,[46] revealing a desire for a body in the process of transience.

In addition, Ambrosio takes advantage of Matilda's isolation in the hospital room. Even though he is oblivious to his (ab)use of power at this point, he creates obedience through separation:[47] the only witness able to reveal Ambrosio's crime is Matilda herself, who at this point, however, Ambrosio presumes will die soon. He becomes more aware of his power when they share their affection for each other once again the next morning. It is then that his initial vice is slowly "normalised" because Ambrosio "no longer reflected with shame upon his incontinence, or dreaded the vengeance of offended heaven" (166). The Gothic motif of transgressing boundaries here results in a reshaping of norms, altering the meaning of right and wrong, as Ambrosio "enjoys a kind of judicial privilege with its own laws, its specific offenses, its particular forms of judgment".[48] As such, this scene demonstrates Ambrosio's breaking out of his former way of life, triggered by the proximity of Matilda's death. He experiences his inherent power through his ability to rearrange norms. Consequently, this scene can arguably be seen as a starting point for the monk's change from saint to sinner, since he "promptly embarks on a lurid career of […] seduction, rape [and] necrophilia",[49] as his later encounters with Antonia reveal.

Ambrosio's evolving sexual desire, as well as his increasing normalization of perversion, is revealed as his awoken passion makes him furtively enter the house of his primary target of satisfaction: Antonia. Having observed her with Matilda's 'magic mirror', and having acquired knowledge about her actions to approach her more easily, Ambrosio uses "dark arts"[50] to make her unconscious, to put her in a deathlike state in order to possess her and her body (see 220).

According to Foucault, "hierarchical observation" is one major aspect of power structures. It is described as "eyes that must see without being seen; using techniques of subjection and methods of exploitation" that are "secretly preparing a new knowledge of man".[51] With the help of the mirror, Ambrosio is able to watch Antonia undress and to gaze at her naked body in secrecy when she is about to take a bath (see 200). According to Laura Mulvey, this voyeuristic 'male gaze' features an active male and passive female role.[52] In addition, surveilling Antonia can "itself [be seen as] a source of pleasure".[53] Combined with the clergyman's ability to watch Antonia and to prepare his approach on her, this puts him in a superior position.

Ambrosio's observation of Antonia is again a step further in the direction of the sinner. After the initial vice committed with Matilda, his spying on Antonia is his first deliberate attempt to give in to his desires. Once Ambrosio has accumulated enough information, he enters Antonia's domicile in order to have intercourse with her. When Ambrosio has cast his spell to put Antonia in a heavy sleep, "he considered her to be absolutely in his possession, and his eyes flamed with lust and impatience" (220). The monk acts more deliberately, because compared to the secrecy of breaking his vows at Matilda's deathbed, Ambrosio now disregards the lack of consent and puts Antonia in a temporal state similar to death (see 221). Furthermore, despite the interruption of his attempt by Antonia's mother, he "believe[s] that his fame [is] too firmly established to be shaken by the unsupported accusations of two unknown women [Antonia and her mother]" (219). Adding to his previous methods of surveillance, he now uses the power of his rank to avert the revelation of his crime. He relies on his high position in the Church, and on being more trustworthy than the witnesses. The monk's serenity, however, does not originate from his Christian faith but rather from his certainty that he will go unpunished.

Moreover, his abandonment of formerly cherished virtues is also mirrored when "[h]is desires were raised to that frantic height by which brutes are agitated" (220). Ambrosio lacks "reason and the clearly demarcated sense of self and world it sustains [after] being invigorated by passion".[54] His duties as a clergyman, his vocation, do not reflect his values anymore. The usage of the word 'brute' also symbolises his change, as it is connected to the Gothic's transgressing of taboos, because he

> with growing urgency discovers the need to violate, defile, to soil and profane the being who has come to represent for him the sum of erotic pleasure precisely because she is most clothed in the aura of the Sacred, and most protected by taboo.[55]

Although Ambrosio's plan cannot be executed, his sexual deviance can now be categorised as a variation of necrophilic fantasy. Even though he does not actually kill his victim, he causes her to be in a transient state similar to death and feels his desire increase by the thought of possessing her temporarily 'lifeless' body. Consequently, his necrophilia can be interpreted as a fantasy of sexual intimacy with a dead person.

The climax of Ambrosio's crimes arrives when he sedates Antonia again but this time stages her death by burying her in the sepulchre. First, when considering structures of power in connection to Antonia's simulated death, norm setting and the acquisition of knowledge must be considered. Furthermore, her deathlike state involves features of "constant supervision, [and] the elimination of anything that might disturb or distract".[56] With Antonia hidden in the sepulchre, "[b]y the side of three putrid half-corrupted bodies" (277), Ambrosio is able to be alone with her long enough to commit his crime, preventing interventions that thwarted previous attempts. As such, the sepulchre serves as the perfect place to isolate Antonia from the public and can thus be seen as an example of Foucault's description of creating "a useful space"[57] to execute power. Isolated from the outside world, the enclosed space of the sepulchre provides Ambrosio with absolute power over Antonia's docile and submissive body, symbolising the

> opening up of sepulchral depths, the fascination with what may lie hidden in the lower dungeons of institutions and mental constraints ostensibly devoted to discipline and chastity. What does lie hidden there

is always the product of erotic drives gone berserk, perverted and deviated through denial.[58]

The grave, therefore, supports Ambrosio's power, and the inherent sexualised atmosphere eases the path for his subliminal mind to dominate his psyche and actions and hence Antonia. Her sedation does not merely cause her to appear as if she were in a state of transience, her lifeless body is treated as such. Ambrosio's necrophilia can at this point be categorised as a new form of necrophilia: necrophilic homicide.

Finally, waiting for Antonia to wake from 'death' adds another sexual deviance to Ambrosio's sexual perversion, because "the resistance, which he expected from her, seemed to give fresh edge to his fierce and unbridled desires" (278). He eagerly awaits Antonia fighting against his attempts to abuse her, disregarding the lack of consent. He falsely justifies rape through his conviction of superiority over the young woman and his own set of norms. Regarding himself as a lover who intends to affectionately show Antonia the pleasures he has been denied so far, Ambrosio is not even fully aware of his crime and consequently articulates astonishment about Antonia's sustained struggle against him and the fear she expresses (see 279).

As Ambrosio's 'necrophilic evolution' shows, he takes the path from saint to sinner. He experiences possibilities of manipulating and shaping people for his pleasure. After having realised his superiority over Matilda in a spontaneous interaction, he increases his active participation by deliberately sedating Antonia and bringing her to the sepulchre, where his "impossible object"[59] is isolated from society. Abusing his power to put her in a transient state appears as his only way to find satisfaction. His desires manifest themselves in an altered and distorted view of social norms, justifying that the desire for the transient body has become his ultimate desire. These sexual obsessions are presented in harmful actions, in this case, necrophilia and rape, expressing domination and possession of someone.

3.2 A Mother's Love: The Transient Infant

In contrast to Ambrosio's 'necrophilic evolution', Agnes's storyline portrays her love for her deceased child as nonnecrophilic because it is of a different origin; it is maternal love. When Agnes thinks that her reunion with her loved one, Raymond, is impossible, she decides to join a convent to live a life in celibacy. Raymond, however, continues to look for Agnes, and when he finds her, "in an unguarded moment, the honour of Agnes was sacrificed to [his] passion", (138) leaving her with child. Soon, she cannot hide her pregnancy and has to confess her breaking of the vows to the prioress and is faced with a "penance adjudged to the crime [...] most cruel, most inhuman!" (257): imprisonment and isolation in the sepulchre. Here, Agnes suffers from malnutrition and is unable to nourish her newborn sufficiently, resulting in its early death. Despite the transient state of her child, Agnes holds onto it, caressing and fondly kissing it until she is rescued from her devastating situation (see 301).

Lewis's depiction of Agnes's situation can be seen as a contrast to the Gothic's "destructive patriarchy",[60] which is represented by the monk's power. Yet in this account it is not Agnes who is the female in power, but the prioress of the convent, who punishes Agnes and sends her to the catacombs with little nourishment (see 298). This relation exemplifies that not only is Ambrosio able to control others, but that a female whose actions are equally severe because she abuses her power to rule over Agnes is as well. Agnes, on the other hand, embodies a docile body,[61] enclosed in the catacombs, the victim of the prioress's power and subordinated by her rank.[62] The concept of patriarchy is hence eliminated in this regard, for the prioress uses similar mechanisms of executing power as Ambrosio: creating a "useful space",[63] separating the victim and causing (actual) death. Due to Agnes's malnutrition and inability to nourish her child, her infant is unable to stay alive for long. Its death can at this point even be considered infanticide, because "British literary narratives shift infanticide and child murder away from the biological mother",[64] in this case to "*her* [Agnes's] Mother Superior",[65] the prioress. Following this line of argumentation, this can also be linked to the concept of power, since "the infanticidal mother is characterized as selfish, powerful, and dangerous".[66]

Nevertheless, Agnes is not merely depicted as an incapable mother. According to Francus, the descriptions of dead infants in literature are uncommon in the eighteenth century[67] in order to veil the existence of infanticides.[68] Lewis, however, describes the transient infant in detail. Surrounded by graves and dead bodies, Agnes explains that she

> placed it on my [Agnes's] bosom, its soft arm folded round my neck, and its pale cold cheek resting upon mine. Thus did its lifeless limbs repose, while I covered it with kisses, talked to it, wept and moaned over it without remission, day or night. [...]. It soon became a mass of putridity, and to every eye was loathsome and disgusting object; to every eye but a mother's. In vain did human feelings bid me recoil from this emblem of mortality with repugnance: I withstood, and vanquished that repugnance. I persisted in holding my infant to my bosom, in lamenting it, loving it, adoring it! (301-302)

Agnes cannot part with her child. She finds too much comfort in its presence, even though it entails holding a corpse and kissing the decaying body. By describing this scene in such detail, Agnes is portrayed as a caring mother, loving her transient child beyond life's boundaries.

However, according to Miller, Agnes "responds inappropriately to the space of dissolution by overattaching to the physical body of her dead infant in a different form of necrophilia".[69] For Miller, "necrophilia is the only form of love available to Agnes", and her necrophilic "experience is sympathetic, in contrast to Ambrosio's, because it manifests itself as maternal love".[70] However, if the defining difference between Agnes's and Ambrosio's love is its nature, one being a mother's care, the other being a lover's sexual desire, the question arises whether, in contrast to Miller's line of argumentation, Agnes's behaviour can truly be classified as necrophilic.

Even though I agree with Miller to a certain extent – after all, Agnes's behaviour "still connects to common stereotypes of necrophilia: chiefly, that it is considered 'loathsome and disgusting' to outsiders whereas the living participant finds comfort in it"[71] – her emotional reaction seems to be rather a manifestation of the concept of motherhood at the beginning of the eighteenth century and as such not "deviant but maternal".[72] Toni Bowers describes the representation of motherhood at this time as "failed authority and abdicated responsibility", with "inadequate maternal characters [in novels]: passive and ineffectual, devious and selfish, silent or absent when most needed".[73] Agnes does not fulfil these characteristics because she cares for her child as long as possible, nurturing it to the limit of her bodily abilities and even comforting it after it passes away. Lewis's depiction of Agnes as a mother who loves her child beyond life's boundaries can therefore rather be seen as a new understanding of motherly responsibilities.

Furthermore, even though Miller asserts that Agnes's behaviour exhibits some type of necrophilia[74] and her necrophilic love "is all that can sustain her during her imprisonment",[75] neither does Agnes take pleasure from her child's transience nor does the corpse evoke a feeling of sexual desire in her. Taking another look at the definitions of necrophilia, it becomes clear that considering Agnes's love for her infant as necrophilic is problematic. For once, Rosman and Resnick's variations cannot be applied here, because the relation between mother and child lacks "a sexual attraction to corpses"[76] that would be necessary for all three forms of necrophilia identified: necrophilic fantasy, "regular" necrophilia and necrophilic homicide. Equally, this applies to Downing's definition.[77] When considering the etymological definition, which focuses less on the sexual aspect, it refers at least to fondness for the dead, which is not the case here, either. Even though affectionate for her newborn after its death, neither does Agnes feel aroused by the corpse, nor is she in any way fond of the dead, for otherwise, she would feel excitement. The emotion applicable to Agnes is mourning, which, though it is part of the idea of love,[78] does not refer to a sexual relationship with the mourned. Therefore, the crucial aspects of necrophilia do not apply to Agnes and her child, and as such this challenges Miller's interpretation of a "sympathetic"[79] variation of necrophilia.

In addition, Miller refers to Agnes's emotions towards her dead child as "inappropriate[]" and "overattaching".[80] The latter is applicable only when considering eighteenth-century attitudes towards grieving over one's dead child. In this regard, Margaret R. Hunt states, "there was also a good deal of callousness when it came to the deaths of children" because "[t]he deaths of children were *so* common that many people thought parents should submit to the will of God and 'get over' their grief".[81] For an eighteenth-century audience, therefore, Agnes's behaviour and intense mourning over the loss of her newborn was presented in unusual detail and length. Yet the overattachment is related less to an exaggeration of emotions in general or an unnatural attachment but rather to the frequency of the era's infant mortality. Today, consideration of the parents is practiced after an infant's passing. When an infant dies, its mother has the option to stay in the hospital with her deceased child in order to bid it farewell and, depending on the respective law, is even allowed to take it home for a specific amount of time. [82] Mothers are even strongly encouraged to see and touch their deceased child in order to realise the loss, and some talk to it and caress it as if it were still alive.[83] Agnes does not hence behave "inappropriately"[84] as Miller claims but rather expresses part of a natural process of coping with loss.

Consequently, Agnes's maternal love for her dead infant needs to be strongly distinguished from the sexualised variations of necrophilia shown by Ambrosio. Even though the infant's death is indirectly connected to power, since Agnes is the victim of mistreatment and is imprisoned in the sepulchre, it is not Agnes's execution of power over her infant that causes it to transgress the boundaries of life. In comparison with Ambrosio, the two characters appear in juxtaposition to each other. As initially pious characters, both Ambrosio and Agnes break their vows through sexual defilement. However, whereas Ambrosio's action goes unpunished and triggers his physical, necrophilic desire for female bodies in transience, Agnes is severely punished for her 'crime'. Her enclosure leads to her being unable to nourish her newborn child, and she ultimately has to face the transience of life as well as her failure as a nun, woman and mother. By including maternal love for the transient body, the concept of the male as the holder of power is relativised, because the prioress is also in power and responsible for the infant's death. In addition, Agnes represents a new form of motherhood, caring for her child to the extent that is often disregarded in the literature of the time.

4. Conclusion

Affection for the transient body, as the analysis of *The Monk* has shown, cannot be regarded as a concept following a single explanation or originating from a sole form of desire. Although indeed closely connected to power structures, love for the transient body varies in representation as well as its sympathy, influencing an (in)acceptance of the relation between a person and the body in the state of transience. The applicable scenes in *The Monk* demonstrate that transient bodies, either close to the state of dying or those that are actually dead, trigger different forms of desire. On the one hand, this desire can lead to perverted forms, such as necrophilia. On the other hand, a mother's love for the transient body after an infant's death is culturally accepted.

Ambrosio's increasing connection of (sexual) desire and bodily affection with corporal transience and death ultimately results in his ability to approach the women he desires only via power and mental and physical superiority. It is a mixture of making the woman's body obedient and reducing other influences on it.[85] When looking at scenes involving Ambrosio, it is apparent that the power of his desire to possess and hurt people dramatically increases throughout the novel. Whereas in the first deathbed scene with Rosario/Matilda it is Ambrosio who is seduced and who still shows reluctance when it comes to breaking his vows, he is the one who becomes the driving force later on. The sexual deviances of necrophilia and rape are the manifestations of his great longing for sexual satisfaction and result in superiority over his victims. In this end, his formerly Christian values have vanished, for "Ambrosio's desire […] is destructive; it doesn't bind or build unities but rather shatters and destroys".[86]

By contrast, Agnes's wish is to hold onto her newborn in the catacombs of the convent, without any sexual thoughts for her child. Her behaviour does not express necrophilic tendencies but rather maternal love and mourning. Her feeling for the transient body is a process of understanding the loss she just experienced. Only her emotional connection to her infant makes her care for it beyond its passing.

The emotions ignited by a transient body can, therefore, be linked to the proclivity for power. It appears directly for Ambrosio and indirectly for Agnes, who herself becomes a victim of power and as a result loses her child. However, the love for the transient is not bound to extreme forms of desire, such as necrophilia, but depends on the juxtaposition of reason and passion.

Notes

[1] Haggerty, George E. (2009). "Queer Gothic." *A Companion to the Eighteenth-Century English Novel and Culture*. Eds. Paula R. Backscheider and Catherine Ingrassia. Oxford: Blackwell, 383-398, 395.

[2] "Transient." *Merriam-Webster.com*. Merriam-Webster, 2011. Web. 21 February 2018.
[3] Freud, Sigmund. "On Transience." *Freud's Requiem*. Riverhead Books, 2015. N. pag. Web. 25 February 2018. <www.freuds-requiem.com/transience.html>.
[4] Botting, Fred (2014). *Gothic*. 2nd ed. London: Routledge, 1.
[5] *Ibid.*, 2.
[6] *Ibid.*, 3.
[7] Baker, Brian (2007). "Gothic Masculinity." *The Routledge Companion to Gothic*. Eds. Catherine Spooner and Emma McEvoy. London: Routledge, 164-173, 165.
[8] See Haggerty (2009), 388.
[9] Botting (2007), 2.
[10] See *ibid.*, 58.
[11] See *ibid.*, 9.
[12] Haggerty (2009), 395.
[13] "Necrophilia." http://etymonline.com. Douglas Harper. 2001-2014. Web. 25 February 2018.
[14] Downing, Lisa (2003). *Desiring the Dead: Necrophilia and Nineteenth-Century French Literature*. Oxford: European Humanities Research Centre, 5.
[15] See "Necrophilia."
[16] See Rosman, Jonathan P., and Phillip J. Resnick (1989). "Sexual Attraction to Corpses: A Psychiatric Review of Necrophilia." *Bulletin of the American Academy of Psychiatry and the Law* 17.2, 153-163, 154.
[17] *Ibid.*, 158.
[18] See "Rape." *Merriam-Webster.com*. Merriam-Webster, 2011. Web. 24 February 2018.
[19] See Foucault, Michel (1997). *Discipline and Punish: The Birth of the Prison*. New York: Vintage Books, 145.
[20] Botting (2014), 4.
[21] See Foucault (1997), 178-180.
[22] *Ibid.*, 184.
[23] See Weber, Max (1947). *The Theory of Social and Economic Organization*. Glencoe: Free Press, 328.
[24] Foucault (1997), 171.
[25] *Ibid.*, 136.
[26] *Ibid.*, 143.
[27] Oliga, John C. (1996). *Power, Ideology, and Control*. New York: Plenum, 83.
[28] Haggerty (2009), 389.
[29] See Foucault, Michel (1978). *The History of Sexuality*. New York: Pantheon Books, 112.

[30] Francus, Marilyn (2012). *Monstrous Motherhood: 18th-Century Culture and the Ideology of Domesticity*. Baltimore: The Johns Hopkins University Press, 71.
[31] *Ibid.*, 46.
[32] Foucault (1997), 171.
[33] See Francus (2012), 72.
[34] *Ibid.*
[35] See Foucault (1997), 143.
[36] *Ibid.*, 166.
[37] Francus (2012), 79.
[38] Downing (2003), 11.
[39] Foucault (1997), 164.
[40] See Botting (2014), 7.
[41] See Lewis, Matthew (2009 [1796]). *The Monk*. Ware: Wordsworth Editions Limited, 14-15. Further references to this edition will be included in the text.
[42] Miller, Laura (2013). "Between Life and Death: Representing Necrophilia, Medicine, and the Figure of the Intercessor in M. G. Lewis's *The Monk*." *Sex and Death in Eighteenth-Century Literature*. Ed. Jolene Zigarovich. London: Routledge, 203-223, 209.
[43] *Ibid.*, 213.
[44] *Ibid.*, 209.
[45] *Ibid.*
[46] See Downing (2003), 5.
[47] See Foucault (1997), 143.
[48] *Ibid.*, 178.
[49] Preu, James A. (1958). "The Tale of Terror." *The English Journal* 47.5, 243-247, 245.
[50] Botting (2014), 2. The 'magic mirror', activated with the right spell, shows any person's immediate actions and is initially used by Matilda to gain knowledge about Ambrosio (Lewis 199). The 'dark arts' refer to magic that Matilda enables Ambrosio to use, for instance the myrtle that opens all locked doors and, in addition, puts the desired person into a heavy sleep (205).
[51] Foucault (1997), 171.
[52] See Mulvey, Laura (1999). "Visual Pleasure and Narrative Cinema." *Film Theory and Criticism: Introductory Readings*. Eds. Leo Braudy and Marshall Cohen. New York: Oxford University Press, 833-844, 835-837.
[53] *Ibid.,* 835.
[54] Botting (2014), 7.
[55] Brooks, Peter (1973). "Virtue and Terror: The Monk." *English Literary History* 40.2, 249-263, 259.
[56] Foucault (1997), 150.
[57] *Ibid.*, 144.

[58] Brooks (1973), 259.
[59] Botting (2014), 72.
[60] See Kilgour, Maggie (1995). *The Rise of the Gothic Novel*. London: Routledge, qtd. in Francus, Marilyn (2012). *Monstrous Motherhood: 18th-Century Culture and the Ideology of Domesticity*. Baltimore: Johns Hopkins University Press, 80.
[61] See Foucault (1997), 136.
[62] See *ibid.*, 145.
[63] *Ibid.*, 144.
[64] Francus (2012), 77.
[65] Kahane, Claire (1980). "Gothic Mirrors and Feminine Identity." *The Centennial Review* 24.1, 43-64, 46. (Emphasis in the text).
[66] Francus (2012), 74.
[67] See *ibid.*, 81.
[68] See *ibid.*, 77.
[69] Miller (2013), 216.
[70] *Ibid.*
[71] See *ibid.*, 217.
[72] See *ibid.*
[73] Bowers, Toni (1996). *The Politics of Motherhood: British Writing and Culture, 1680-1760*. Cambridge: Cambridge University Press, 16.
[74] See Miller (2013), 217.
[75] See *ibid.*, 216.
[76] Rosman and Resnick (1989), 153.
[77] See Downing (2003), 5.
[78] See Lutz, Deborah (2006). *The Dangerous Lover: Gothic Villains, Byronism, and the Nineteenth-Century Seduction Narrative*. Columbus: Ohio State University Press, 38.
[79] See Miller (2013), 216.
[80] *Ibid.*
[81] Hunt, Margaret R. (2010). *Women in Eighteenth-Century Europe*. London: Routledge, 92. (Emphasis in the text).
[82] For instance, German law allows parents to take home the deceased infant for usually 36 hours, depending on the federal state; see Initiative Regenbogen (2018). Web. 27 July 2018. <http://initiative-regenbogen.de/bestattungsgesetze.html>.
[83] Brachmann, Diana (midwife). Personal Interview. 27 July 2018.
[84] Miller (2013), 216.
[85] See Foucault (1997), 141.
[86] Jones, Wendy (1990). "Stories of Desire in *The Monk*." *ELH* 57.1, 129-150, 137.

Bibliography

Baker, Brian (2007). "Gothic Masculinity." *The Routledge Companion to Gothic*. Eds. Catherine Spooner and Emma McEvoy. London: Routledge 164-173.
Botting, Fred (2014). *Gothic*. 2nd ed. London: Routledge.
Bowers, Toni (1996). *The Politics of Motherhood: British Writing and Culture, 1680-1760*. Cambridge: Cambridge University Press.
Brachmann, Diana (midwife). Personal Interview. 27 July 2018.
Brooks, Peter (1973). "Virtue and Terror: The Monk." *English Literary History* 40.2, 249-263.
Downing, Lisa (2003). *Desiring the Dead: Necrophilia and Nineteenth-Century French Literature*. Oxford: European Humanities Research Centre.
Ellis, Lee, and Charles Beattie (1983). "The Feminist Explanation for Rape: An Empirical Test." *The Journal of Sex Research* 19.1, 74-93. Web. 27 February 2018.
Foucault, Michel (1978). *The History of Sexuality*. New York: Pantheon Books.
--- (1997). *Discipline and Punish: The Birth of the Prison*. New York: Vintage Books.
Francus, Marilyn (2012). *Monstrous Motherhood: 18th-Century Culture and the Ideology of Domesticity*. Baltimore: Johns Hopkins University Press.
Freud, Sigmund. "On Transience." *Freud's Requiem*. Riverhead Books, 2015. n. pag. Web. 25 February 2018. <www.freuds-requiem.com/transience.html>.
Haggerty, George E. (2009). "Queer Gothic." *A Companion to the Eighteenth-Century English Novel and Culture*. Eds. Paula R. Backscheider and Catherine Ingrassia. Oxford: Blackwell 383-398.
Hunt, Margaret R. (2010). *Women in Eighteenth-Century Europe*. London and New York: Routledge.
Initiative Regenbogen (2018). Web. 27 July 2018. <http://initiative-regenbogen.de/bestattungsgesetze.html>.
Jones, Wendy (1990). "Stories of Desire in *The Monk*." *ELH* 57.1, 129-150.
Kahane, Claire (1980). "Gothic Mirrors and Feminine Identity." *The Centennial Review* 24.1 43-64.
Lewis, Matthew (2009 [1796]). *The Monk*. Ware: Wordsworth Editions Limited.
Lutz, Deborah (2006). *The Dangerous Lover: Gothic Villains, Byronism, and the Nineteenth-Century Seduction Narrative*. Columbus: Ohio State University Press.
Miller, Laura (2013). "Between Life and Death: Representing Necrophilia, Medicine, and the Figure of the Intercessor in M. G. Lewis's *The Monk*." *Sex and Death in Eighteenth-Century Literature*. Ed. Jolene Zigarovich. London and New York: Routledge, 203-223.

Mulvey, Laura (1999). "Visual Pleasure and Narrative Cinema." *Film Theory and Criticism: Introductory Readings*. Eds. Leo Braudy and Marshall Cohen. New York: Oxford University Press, 833-844.

"Necrophilia." http://etymonline.com. Douglas Harper. 2001-2014. Web. 25 February 2018.

Oliga, John C. (1996). *Power, Ideology, and Control*. New York: Plenum.

Preu, James A. (1958). "The Tale of Terror." *The English Journal* 47.5, 243-247.

"Rape." *Merriam-Webster.com*. Merriam-Webster, 2011. Web. 24 February 2018.

Richardson, Samuel (1985 [1748]). *Clarissa, or the History of a Young Lady*. New York: Viking.

Rosman, Jonathan P., and Phillip J. Resnick (1989). "Sexual Attraction to Corpses: A Psychiatric Review of Necrophilia." *Bulletin of the American Academy of Psychiatry and the Law* 17.2, 153-163.

"Transient." *Merriam-Webster.com*. Merriam-Webster, 2011. Web. 21 Feb 2018.

Walpole, Horace (1982 [1764]). *The Castle of Otranto*. Oxford: Oxford University Press.

Weber, Max (1947). *The Theory of Social and Economic Organization*. Glencoe: Free Press.

Lisa Ahrens (Paderborn)

Transient Bodies at the Threshold of Conversion: Physical Reflections of New Religious Identities

1. Introduction

The body plays an essential role in the construction of religious identity. This becomes particularly obvious when the individual is not socialised into a particular religious identity through his or her upbringing, but when she or he consciously chooses a new religious affiliation and undergoes a process of conversion. This transformation is often accompanied by and consequently represented through embodied religious practices like praying, fasting or wearing hijab, the Muslim veil. Quite significantly, such practices carry meaning not only for the individual, but also more generally for society as they manifest religion and religious identities in secular public space. The following paper analyses how representations of the transient body and embodied religious practices in novels by British Muslim writers mirror constructions of religious identities and engage in the wider discourse of secularism and religion as apparent binary oppositions in public space. For that purpose, it will first of all illustrate the concept of British Muslim identities within British society, focusing especially on conversion as a period of transience and the changing perceptions of the transient body linked to it. It will then offer a close reading of selected scenes from Robin Yassin-Kassab's *The Road from Damascus* (published in 2008) and Leila Aboulela's *Minaret* (published in 2005), which represent this issue.

2. 'Embodied Faith': Religion, the Body, and Discourse

Geoffrey Nash remarks that "the construction of a Muslim diasporic identity is a recent phenomenon".[1] Previously, the spectrum of key identity signifiers in Europe was limited mainly to gender, ethnicity, or class. A reason for this can be found in Ziauddin Sardar and Waqar Ahmad's study of British Muslims, which claims that in a secular or at best Christian society like Britain, religion – and particularly a Muslim religious affiliation – has been "largely marginalised and relegated to the private sphere".[2] As 'embodied faith', the body plays a significant role in this respect as it makes religion visible in the public sphere.[3] In fact, Anne-Marie Korte suggests that religion's "embodied (re)appearance might be considered an unexpected countering of modernity's increasing discomfort with religion's non-rational aspects and aspirations".[4] Her remark implies that the emergence of a (Muslim) religious presence in the public sphere constitutes a shift which sets religion as an identity signifier at the centre of attention, thereby broadening the spectrum of key identity signifiers. This is also emphasised by Stefano Allievi, who remarks that "[a] public space which used to be described in terms of secularization is now increasingly described as a territory in which a 'return of religions' is one of the main ongoing processes".[5] Thus, not only do British Muslims choose to define themselves in terms of their religious affiliation rather than, for instance, their ethnic background, but they also communicate this more openly in the public sphere by engaging in embodied religious practices. Indeed, Nasar Meer uses the term 'Muslim consciousness' to describe British Muslims' increasing negotiation of and dynamic interaction with their religious identity.[6] Consequently, the body increasingly turns into "a site of interaction, appropriation and reappropriation".[7]

It is possible to contextualise the relationship between religion and the body or embodied practices within Michel Foucault's understanding of power. According to Deborah Lupton, the body is "the ultimate site of political and ideological control, surveillance and regulation".[8] Foucault suggests that there are different varieties of power, such as sovereign power, disciplinary power or biopower.[9] The form which is of particular relevance for the present study is disciplinary power. In *Discipline and Punish*, Foucault argues that disciplinary power uses division and supervision to create a "constant division between the normal and the abnormal, to which every individual is subjected".[10] As a result, those mechanisms control and regulate individuals' behaviour and, even more importantly, make individuals control themselves through the internalisation of norms. Foucault uses the prison to illustrate how disciplinary power works, but one should keep in mind that in fact all practices or institutions – including religion – function in a manner which shapes a person's behaviour and mind-set. What plays an important role here is discourse. Quite significantly, 'discourses' can be understood to include not only language or speech acts, but also practices.[11] Foucault links discourses to a 'regime of truth' which he conceives of as discourses which are generally accepted as true and therefore have a normative function with regard to acceptable and inacceptable behaviour.[12]

Foucault argues that the body must be seen as the focus of a number of discursive pressures, as it is "the site on which discourses are enacted and where they are contested".[13] Thus, discourses can be said to produce norms and standards which separate embodied practices into those which are acceptable and those which are unacceptable. This implies that discourses work rather implicitly and are naturalised norms, which are expressed in particular embodied practices. In this sense, religion and secularism can serve as discourses which structure conceptions of the body and the practices related to it.

According to Esra Mirze Santesso, religion's exclusion from the public sphere is also evident in postcolonial and literary discourse.[14] Claire Chambers notes that in the past, particularly "from the mid-1990s to the 2000s", literary representations of British Muslims [15] often reaffirmed 'Western' conceptions about Islam and British Muslims: [16] Protagonists with an openly displayed Muslim affiliation appeared rather infrequently, and when they did there was usually an unequivocal link between Islam and terrorism, as well as the use of stereotypical characters and motifs, such as honour killings or a hostility towards nonreligious values.[17] Referring to Robert Young, Santesso traces this back to "an absolute division between the material and the spiritual", which is brought about by Western constructions of secularism and religion as apparent binaries. [18] This distinction holds significant implications for British Muslims: Their identities as both British and Muslim are considered mutually exclusive, "rais[ing] questions of loyalty". [19] However, it is possible to observe the rise of a Muslim consciousness in literature as well: The shift from the perception of religious affiliation as a secondary concern to a more central element can be observed not only in society in general, but also in literature. Establishing religion as a central topic, representatives of this development explicitly address the tension between religion, secularism and questions of belonging. Still more importantly, novels like *The Road from Damascus* and *Minaret*, which are at the centre of the present paper, portray this development through the religious conversion of their main protagonists and their changing bodily practices.

3. Transcending Bodily Limits: Conversion and the Transient Body in *The Road from Damascus*

The protagonists of *Minaret* and *The Road from Damascus* both start out as nonreligious or even atheist before they develop a Muslim identity. In fact, the processes of conversion which they undergo are of particular importance here as they not only facilitate the reconstruction of their identities, but also of conceptions of the body. Indeed, the converts' bodies become transient bodies supporting the transformative process they experience during that period. Conversion is a conscious choice. Daniel Winchester notes that conversion has enormous impact on the individual's sense of self. Quite significantly, he identifies a productive link between embodied religious practice – and thus, the individual's interaction with and use of his or her own body – and this new identity. What this implies is that those practices and perceptions of the body are not the *result* of a new religious affiliation, but instead become important, even *constitutive* elements in developing a new sense of self.[20] Similar views are expressed by Thomas P. Kasulis and Nüfer Göle. In his capacity as editor of Yuasa Yasuo's mind-body theory, Kasulis remarks that "practices may be said to precede the beliefs",[21] thereby emphasising the productive nature of embodied religious practices. This opinion is shared by Göle, who suggests that "there is a strong correlation between the reinforcement of faith [through bodily practices and rituals] and the construction of identity".[22]

In contrast to those who are born into a particular religious group, people who convert often do so "during times of personal strain".[23] This is also true for the protagonists of Aboulela's and Yassin-Kassab's novels. At the beginning of Aboulela's *Minaret*, for instance, the main protagonist, Najwa, lives a privileged and secular life in Sudan before her father's political activities force her to flee the country and move to England in 1985. There she lives in comparative poverty but takes on a Muslim identity. In her analysis of Aboulela's first novel, *The Translator* (1999),

Heather Hewett observes that the religious conversion of one of the protagonists "is triggered by his physical struggles" and his awareness of his body's transience, particularly the "experience of his own physical vulnerabilities and, by extension, death".[24] Indeed, similar tendencies can be identified in *Minaret*. Aware of the fact that "[w]*e all have an end we can't escape*", Najwa wishes for "a restoration of innocence. I yearned to go back to being safe with God".[25] It seems to be Najwa's fear of her own transience which results from what she perceives as sins – for instance, embodied practices linked to her family's secular lifestyle like close-fitting clothes (see 23), indulging in food (see 123), excessive materialism (see 52), or her sexual relationship with her former boyfriend (see 174) – which makes her seek religion's comfort.

In *The Road from Damascus*, conversion is represented as a significant transition phase as well. Initially, Sami, the novel's second-generation immigrant protagonist, refuses everything religious as "backwardness".[26] Seeing his Muslim background as an obstacle to his belonging to Britain, he actively denies his origin (see 61) and instead holds on to the atheism his father instilled in him. It is in a moment of personal and professional crisis that he develops a tentative Muslim identity which is based on agnosticism.[27]

Sami's conversion is accompanied by moments in which he transcends the limits of his body in order to gain new insights from which he ultimately develops a new, tentative religious identity. A person who plays a crucial role in this context is Mustafa, his late father. Mustafa was a well-known academic who specialised in Arabic literature. More importantly, however, he despised religious belief and was a radical atheist who did not accept any other worldview than his own. His ideological convictions even made him betray his wife's religious brother to the Syrian secret police during conflicts between the secular Syrian government and the Muslim Brotherhood in the 1980s. Initially unaware of his father's betrayal, Sami aspires to follow in his father's footsteps and seems intensely influenced by secular discourses, as it is Mustafa's secular or atheist 'grand narrative' which controls and shapes Sami's behaviour and his perception of his body. According to Jean-François Lyotard, such grand narratives are used to legitimise (exclusionary) power structures, for instance, by establishing particular discourses – such as secularism – as an apparently universal truth.[28]

The effect of the secular grand narrative becomes obvious by the exclusionary lines Sami draws: He divides embodied practices and habits into those which are secular and acceptable and those which are religious and therefore unacceptable. For instance, he does not want to be seen with his wife, who has decided to wear the hijab, because he is afraid that people might consider him a religious person who forces his wife to wear the veil, and he speaks dismissively of people who engage in religious practices such as praying (see 58, 100). In the course of the novel, Sami slowly realises that his father's 'grand narrative' is only one of many possible narratives, and that it is rather unlikely that one is able to identify a single, ultimate truth. It is this realisation which causes him to develop a religious identity that is by no means conventional or traditional, but rather tentative and based on "a doctrine of radical unknowing" (347).

Sami's development of such an identity is gradually brought about by two moments in which his body and mind interact productively with one another and which represent different stages of his development. Not only do they draw attention to the bodily and mental transitions taking place at a time of profound change in his life, but they lead to insights which instigate a process of constructing a new religious identity. Interestingly, both moments are linked to a hallucination which allows him to momentarily transcend his bodily limits and at the same epitomises the changes his religious conversion will soon bring about: On both occasions, he sees an "apocalypse horse" whose face looks like that of his dead father, Mustafa (166). While the second moment takes place during a neuroscientific experiment, the first one occurs during a night out when Sami is under the influence of drugs. At first glance, Sami resorts to substance abuse in order to compensate for the discrepancy between his father's expectations, which require him to reject any religious interests and become an academic, and his reality, which sees him being told by his PhD supervisor to abandon his academic career. However, as will soon become obvious, the drugs also make him realise that his father's secular grand narrative is by no means fixed and universal. Thus, by moving across the limits of his body, Sami becomes aware of the transient nature not only of his physical experience, but also of the grand narrative which has shaped his life.

Following the consumption of various illegal substances, Sami seems to be reduced to mere physicality and loses access to rational thinking. The heterodiegetic narrator reveals that by taking drugs, Sami wants "to derange himself. To purify himself" (157), which hints at the still rather unconscious need to alter his mind-set. Sami's perception seems to be narrowed down to his body and senses when the narrator describes how Sami's throat and stomach feel, recounts stages of his digestion, and portrays the sensation of the night air on his body (see 157). The drugs also seem to influence his sense of self, which is illustrated by his remark that "I am no longer Sami Traifi […]. I'm nothing. I am. I am attaining nothing" (157), and that in the meantime, he is only "Sami's body" (164).

It is at this point that Sami is confronted with the apocalypse horse for the first time, an encounter which will soon be followed by a second appearance the same night. Thus, he may have temporarily escaped from his personal and professional problems, but he now seems to be confronted with their source: The belief in his father's atheist convictions, which generate exclusionary boundaries between religion and secularism. The significance of the drug-induced appearance of the apocalypse horse is foregrounded further in a prison cell later that night. The narrator suggests that Sami feels like "he was on the verge of something. The lifting of a veil. The Greek word for it is apocalypse" (181). The quote links the hallucinated apparition of his father as an apocalypse horse to a new insight soon to be gained, and indeed, the horse resurfaces again that night, but this time Sami tells it to go away (see 183). Thus, his intoxicated state seems to have brought him to a point where the exclusionary boundaries mentioned above are renegotiated.

Quite significantly, Sami now realises two things. First, he comprehends that his father has really died, which reminds him of the human body's transience: He remembers that "he too was bones and meat and vibrating pulp within a peel. That the body was coming to its end" (183). Second, this insight prompts him to reevaluate his attitude towards religion. The narrator remarks that Sami is now ready

> to examine all the superstitions he'd built around his father's ghost. The God fiction, for instance. […] What if he were to believe, positively, in a God, in the unseen? To believe that death was not death but another kind of life? Would that be wrong? […] No, not wrong. Perhaps not right either. But not wrong. (183)

Thus, having noticed the transience and constructedness of the body, Sami seems to become aware of the transience of the exclusionary boundaries between secularism and religion as well. This experience clearly highlights a spiritual, transcendent dimension which can be accessed once physical limits have been overcome and which takes the individual beyond time and space.

From being 'nobody' he begins to develop a religious identity. Interestingly, this process initially sees Sami rely on a number of embodied religious practices before he becomes more self-sufficient and actively constructs a rather unconventional religious identity. Following his encounters with the apocalypse horse, he changes his outward appearance and adopts religious habits, which gives his new identity a physical presence in the public sphere. At the same time, his bodily changes also mirror Sami's status as a transient body who lives through a significant transition period. Perhaps the most visible transformation results from Sami's decision to grow a beard. This change of appearance does not simply accompany the construction of a new identity, it represents a reassessment of the boundaries between religion and secularism, the metaphysical and the physical. Thus, the narrator explains that Sami used to spend a lot of time on "scraping at his face to make it smooth and secular [...]. As if facial hair signified evils beyond itself" (209). He then goes on to radically change other aspects of his life and body as well: He stops drinking alcohol, smoking cigarettes, and using drugs, and consequently, "clarity needled and prickled him" (253). In addition, Sami also concentrates on healthy eating, he deprives himself of sleep, and he begins to fast (see 255).

Now that he has adopted a more religious appearance and lifestyle, he experiences another religious epiphany, which represents the second decisive moment in his religious conversion. In need of money, Sami participates in an experiment which aims at identifying and measuring a person's religious experience in the brain (see 276-282). During the experiment, Sami is given shocks which trigger epileptic fits and once again make him transcend the limits of his body into a transient state of mere mental consciousness or awareness. Similarly to the previous occasion when he was under the influence of drugs, the apocalyptic horse with his father's face reappears, but this time Sami does not simply tell it to go away but instead kills it with a sword (see 281). He is now much more determined in his rejection of his father's dominant hegemonic perspective; in fact, Sara Illot suggests that with regard to Sami's father, "the moment of death simultaneously signifies the death of grand narratives and meaning". [29] Thus, both the drugs and the experiment can be seen as external sources of control which manipulate the body in order to transcend its limits. In both cases, the body is a vehicle which is used to experience a move beyond the purely physical world into a transcendent state, thereby generating spiritual transformations and new identity positions.

So far, it has become clear that the body plays a crucial role in renegotiating preconceptions of a religious or secular worldview. Transcending bodily limits provides Sami with new insights and perspectives and, considering his first drug-instilled experience, challenges his sense of self. Thus, it paves the way for actively constructing a new religious identity. When Sami prays in a London mosque, he does so feeling comfortable and at ease for the first time. Quite strikingly, like the previous occasions analysed in the present essay, this experience also sees Sami's consciousness transcend time and place. However, this time Sami's body is not represented as a passive vehicle used to instigate spiritual insights. Instead, he uses his body actively to create a religious experience which seems to redefine his sense of self, thereby contributing to the construction of a religious identity: The narrator reports that Sami

> sidesteps the idea of himself. Sami Traifi, inhaling abstraction, inhaling void. He touches thumbs to earlobes. Folds hand on solar plexus.
> 'Bismillah ur-Rahman ur-Raheem,' he starts. Immediately he's crowded by idle memories, and by his voice, the proof of himself. Breathes a while longer, inhaling abstractions. Starts, 'All praise is due to God alone, the Sustainer of all the worlds.' Shudders and stops. When he isn't following a leader he remembers fragments only. Breathes some more. Just relax. Notices here that he's broken into two separate pieces: the piece that advises the other piece to relax. The two pieces in fact not two selves but two functions of the words. Speaker and speakee. The order to relax has made him briefly disappear. He speaks from below or above his reason. (330)

What the passage above clearly illustrates is that actively moving his body seems to have an impact on Sami's sense of self – a practice which is particularly significant given that movement implies a transition. As the prayer goes on, he feels that he "splinters" and feels part of "something overarching and complete" as he "bows, stands, prostrates, kneels. Stands. Folds hands" (330). The narrator explains that afterwards, Sami "kneels for five minutes, returning to himself" (330). Once again, notions of time and space seem to be broken up, and Sami appears to be in a state which very briefly makes him escape from his body's transient nature.

This account of Sami's state of mind, intertwined with descriptions of his movements, suggests that praying, as an embodied religious practice, creates this experience of transcendence. Thus, means of external control such as the drugs and the epileptic shocks are represented as tools to work on the body so as to liberate it from Mustafa's exclusively secular or atheist discourse. Then, Sami's independent prayer illustrates how he himself generates an experience which allows him to reconstruct both the boundaries between religion and secularism and his sense of self through embodied practices. As the narrative progresses, it becomes transparent that his religious identity is not based on the adherence to one single 'truth' or grand narrative. In fact, Claire Chambers comes to conclude that *The Road from Damascus* "represents sacred and secular alternatives as being anything but neatly separated from each other".[30] Instead, Sami "develop[s] a trembling, contingent faith" which leaves open more questions than it answers (348). In fact, the embodied practices and bodily changes which accompany Sami's religious conversion – a period which foregrounds his status as a transient body – contribute profoundly to his growing awareness of the transience of dominant grand narratives. Thus, the body can contribute to a critical interaction with those boundaries and grand narratives rather than fixing or strengthening them.

4. Effacement of the Self: Conversion and the Transient Body in *Minaret*

Aboulela's *Minaret* chooses a different approach to religious conversion and the significance it carries for the convert's transient body. In contrast to Yassin-Kassab's novel, the body and religion are not represented as mutually productive, but inherently separate. The narrative is shaped by a strong contrast between religion and secularism, the first of which is presented positively and the second negatively. Najwa starts out as a nonreligious person who feels an undefinable longing, which later turns out to be a yearning for her Muslim faith. As a secular person, Najwa is seen dancing, swimming, and moving freely. She does not pray, and her only reason for fasting during Ramadan is losing weight (e.g., see 23-25; 160). Thus, the narrative creates a link between secularism and the neglect of religious embodied practices in favour of an actively used and publicly visible body. This changes when Najwa commits to a religious lifestyle after she has broken up with her boyfriend Anwar, a determined atheist (see 236-237). She develops a religious identity which reduces or almost erases her physicality, and the narrative thereby promotes the impression that meaning can be found only in religion, illustrating the power of religious discourses over Najwa's body and her sense of self.

When she enters a London mosque for the first time, Najwa sees a girl who reads the Qur'an. She is fascinated by her "detachment that was almost angelic" (237). The term 'detachment' here might suggest a similarity to Sami's state of transcendence. However, it soon turns out that the two protagonists seek different forms of detachment. While Sami is looking for detachment from his father's exclusionary worldview and from its impact on himself, Najwa's detachment is supposed to hide and separate her from anything nonreligious, and thus, a secular lifestyle. A sense of separation is also evoked by Najwa's change of identity. It appears almost radical when she talks about "the Najwa who danced at the American Club disco in Khartoum or Najwa, the maid Lamya hired by walking into the Central Mosque one afternoon" (111). Thus, Najwa seems to have split her identity into a secular and a religious one. Quite significantly, it is her body and a number of embodied practices which become constitutive of her new religious identity.

This becomes evident by Najwa's attempts at detaching herself from society and her ultimate "wholesale refusal of Western standards and practices".[31] Sami in *The Road from Damascus* uses embodied religious practices to defy fixed boundaries: He grows a beard to manifest his new religiousness physically in the public sphere, and he prays to transcend his body and, by challenging the exclusionary discourses which have hitherto shaped both his body and his worldview, also his mind. Najwa, on the other hand, wants to escape from the public gaze. In this sense, Sami uses his beard to actively communicate his religious identity to the (secular) outside world and 'claim' space within it, whereas Najwa's hijab seems to represent the opposite: Rather than using it to claim space, she employs her veil in a way which supports her retreat from the public sphere and thereby a seemingly rigid separation of religion and secularism. It is only when she transcends the secularly connoted public visibility that she truly develops a religious identity. Tellingly, her renunciation of the public gaze is represented as a struggle, which emphasises the hierarchical positions secularism and religion have occupied in her life so far. The physical transformation which seems to contribute most prominently to Najwa's new religious identity is linked to clothes, particularly the hijab. The first hijabs she tries on are her late mother's. Initially, Najwa feels rather uncomfortable and remarks, "I didn't look like myself. Something was removed, streamlined, restrained; something was deflated. And was this the real me? Without the curls I looked tidy, tame; I looked dignified and gentle" (245). Quite significantly, her discomfort results from her impression that her mother's hijab makes her look older and less attractive (see 245). Thus, at this point Najwa still seems to see herself through the 'public gaze' ("I threw it [the hijab] on the bed. I was not ready yet", 245). In this respect, it is possible to say that this 'public gaze' represents for Najwa what Sami's father's secular grand narrative implies for him: a standard against which identities are constructed.[32]

It is not until she has tried on one of her mother's tobes that Najwa experiences an epiphany which becomes constitutive of her religious identity. Often referred to as "Sudan's national costume",[33] a tobe "is a rectangular piece of cotton fabric measuring two metres wide and four to seven metres in length which a woman drapes around her head and body whenever she exits her home".[34] It is perhaps because the tobe creates a physical transformation which goes beyond the hijab that Najwa now feels like "another version of myself, regal like my mother, almost mysterious. Perhaps this was attractive in itself, the skill of concealing rather than emphasizing, to restrain rather than to offer" (246). What is striking here is that Najwa's insight reverses the established standard mentioned above. However, as opposed to Sami, who comes to challenge his father's standard but does not substitute it with a new one, Najwa immediately constructs new binaries: concealing or emphasising, restraining or offering.

Thus, in contrast to Sabine Schmidt's reading of *Minaret*, which conceives of Najwa's hijab as "a symbol of her faith",[35] the present study argues that Najwa is not represented as using her hijab or her tobe[36] as a signifier of her religious identity, like Sami is with regard to his beard. Instead, she employs it to hide behind it. When she remarks that "[w]ithout it, our nature is exposed", there seems to be a sense of danger and vulnerability attached to the public gaze (186). This is also emphasised by Ulrike Tancke, who refers to Najwa's faith as "an act of self-protection" or "a carapace" and suggests that "wearing the hijab protects her [Najwa], not primarily from the male gaze, but from the diffusion of her identity".[37]

Even more explicitly, Najwa suggests that she becomes "invisible" when wearing her veil, and that before, as a secular person, people only cared about her appearance (247). From then on, her religious conversion grows more intense, which is highlighted by Lindsey Moore, who argues that Najwa's decision to wear the hijab "encourages her to reconceptualise the relationship between self and world":[38] Najwa reveals that she feels regret about her secular lifestyle, that

> tears ran down my face. I sweated and felt a burning along my skin, in my chest. This was the scrub I needed. Exfoliation, clarifying, deep-pore cleanse – words I knew from the beauty pages of magazines and the counters of Selfridges. Now they were for my soul not my skin. (247)

This account clearly emphasises her withdrawal from what is presented throughout the narrative as a secularly connoted physical world and her own physicality. Thus, her awareness of her body's transience and the superficiality of appearances seems to have altered Najwa's perspective: It is her soul which becomes her prime concern, and her withdrawal from anything physical and secular seems necessary in order to grow spiritually.

Najwa's experience of prayer points in a similar direction. Her first attempt at praying at the mosque is rather unsuccessful, as the following passage reveals:

> I was wearing what I believed to be my most modest dress. It had long sleeves and fell to below my knees. When I bent down to pray, my calves and the backs of my knees were bare. Someone came up from behind me and threw a coat over my back. I guessed it was one of the elderly ladies. I sensed the difficulty, the heave with which she got off the floor and approached me. The coat slipped when I straightened up. There was the shame that I needed it, then the silly inevitability of it

> slipping off. I heard a sigh behind me, whispers in a language I couldn't understand – Turkish, Urdu? When I finished praying, I could not meet the eyes of whoever owned the coat. It lay in a heap behind me. I sat hunched on the floor, knowing I wasn't good, knowing I was far away and just taking the first step in coming here still wasn't enough. (237-238)

Once again, Najwa's religiousness seems to coincide with an absorption of her physicality as she is covered to hide her body. Unlike Sami, whose bodily movements during prayer expand his perspective, Najwa sees her visible body as proof of her failure, and thus it has to be transcended. The examples cited here, particularly the last one, also transport value judgments: Not only is religion linked to 'being good', but it is also contrasted to Najwa's physical visibility, which is related to her secular lifestyle. Critics have noticed that Aboulela's œuvre seems to promote an "ideology of singleness and separation",[39] and this tendency can certainly be observed in *Minaret*, where it is the protagonist's interaction with her body that illustrates the narrative's promotion of boundaries. Transience is ultimately represented as a status which must be overcome in order to achieve spiritual strength.

5. Conclusion

It can be said that the novels differ significantly in their representation of the body and embodied practices. In Yassin-Kassab's novel the protagonist's control of his transient body is productive and supports the renegotiation of exclusionary boundaries. At the same time, in making use of his body through religious practices, Sami is able to construct a new, more balanced sense of self which refrains from considering one discourse or perspective as more dominant than another. In Aboulela's narrative, on the other hand, control seems to be oppressive and limiting. This is mirrored in the religious identity Najwa develops, which clearly excludes anything nonreligious and physical and therefore maintains the dominance of exclusively religious discourses at the expense of a balanced outlook. For Najwa, conversion is a transition phase which decreases her body's visibility and even seems to lead her towards self-effacement. At the same time, the text equates her growing invisibility in society's perception with spiritual growth. Thus, in contrast to Sami, Najwa ultimately strives for permanence and fixed grand narratives which allow her to transcend her physicality. While *The Road for Damascus* foregrounds the transience of the body and dominant discourses, *Minaret* seems to reject transient positions or in-between states.[40]

Nevertheless, both novels emphasise the body's function as a site of ideologically charged discourses. Thus, Daniel Winchester's claim mentioned at the beginning of this study can be extended to literary representations of conversion as well: The way the protagonists interact with and use their bodies reflects the religious identities they develop, and embodied practices can therefore be considered constitutive and productive elements in terms of identity.

Notes

[1] Nash, Geoffrey (2012). *Writing Muslim Identity*. London: Continuum, 7.
[2] Sardar, Ziauddin, and Waqar I. U. Ahmad (2012). "Introduction." *Muslims in Britain: Making Social and Political Space*. Eds. Sardar and Ahmad. Abingdon: Routledge, 1-16, 3.
[3] Korte, Anna-Marie (2017). "Embodied Faith as Bone of Contention: Introduction to 'Bodies and Rituals.'" *Contesting Religious Identities: Transformations, Disseminations and Meditations*. Eds. Bob Becking, Anna-Marie Korte and Lucien Liere. Leiden: Brill, 195-202, 197.
[4] *Ibid.*
[5] Allievi, Stefano (2005). "Conflicts, Cultures, and Religions: Islam in Europe as a Sign and Symbol of Change in European Societies." *Islam and the New Europe: Continuities, Changes, Confrontations*. Eds. Sigrid Nökel and Levent Tezcan. Bielefeld: Transcript, 18-44, 19.
[6] Meer, Nasar (2012). "Misrecognizing Muslim Consciousness in Europe." *Misrecognition and Ethno-Religious Diversity*, special issue of *Ethnicities*, ed. by Nasar Meer, Wendy Martineau and Simon Thompson, 12.2, 178-196, 180.
[7] Coupland, Justine, and Richard Gwyn (2003). "Introduction." *Discourse, the Body, and Identity*. Eds. Coupland and Gwyn. Basingstoke: Palgrave Macmillan, 1-18, 4.
[8] Lupton, Deborah (1994). *Medicine as Culture*. London: Sage, 23.
[9] Lilja, Mona, and Stellan Vinthagen (2014). "Sovereign Power, Disciplinary Power and Biopower: Resisting What Power with What Resistance?" *Journal of Political Power* 7.1, 107-126, 107-108.
[10] Foucault, Michel (1995). *Discipline and Punish: The Birth of the Prison*. Trans. Alan Sheridan. New York: Random House, 199.

[11] Hall, Stuart (2003). "The Work of Representation." *Representation: Cultural Representations and Signifying Practices*. Ed. Hall. London: Sage, 13-74, 44-49.

[12] Foucault, Michel (1980). *Power/Knowledge: Selected Interviews and Other Writings 1972-1977*. Trans. Colin Gordon, Leo Marshall, John Mepham and Kate Soper. Ed. Colin Gordon. New York: Pantheon Books, 131.

[13] Mills, Sara (2003). *Michel Foucault*. London: Routledge, 81.

[14] Santesso, Esra Mirze (2013). *Disorientation: Muslim Identity in Contemporary Anglophone Literature*. Basingstoke: Palgrave Macmillan, 5.

[15] Examples of such works are Monica Ali's *Brick Lane* (2002), Nadeem Aslam's *Maps for Lost Lovers* (2004) and Hanif Kureishi's *The Black Album* (1995).

[16] Chambers, Claire (2011). "Recent Literary Representations of British Muslims." *Mediating Faiths: Religion and Socio-Cultural Change in the Twenty-First Century*. Eds. Michael Bailey and Guy Redden. Farnham and Burlington: Ashgate, 175-188, 175.

[17] *Ibid.*

[18] Santesso (2013), 5.

[19] Sardar and Ahmad (2012), 3.

[20] Winchester, Daniel (2008). "Embodying the Faith: Religious Practice and the Making of a Muslim Moral Habitus." *Social Forces* 86.4, 1753-1780, 1755, 1763.

[21] Kasulis, Thomas P. (1987). "Editor's Introduction." *The Body: Toward an Eastern Mind-Body Theory*. By Yuasa Yasuo. Trans. Nagatomo Shigenori and Thomas P. Kasulis. Ed. Kasulis. Albany: State University of New York Press, 1-16, 7.

[22] Göle, Nıüfer (2017). "Contesting Islam: The Making and Unmaking of Religious Faith." *Contesting Religious Identities: Transformations, Disseminations and Meditations*. Eds. Bob Becking, Anna-Marie Korte and Lucien Liere. Leiden: Brill, 203-218, 207.

[23] Long, Theordore, and Jeffrey K. Hadden (1983). "Religious Conversion and the Concept of Socialization: Integrating the Brainwashing and Drift Models." *Journal for the Scientific Study of Religion* 22.1, 1-14, 1.

[24] Hewett, Heather (2009). "Translating Desire: Exile and Leila Aboulela's Poetics of Embodiment." *Expressions of the Body: Representations in African Text and Image*. Ed. Charlotte Baker. Bern: Peter Lang, 249-275, 261.

[25] Aboulela, Leila (2006). *Minaret*. London: Bloomsbury, 242. (Emphasis in the text). Further references to this edition will be included in the text.

[26] Yassin-Kassab, Robin (2009). *The Road from Damascus*. London: Penguin, 2. Further references to this edition will be included in the text.

[27] Rashid, Catherine (2012). "British Islam and the Novel of Transformation: Robin Yassin-Kassab's *The Road from Damascus*." *Journal of Postcolonial Writing* 48.1, 92-103, 101.

[28] Lyotard, Jean-François. *The Postmodern Condition: A Report on Knowledge*. Trans. Geoff Bennington and Brian Massumi. Manchester: Manchester University Press, xxiv, 37.

[29] Illot, Sara (2009). *New Postcolonial British Genres: Shifting the Boundaries*. Basingstoke: Palgrave Macmillan, 32.

[30] Chambers, Claire (2012). "'Sexy Identity-Assertion': Choosing Between Sacred and Secular Identities in Robin Yassin-Kassab's *The Road from Damascus*." *Culture, Diaspora, and Modernity in Muslim Writing*. Eds. Rehana Ahmed, Peter Morey and Amina Yaqin. New York: Routledge, 117-131, 122.

[31] Nash, Geoffrey (2007). *The Anglo-Arab Encounter: Fiction and Autobiography by Arab Writers in English*. Bern: Peter Lang, 136.

[32] Seda Canpolat argues that even though Najwa's "embodied piety [through the hijab] shields her from the sexist gaze, it cannot protect her from racist abuse", thereby characterising the public gaze as both racist and sexist. (Canpolat, Seda [2016]. "Gazing the Muslim Woman in Fadia Faqir's *My Name Is Salma* and Leila Aboulela's *Minaret*." *Contemporary Women's Writing* 10.2, 216-235, 218.) In the context of the present article, however, the public gaze is conceived of as secular.

[33] Brown, Marie Grace (2015). "Fashioning Their Place: Dress and Global Imagination in Imperial Sudan." *Gender, Imperialism and Global Exchanges*. Eds. Stephan F. Miescher, Michele Mitchell and Naoko Shibusawa. Chichester: Wiley-Blackwell, 115-131, 115.

[34] *Ibid*.

[35] Schmidt, Sabine (2016). *Beyond the Veil: Culture, Religion, Language and Identity in Black British Muslimah Literature*. Trier: WVT, 118.

[36] For most of the narrative Najwa is seen wearing a hijab rather than a tobe.

[37] Tancke, Ulrike (2011). "'Original Traumas': Narrating Migrant Identity in British Muslim Women's Writing." *Postcolonial Text* 6.2, 1-15, 9.

[38] Moore, Lindsey (2012). "Voyages Out and In: Two (British) Arab Muslim Women's Bildungsromane." *Culture, Diaspora, and Modernity in Muslim Writing*. Eds. Rehana Ahmed, Peter Morey and Amina Yaqin. New York: Routledge, 68-84, 77.

[39] Steinitz, Tamar (2013). "Back Home: Translation, Conversion and Domestication in Leila Aboulela's *The Translator*." *Interventions* 15.3, 365-382, 367.

[40] I am very grateful to Merle Tönnies for her inspirational and insightful thoughts which helped me finalise this idea.

Bibliography

Aboulela, Leila (2006). *Minaret*. London: Bloomsbury.
Ali, Monica (2004). *Brick Lane*. London: Black Swan Books.

Allievi, Stefano (2005). "Conflicts, Cultures, and Religions: Islam in Europe as a Sign and Symbol of Change in European Societies." *Islam and the New Europe: Continuities, Changes, Confrontations*. Eds. Sigrid Nökel and Levent Tezcan. Bielefeld: Transcript, 18-44.

Aslam, Nadeem (2005). *Maps for Lost Lovers*. London: Faber & Faber.

Brown, Marie Grace (2015). "Fashioning Their Place: Dress and Global Imagination in Imperial Sudan." *Gender, Imperialism and Global Exchanges*. Eds. Stephan F. Miescher, Michele Mitchell and Naoko Shibusawa. Chichester: Wiley-Blackwell, 115-131.

Canpolat, Seda (2016). "Gazing the Muslim Woman in Fadia Faqir's *My Name Is Salma* and Leila Aboulela's *Minaret*." *Contemporary Women's Writing* 10.2, 216-235.

Chambers, Claire (2011). "Recent Literary Representations of British Muslims." *Mediating Faiths: Religion and Socio-Cultural Change in the Twenty-First Century*. Eds. Michael Bailey and Guy Redden. Farnham and Burlington: Ashgate, 175-188.

--- (2012). "'Sexy Identity-Assertion': Choosing between Sacred and Secular Identities in Robin Yassin-Kassab's *The Road from Damascus*." *Culture, Diaspora, and Modernity in Muslim Writing*. Eds. Rehana Ahmed, Peter Morey and Amina Yaqin. New York: Routledge, 117-131.

Coupland, Justine, and Richard Gwyn (2003). "Introduction." *Discourse, the Body, and Identity*. Eds. Coupland and Gwyn. Basingstoke: Palgrave Macmillan, 1-18.

Foucault, Michel (1980). *Power/Knowledge: Selected Interviews and Other Writings 1972-1977*. Trans. Colin Gordon, Leo Marshall, John Mepham and Kate Soper. Ed. Colin Gordon. New York: Pantheon Books.

--- (1995). *Discipline and Punish: The Birth of the Prison*. Trans. Alan Sheridan. New York: Random House.

Göle, Nilüfer (2017). "Contesting Islam: The Making and Unmaking of Religious Faith." *Contesting Religious Identities: Transformations, Disseminations and Meditations*. Eds. Bob Becking, Anna-Marie Korte and Lucien Liere. Leiden: Brill, 203-218.

Hall, Stuart (2003). "The Work of Representation." *Representation: Cultural Representations and Signifying Practices*. Ed. Hall. London: Sage, 13-74.

Hewett, Heather (2009). "Translating Desire: Exile and Leila Aboulela's Poetics of Embodiment." *Expressions of the Body: Representations in African Text and Image*. Ed. Charlotte Baker. Bern: Peter Lang, 249-275.

Illot, Sara (2015). *New Postcolonial British Genres: Shifting the Boundaries*. Basingstoke: Palgrave Macmillan.

Kasulis, Thomas P. (1987). "Editor's Introduction." *The Body: Toward an Eastern Mind-Body Theory*. By Yuasa Yasuo. Trans. Nagatomo Shigenori and Thomas P. Kasulis. Ed. Kasulis. Albany: State University of New York Press, 1-16.

Korte, Anna-Marie (2017). "Embodied Faith as Bone of Contention: Introduction to 'Bodies and Rituals.'" *Contesting Religious Identities: Transformations, Disseminations and Meditations.* Eds. Bob Becking, Anna-Marie Korte and Lucien Liere. Leiden: Brill, 195-202.

Kureishi, Hanif (2010). *The Black Album*. London: Faber & Faber.

Lilja, Mona, and Stellan Vinthagen (2014). "Sovereign Power, Disciplinary Power and Biopower: Resisting What Power with What Resistance?" *Journal of Political Power* 7.1, 107-126.

Long, Theordore, and Jeffrey K. Hadden (1983). "Religious Conversion and the Concept of Socialization: Integrating the Brainwashing and Drift Models." *Journal for the Scientific Study of Religion* 22.1, 1-14.

Lupton, Deborah (1994). *Medicine as Culture*. London: Sage.

Lyotard, Jean-François (1984). *The Postmodern Condition: A Report on Knowledge*. Trans. Geoff Bennington and Brian Massumi. Manchester: Manchester University Press.

Meer, Nasar (2012). "Misrecognizing Muslim Consciousness in Europe." *Misrecognition and Ethno-Religious Diversity*, special issue of *Ethnicities*, ed. by Nasar Meer, Wendy Martineau and Simon Thompson, 12.2, 178-196.

Mills, Sara (2003). *Michel Foucault*. London: Routledge.

Moore, Lindsey (2012). "Voyages Out and In: Two (British) Arab Muslim Women's Bildungsromane." *Culture, Diaspora, and Modernity in Muslim Writing*. Eds. Rehana Ahmed, Peter Morey and Amina Yaqin. New York: Routledge, 68-84.

Nash, Geoffrey (2007). *The Anglo-Arab Encounter: Fiction and Autobiography by Arab Writers in English*. Bern: Peter Lang.

--- (2012). *Writing Muslim Identity*. London: Continuum.

Rashid, Catherine (2012). "British Islam and the Novel of Transformation: Robin Yassin-Kassab's *The Road from Damascus*." *Journal of Postcolonial Writing* 48.1, 92-103.

Santesso, Esra Mirze (2013). *Disorientation: Muslim Identity in Contemporary Anglophone Literature*. Basingstoke: Palgrave Macmillan.

Sardar, Ziauddin, and Waqar I. U. Ahmad (2012). "Introduction." *Muslims in Britain: Making Social and Political Space*. Eds. Sardar and Ahmad. Abingdon: Routledge, 1-16.

Schmidt, Sabine (2016). *Beyond the Veil: Culture, Religion, Language and Identity in Black British Muslimah Literature*. Trier: WVT.

Steinitz, Tamar (2013). "Back Home: Translation, Conversion and Domestication in Leila Aboulela's *The Translator*." *Interventions* 15.3, 365-382.

Tancke, Ulrike (2011). "'Original Traumas': Narrating Migrant Identity in British Muslim Women's Writing." *Postcolonial Text* 6.2, 1-15.

Winchester, Daniel (2008). "Embodying the Faith: Religious Practice and the Making of a Muslim Moral Habitus." *Social Forces* 86.4, 1753-1780.

Yassin-Kassab, Robin (2009). *The Road from Damascus*. London: Penguin.

Alessandra Boller (Siegen)

"It's Easier to Talk Like This in the Dark": The Body with AIDS in Colm Tóibín's *The Blackwater Lightship*

1. Introduction: Hide and Seek

The novel *The Blackwater Lightship*, written by the acclaimed Irish author Colm Tóibín, was published in 1999 and thus at a fruitful time for narratives "distinguished by a sociological purpose".[1] After decades of censorship (beginning in the 1930s) and of centring the particularities of Ireland and 'Irishness', fiction started to address taboo topics which especially the Roman Catholic Church wanted to keep concealed. Already in the 1980s, "there were signs that a desire to take a different perspective on Irish history and its current condition was beginning to take hold of the popular and political imagination".[2] Gerry Smyth identifies "new political, social and cultural languages"[3] which gave voice to the rapidly changing reality of Ireland in the 1990s. New fiction written by emerging literary voices became connected to a wider processing of social and historical issues when the "wounded, traumatised subject"[4] became a representative character, and suppressed minorities, such as homosexual people and (abused) women, and their often suffering bodies moved to the centre of attention in both fiction and the media.

Together with writers such as Patrick McCabe, Emma Donoghue, Anne Enright and Roddy Doyle, Colm Tóibín is one of the most prominent and innovative members of the group of "new Irish novelist[s] [who were] concerned to narrate the nation as it has been and is, rather than how it should be or might have been".[5] As such, Tóibín's *The Blackwater Lightship* is a (culturally) significant contribution not just to Irish literature but also to the debates that shaped public discourse in the nineties. Critics have labelled it "one of the cultural landmarks of Irish homosexuality in recent history"[6] and one of the "milestones in

Irish gay rights".[7] It features characters stemming almost exclusively from marginalised groups, and it was the first novel dealing with a homosexual man, Declan, suffering and dying from AIDS in Ireland.

Set off by the reality of Declan's transient body and his wish to spend time with his family/ies, the novel tells the individual stories of three generations. Declan's estranged family members have to resume their communication while being forced to come to terms with his impending death as well as with their prejudices and personal problems. Declan's body appears overly visible: It clearly displays its infection and lack of physiological functioning in the wake of AIDS, a syndrome that society in the 1980s and early 1990s ascribed a particular meaning to. As such, Declan's pathological body reveals frictions within the family, but it also stands between the poles of past and present, progress and stagnation. Thus, the engagement with the transience of this particular body and with the family, often regarded as a synecdoche of Ireland, leads to a reassessment of personal attitudes and opinions and simultaneously promotes an engagement with the nation's ongoing issues and contributes to a reassessment of its history/ies.

Tóibín's novel exemplifies that literary and cultural texts are not only "one of the means by which our societies generate their knowledges of self, society and the natural world"[8] but that they can also be regarded as agents in a complex network. In Tóibín's novel, the Irish narrative of modernisation, a tale also connected to the decriminalisation of homosexuality in a deeply conservative society, is interrelated with the cultural narrative of AIDS as well as with media and political narratives. Declan's case raises readers' awareness of AIDS and its effects; it forces them to see how Irish society and the Catholic Church tried to keep the homosexual community an invisible and deviant minority [9] by associating supposedly deviant behaviour with punishment by disease.

However, even though the narrative revolves around Declan and his serious medical condition, he remains impalpable, hazy and mostly silent. Therefore, despite all the positive reviews the novel received, Tóibín was criticised for not accrediting Declan with a strong voice.[10] However, I argue that Declan's lack of voice has a cultural significance and reason and is eventually linked to different notions and levels of transience. The interplay of voice and silence, a common technique in 1990s Irish writing,[11] brings to the fore what is left unsaid and how it is left unspoken. Declan's puzzling elusiveness and the simultaneous (over)representation of his transient body trigger readers' thorough engagement with the novel's topics and politics. By oscillating between notions of visibility and invisibility, voice and silence, and metaphoric and graphic depictions of decay and death, Tóibín renders homosexuality visible while simultaneously revealing and criticising the Irish code of silence.

2. Pathological States

Lois McNay's claim that "it is impossible to know the body outside of the meaning of its cultural significance"[12] proves to be entirely true when the body with AIDS is considered in the context of Irish society, culture and history. This body stands at the intersection of various discourses, and although it shines a light on different forces and struggles and seems to occupy a central position, it was rendered almost invisible in pre-1990s Ireland, where "a systematic control and repression of homosexuality through the law, medicine and religious doctrine had been the only visible cultural identity for gay men".[13] This context[14] explains the huge impact and political significance of *The Blackwater Lightship*, whose author "help[ed] transform public perceptions on homosexuality and the family"[15] when he foregrounded the transience of individual lives and societal structures.

Guillermo Severiche argues that AIDS, when expressed in language, becomes a discursive construction and a powerful cultural artefact. "[T]he idea that disease in literary discourse functions as a sociopolitical device"[16] ties in with the tradition of seeing the personal as the social body – an idea which also thrusts itself upon the reader of Tóibín's novel. In addition to affecting the body, the AIDS syndrome has for a long time also imposed various meanings on the person suffering from it. The cultural narratives of AIDS and cancer, a disease also crucial in the novel because Declan's and Helen's father died from it, are entirely different from one another. Especially during the first decades of its spread, AIDS was linked to shame, culpability and moral punishment, while the rhetoric of cancer was and still is characterised by terms such as 'courage', 'bravery' and 'fighting'. Thus, the "body with AIDS has been seen as the site of death and contagion, of prejudice and moral penalties",[17] and the once-lethal syndrome was also dreaded because of the social death it could effect.

In contrast to many other Western countries, which launched campaigns that simultaneously targeted people's fear and raised awareness of the importance of prevention, the Irish Catholic reaction was marked by "denial about the threat posed by AIDS"[18] and preached abstinence instead of informing the public about the protective functions provided by condoms, which were still mostly forbidden in Ireland. Both the state's and Church's role in the spread of HIV thus should not be underestimated: Sexual-health promotion was still largely prohibited, and the Church, having a huge influence on education, was unwilling "to initiate sex education in church-run schools".[19] Jennifer M. Jeffers exemplifies the Church's attitude by citing father Michael Kennedy's 1995 "'sin and damnation' sermon", which sanctified a "misogynistic heterosexuality".[20] Moreover, she also accuses the Catholic Church of having been directly interwoven in the spread of HIV in Ireland.[21] The rhetoric of sin ties in with the discursive connection of AIDS to specific 'risk groups',[22] which shaped public discourse in the 1980s especially, the decade associated with AIDS paranoia. Therefore, the majority displayed hostility for the potential bearers of a threatening disease "inscribed within a cultural discourse of stigma, sexual guilt, and punishment".[23] The highly problematic connection between AIDS and gay sexuality was deeply anchored in people's minds in all Western societies and thus was associated with homophobic beliefs, which "have for long damaged the self-image and dignity of homosexuals, many of them sharing personal histories of repression, secrecy, and self-hatred".[24] Well into the 1990s, it was still "commonly assumed that the body [was] contagious and that the causes of the illness were illicit. AIDS then [became] a cultural marker which [made] visible social codes that [were] usually hidden or repressed".[25] This also entailed a lack of "sympathy for [AIDS patients'] predicament and suffering"[26] because they had to "carry an additional burden of shame and rejection"[27] as soon as they were identified as a 'person with AIDS'.

Because of this then-prevalent focus, Tóibín's creation of a counterbalance is noteworthy: His thematisation of AIDS as a medical event just like any other is progressive[28] but simultaneously discloses that AIDS remains unspeakable in the 'real world' beyond the borders of the hospital. "Within a staunchly Catholic paradigm, little (if any) space remained for dissident voices; indeed, preserving a homogeneous, properly Catholic story meant criminalising homosexuality in Ireland until 1993".[29] The significance of Declan's lack of voice thus has to be understood in the context of the cultural narrative of AIDS in general and the unrepresentability of homosexual characters suffering from AIDS in pre–Celtic Tiger Irish society.

3. The Transient Body at the Centre of Attention

Tóibín's novel, set before the decriminalisation of homosexuality in 1993, spans a long weekend, and the events are set into motion when Declan demands to spend time at his grandmother's house in Cush, County Wexford, together with his family and friends. His grandmother, Dora, his mother, Lily, and his sister, Helen, make up his biological but estranged and dysfunctional middle-class family, who learn of his infection with HIV and, in Lily and Dora's case, of his homosexuality only once he is suffering from AIDS. Tóibín's political commentary and criticism is related from a point of view which a mainstream Irish readership can identify with: While the story is narrated by an apparently rather detached heterodiegetic voice, Helen, who is mostly open-minded despite being partially rooted in traditional thought structures, serves as the novel's focaliser. The novel's relevance is not diminished by this technique, which actually helps convey the "incomprehension that many gays have experienced"[30] as readers are confronted with the external reactions of other characters and with Helen's thoughts and ambivalent feelings, which might mirror their own.[31]

Declan's gay friends Paul and Larry, who are also well acquainted with his medical history and the needs of his body, form a caring and functional (family) unit and thus an alternative to Declan's dysfunctional biological family. This well-working model, which seems to depict the gay community as a better family, can be regarded as an attack on marriage and the traditional family,[32] the cornerstones of Irish society as defined in the Irish constitution. Moreover, this subtle move opens up the possibility of rethinking what counts as family beyond a patriarchal model,[33] and it opposes the homophobia still prevalent in the 1990s, which was interlinked with the "cultural imperative of preserving the Catholic ethos".[34]

In many respects, Declan's visible decline serves as the catalyst[35] within the plot and as a powerful reminder of HIV, AIDS and all their effects. While Declan does not speak much, his overly visible body speaks for him, thus becoming an active agent and gaining centre stage. The visibility of Declan's decaying body is reminiscent of the threat of death and disease but also of transience in general. However, especially upon the novel's first publication, it also forced readers to 'see' what had formerly been rendered mostly invisible by the Church and society. Jeffers, though rather critical of Tóibín's approach, pointedly states that "Declan is unpresentable because socially, culturally, and sexually the reader is not prepared to see him. It is difficult to 'represent' the unseen and the unexplored in our society and culture". [36] Thus, Declan's unrepresentability and the elusiveness of his character can be traced back to the silence, fear and disgust that Irish society displayed towards homosexuals, especially when their bodies bore the marks of AIDS.

Hence, Declan's personality is almost buried beneath the meaning that society projects onto his body. According to Eibhear Walshe, there is "no gay subjectivity beyond his bodily frailty", and the "narrative appears to render him the body upon which mortality, loss of bodily control and illness announces itself".[37] Generally, when the common opportunistic infections of AIDS make the disease and thus also the body's transience visible, [38] the patient is "burdened with excess corporeality",[39] which could lead to a symbolic social death. Hence, AIDS and the stigmatisation it effects seem to overwrite the subject's personality and identity.

When the embeddedness of Declan's fictional case in a wider cultural discourse is taken into account, Georges Canguilhem's discussion of René Leriche's conception of pathology provides crucial insights: "The state of health is a state of unawareness where the subject and his body are one. Conversely, the awareness of the body consists in a feeling of limits, threats, obstacles to health".[40] According to Leriche, health thus is "life lived in the silence of the organs",[41] which makes health a state of unawareness while "[d]isease reveals normal functions to us at the precise moment when it deprives us of their exercise".[42] Thereby, Leriche asserts that only a disturbed or interrupted function brings the inherent workings of a healthy body to the surface and reveals the transience not only of life but also of the state of health which can quickly be taken over by disease. This observation can be taken to an allegorical level once again: The sudden visibility of minoritised bodies, such as the (homosexual) body with AIDS, fuelled the rapid changes of the 1990s and revealed that structures and value systems are not fixed forever. The allegorical body of society, or the entire (heteronormative) population, could not remain in its state of wilful unawareness and was increasingly forced to acknowledge the lives of those relegated to its margins when these 'other' bodies revealed societal functionings and the lack thereof.

The (over)representation of Declan's body thus enables readers to see more, not less, as this technique shows that Irish society mostly was inclined to see the ill body and its negative connotations instead of the individual person. Due to the cultural narrative and the markers of AIDS, Declan cannot stop his body from communicating too much – therefore, he is hidden from view, which stresses the connection between voice and space. Declan's body tells its own story, but it does not betray much about his personal history. The reader never learns about Declan's lifestyle and is informed about a minor aspect of his life only when Paul states that Declan has often visited him and his husband in Brussels until two years earlier, when he became sick. In Brussels, Declan "checked out all [their] friends from the Catholic gay organisation" (174).

> [E]verybody fell for him – and he would bounce up and down with them for maybe two weekends, and then he'd arrive again and we'd know by something he did or said that he hadn't been returning So-and-so's calls, so we learned never to tell anyone he was coming. And then the whole routine would start again […]. (174-175)

Paul's story seems to support stereotypical ideas society held about homosexuality as a promiscuous and thus dangerous form of sexuality. Thus, it also appears to confirm Irish Catholic society's interpretation of sinful, promiscuous behaviour as the reason for Declan's illness. Drawing on the understanding of AIDS as a deserved punishment for the transgression of heterosexual norms and values, Tóibín here provokes a specific reaction, as exemplified by Jeffers: "Declan apparently valued neither abstinence nor fidelity,[43] and the reader is made to assume through Paul's narrative that Declan's reckless behaviour in Brussels led him to contract the AIDS virus".[44] However, Tóibín's narrative, thankfully, does not support the general idea of AIDS as punishment: In contrast to common reactions in the 1990s, none of the other characters reproaches or blames Declan when his dying body finally forces him to reveal both his sexuality and the illness. AIDS is thus not linked to moral faults, and Declan's past becomes irrelevant in the face of impending death.[45] While the odd, almost complete absence of an individual identity behind Declan's body indirectly shows how society perceived homosexual men suffering from AIDS, Tóibín also portrays a wished-for, progressive form of treatment. Declan's friends, his family and the consultant in hospital resist the temptation to draw on metaphorical language which could evoke interpretations of disease as punishment, but instead deal with Declan's opportunistic infections just like any other medical condition instead (see, for instance, 100), thus emptying the discourse from the rhetoric of punishment and shame.

4. Decay and Death

Generally speaking, the body plays a crucial role in the subject's psychical formation; it is the "central object over and through which relations of power and resistance are played out".[46] People who are visibly ill or display their Otherness are metaphorically and physically confined to the margins of society. Therefore, homosexuals, considered 'deviant' people, were pushed to the 'uninhabitable' zones of social life[47] and thus for a long time were hardly visible in mainstream Irish discourse. With AIDS, this practice became even more rigid as infected people were considered the ultimate 'other', and gay men especially were "relegated to a space of non-identity".[48] Tóibín's novel, in contrast, centres on these 'other' bodies that do not fit Irish conceptions of 'normal'. At the same time, the author points to the discrimination against them by using a highly symbolical setting which alludes to the sick body being understood as abject. Declan's suffering body tells a story of marginalisation, but it does so only in his grandmother's remote house, which is located close to an eroding coastline and which stands between past and present. Declan's condition as well as his puzzling and telling lack of voice must be assessed in terms of the symbolic connotations of this specific space, because this interplay discloses the multiple levels of transience addressed in Tóibín's novel: of the body but also of society's traditional structures and mindsets.

Dora's house has been a crucial place for all family members' personal histories, but now it is, despite some renovations, in a general condition of decay (see 55-56). The setting evokes the idea that Declan has to reside at a place where he is at or even beyond the boundaries of society – as soon as his body betrays his then-lethal infection, Declan seems to cross the boundary between life and death.

Furthermore, the house is threatened by the erosion of the nearby cliffs, which remind Helen of death and of the destruction of apocalyptic scope she imagined when she was younger (see 103-104, 216). Facing nature's sublime power, she arrives at the insight that individual persons do not count on a larger scale because of their lives' inevitable transience, which again points to Declan: The fact that he is not graspable as an individual does not diminish the value of the narrative for a whole group of underrepresented people. Helen knows that the world will persist after his death, but it will be changed, just like the place in Cush: The erosion will take something away, but it will not be the end of the world and could eventually include renewal.

But as a new order is yet to come, Declan is still hidden from (the neighbours') view.[49] If Declan is heard, he is often invisible (in his room, crying out), or he is seen but hardly talks. In the house, everything revolves around his body when Declan's friends and family observe the steady deterioration of his condition (see 33, 205). A bruise on his face renders AIDS increasingly visible and forcefully reminds everyone of the transience of health or even relative well-being. This heightened visibility, which symbolises the continuing decline of his body, is accompanied by Declan's partial loss of eyesight and his increasing silence, which opens up a space for readers' pondering on the general suffering experienced by AIDS patients. Eventually, in the face of pain, the loss of self-control and of independence, Declan's tone becomes "abject, childlike, desperate" and his powerlessness is underlined by one of his last sentences in the novel: "Mammy, Mammy, help me, Mammy" (258).

5. Counter-Narratives

While Declan, due to his homosexuality plus the manifestation of death and disease on his body, might still have been unrepresentable in a conservative and repressive society, "Declan's friends [...] express the previously silenced experiences of homosexuals in the Republic. Hence homosexual prejudices are challenged by their personal accounts and family struggles"[50] when they are granted a voice. In regard to Adam Jaworski's observation that many "aspects of the oppressive role of silence in politics can be related to the societal silencing of dominated groups",[51] Larry's and Paul's stories, which function as personal counter-narratives to mainstream family life and discourse and bear witness to marginalisation, are highly significant and raise hope for change.

Larry's coming-out story exemplifies this approach. Before the decriminalisation of homosexuality, he was involved in a gay group in Dublin that was invited to the official residence of Mary Robinson, the first female Irish president, elected in 1990. There he was surprised by the presence of radio and television teams. Panicking at the thought that his parents might see him on the news, he drove to his hometown, Tullamore:

> You see, no one at home knew. [...] I just blurted out, 'You're not to watch the six o'clock news' [...]. I realised that maybe I could tell my mother, but I certainly couldn't tell [my father]. [...] He went into the kitchen, but I still couldn't say anything and suddenly my mother looked at me and said: 'Are you after joining the IRA?' I couldn't believe it. [...] And then I told her. [...] She said that I would always be her son no matter what I did, but I was to [...] go back to Dublin and she would deal with my father [...]. She was all pale and worried-looking. I think she would have been happier if I had been in the IRA. (145-147)

Larry's story, and especially his comparison of homosexuality to joining the IRA, alludes to the high level of secrecy wrapped around homosexuality. The family, the allegedly fundamental unit of society, becomes a space of silence and of fear of rejection[52] for a person who does not conform to the norm because of something commonly evaluated in terms of deviant bodily practices. Besides, his family's inability to talk about 'taboo subjects' (see 146) mirrors Dora and Lily's "incompetence in talking about sexuality"[53] (see 141).

Religious discourse is again evoked when Larry starts talking about his parents' "nice normal" (147) neighbours, a religious family. He is with "[t]heir youngest son [...] at the moment" but has "been with the other three [...] sons. Two of them are married, but that doesn't seem to stop them" (147). Larry's words "[crumble] the façade of heterosexual

Ireland and show [...] same-sex desire as being more common than is generally believed"[54] but simultaneously reveal that it has to remain hidden. Dora's reaction to this aspect of Larry's story is as revealing as Larry's words are; she considers it blasphemous and apparently more shocking than his reference to the IRA. As José Carregal-Romero aptly summarises, her "perplexity and disconcert illustrate a long Irish tradition of silence and shame surrounding sexual transgressions and same-sex desire".[55]

In addition, Tóibín highlights homosexuals' relegation to the shadows with a symbolic setting: Larry relates his experience while sitting in the darkened kitchen and deliberately comments on it by saying that "it's easier to talk like this in the dark" (147). Furthermore, the idea of sinful behaviour, which was especially prevalent before the Celtic Tiger years' more progressive atmosphere, is evoked once more when Larry says that "it's like going to Confession" (147), even though he does not atone for anything. When Lily enters the room and turns on the light, the conversation immediately stops; Dora draws the curtains and Helen wishes for Lily to turn off the light again. The notion of light and darkness thus frames Larry's narrative about 'deviant' behaviour and bodies.

While Larry's as well as Paul's life stories are granted more space, Declan grows ever more silent. When Declan is about to go back to hospital, his presence and visible physical transience determine the atmosphere.

> Declan did not speak, and paid no attention to any of them. [...] They busied themselves passing food, alert all the time of Declan's brooding presence. [...] '[...] leave me alone,' he said without looking up. [...] [N]o one could think of anything to say, and a strange embarrassed sadness descended on the company. [...] Declan held Larry's hand for a moment [...], but he did not turn to look at him, and did not say anything. (249-251)

This passage again centres perceptions, and while Declan hardly speaks, his corporeality communicates. Even though the course of the story leaves no doubt of his fast-approaching death, the increasing realisation of his mortality and transience unites the two family units. Despite the arguments and rejection which characterised the relationship between Lily and Paul, they eventually cooperate and accept the role each plays in Declan's life.[56] Similarly, Declan's biological family members eventually try to come to terms with their past in order to be able to transition into a better future. With this symbolic microcosm, which stands for a changing society, Tóibín thus "reframes heterosexist and homophobic notions of family and community, promoting an ethics of inclusion in the face of a long history of repudiation, silence, and intolerance towards gay men".[57]

With its various (counter-)narratives, the novel thus mirrors a societal and cultural movement in Ireland whose debates on divorce, contraception and the decriminalisation of homosexuality were increasingly held publicly. Marginalised "[g]roups and individuals [...] contributed to the debates which revolved around the body, whilst at times also initiating those debates".[58] The concerns of the people, the debates and the problems as well as the wish for change were inscribed in the non-normative body and eventually discussed through its representation in public. The silence which enwrapped these bodies slowly broke away, also due to the space it conquered in the media.[59]

6. Conclusion: Cultural Work and Non-Transient Effects

Tóibín's *The Blackwater Lightship* comments on the gay male body's "history of invisibility, erasure and criminality"[60] and severs the link between disease and shame. By making the character Declan hardly graspable, by foregrounding his stigmatised body and by relegating it to a remote space, Tóibín holds up a mirror to society, disclosing that homosexuals with AIDS were regarded only in terms of their bodies while their personalities and voices were almost entirely banned from mainstream discourse before the decriminalisation of homosexuality in 1993. These people's position at the margins of society was determined by the threat they seemed to constitute to the body of the population when AIDS, highlighting their transience, rendered them 'walking dead'. Tóibín's novel does not support the reliance on religious instead of medical discourse or the understanding of AIDS as a punishment for sinful behaviour prevalent in the 1980s and early 1990s. On the one hand, the narrative depicts transience and bodily processes, such as general weakness or specific medical issues such as diarrhoea, as part and parcel of everyone's bodily reality. On the other hand, Declan's "excess corporeality"[61] and lack of voice are highlighted by the other marginalised characters' strength and their unique voices. For instance,

Larry relates a personal story which is, due to its references to political figures and historical facts,[62] also anchored in Irish readers' very own reality. His story thus reveals that narrating the nation as it is also means including minoritised groups. It discloses how "Irish narrative also participates in the construction of a modern, more cosmopolitan, and more connected Ireland through the inclusion and active appearance of gay characters".[63]

Tóibín thereby paints the picture of a society which starts to open up by hesitantly including new voices in its discourses. Jeffers states that the "social and political context of the '90s contrasts with the stereotype of Ireland. Economics, politics, sexual preference, and lifestyle choices in Ireland in the 1990s are a reflection of a greater European and global awareness",[64] but the unearthing of various scandals in the 1990s, such as the abuse scandals of the Catholic Church, reveals that it still had to come to terms with its past. The increasing visibility, or audibility, of narratives similar to those in *The Blackwater Lightship*, their emergence from an eroding, conservative society's cracks and fissures, symbolises a crucial step forward.

This idea is also manifest in the novel's multilayered images. Space and voice are essentially intertwined when visibility is linked to the (in)ability to speak and to be heard. Tóibín thus foregrounds the unseen by making it almost entirely unheard. The subtlety of the narrative and its centre, which can be glimpsed at times but then repeatedly passes from view again, demands the reader's engagement because there is so much to unearth that layers have to be peeled away just to find more layers – this is how writing about both personal and national trauma can work. The symbolic setting at the eroding coast and in the decaying house points to loss, and even though the narrative seems to foreground personal issues, it eventually alludes to the problems of the Republic of Ireland as a whole, which engenders the engagement with its past and future. The novel highlights the transience of all things: The connections established between Declan's suffering body and the transience of categorisations and of discriminatory practices provide glimpses of hope and renewal. For example, the erosion can be read as a symbolic dissolving of formerly rigid social boundaries, and in a highly metaphorical act, Dora's house will eventually be modernised, which will require tearing down some of the old walls.

With *The Blackwater Lightship*, "Tóibín [achieved] a cultural centrality for the discourse of AIDS, almost single-handedly, in Irish fiction".[65] Its status as a forerunner becomes even more obvious in retrospect. Dora is convinced that "it will always be" difficult for homosexual men (142), and Terry Eagleton calls Paul's marriage an "extravagant utopian fantasy".[66] However, in 2015, Ireland became the first country to approve gay marriage by a referendum. Moreover, a campaign of the group in favour of gay marriage used personal testimonies not dissimilar to the fictional ones featured in *The Blackwater Lightship*. As Carregal-Romero correctly stresses, "with its inclusion of gay characters telling their life stories, Tóibín's widely read and progressive novel foreshadows the cultural climate surrounding the same-sex marriage referendum".[67] Hence, in this particular framework, Tóibín's subtle and groundbreaking narrative revolving around the body with AIDS, which highlights marginalisation, abjection and transience, also contributed to an engagement with Ireland as a nation that has been labelled 'traumatised'. As part of new Irish fiction, the novel has thus strongly contributed to a new awareness and tangible, hopefully non-transient effects.

Notes

[1] Patten, Eve (2006). "Contemporary Irish Fiction." *The Cambridge Companion to the Irish Novel.* Ed. John Wilson Foster. Cambridge: Cambridge University Press, 259-275, 259.

[2] Smyth, Gerry (1997). *The Novel and the Nation: Studies in the New Irish Fiction*. London: Pluto, 4.

[3] *Ibid.*

[4] Harte, Liam (2009). "'Tomorrow We Will Change Our Names, Invent Ourselves Again': Irish Fiction and Autobiography since 1990." *Irish Literature since 1990: Diverse Voices*. Eds. Scott Brewster and Michael Parker. Manchester: Manchester University Press, 201-215, 207.

[5] *Ibid.*, 177.

[6] Carregal-Romero, José (2016). "The Cultural Narratives of AIDS, Gay Sexuality, and Family in Colm Tóibín's *The Blackwater Lightship*." *Papers on Language and Literature* 52.4, 350-373, 352.

[7] Walshe, Eibhear (2015). "10 Milestones in Irish Gay Rights." *The Irish Times* 16 May 2015: n. pag. <https://www.irishtimes.com/news/social-affairs/10-milestones-in-irish-gay-rights-1.2214151>.

[8] Middleton, Peter, qtd. in Magennis, Caroline (2010). *Sons of Ulster: Masculinities in the Contemporary Northern Irish Novel*. Reimagining Ireland 26. Bern: Peter Lang, 2.

[9] Nolan, Ann (2018). "The Gay Community Response to the Emergence of AIDS in Ireland: Activism, Covert Policy, and the Significance of an 'Invisible Minority.'" *The Journal of Policy History* 30.1, 105-127.

[10] For instance, Terry Eagleton states that Declan is sacrificed and that "one could also read the novel as sidelining gay sexuality". See Eagleton, Terry (1999). "Mothering." *London Review of Books* 21.20. 14 October 1999. n. pag. Web. 11 March 2017. <https://www.lrb.co.uk/v21/n20/terry-eagleton/mothering>. Jennifer Jeffers believes that Declan is punished for irresponsible behaviour and that his body is unrepresented by Tóibín's words and thus excluded from the narrative. Jeffers, Jennifer (2002). *The Irish Novel at the End of the Twentieth Century: Gender, Bodies, and Power*. New York: Palgrave, 119-120. Other critics, such as Eibhear Walshe, instead focus on the lack of identity and of "contemporary Irish gay subjectivity" (qtd. in Carregal-Romero (2016), 368-369). In contrast, José Carregal-Romero believes that "Declan's 'de-sexualisation' does not necessarily translate itself into the erasure of his gay subjectivity" (369). His assertion that Declan has "his own voice" (369) shows that opinions differ on Tóibín's presentation of his central character and on the politics of this portrayal.

[11] Notions of voice and silence (or speechlessness) are prevalent in Irish fiction of that time. For example, there are Roddy Doyle's *The Woman Who Walked into Doors* (for a detailed discussion of the novel's techniques and politics, see Boller, Alessandra (2017). "Women, Violence, and Silence: Roddy Doyle's *The Woman Who Walked into Doors*." *Silence in Modern Irish Literature*. Ed. Michael McAteer. Leiden: Brill, 122-132), Patrick McCabe's *The Butcher Boy* and Emma Donoghue's *The Hood*, which also foregrounds the 'vow of silence' homosexual people were forced to take before 1993.

[12] McNay, Lois (1992). *Foucault and Feminism: Power, Gender and the Self*. Cambridge: Polity Press, 38.

[13] Walshe, qtd. in Carregal-Romero (2016), 361.

[14] Eagleton states that through its setting in Ireland, the story "gains an additional resonance. [Its] suburban goings-on [...] raise questions of tradition and modernity, of pure-hearted rural Gaeldom v. decadent urban gayness, which touch the nerve of a nation increasingly divided between the Treaty of Rome and the Bishop of Rome, between secular modernity and a still powerful church." (Eagleton (1999), n. pag.)

[15] Carregal-Romero (2016), 361.

[16] Severiche, Guillermo (2017). "The Political Embodiment of AIDS: Between Individual and Social Bodies in Colm Tóibín's *The Story of the Night* and *The*

Blackwater Lightship." *Estudios Irlandeses* 12, 115-128, 117. In this regard, Severiche follows Lina Meruane's study *Viral Voyages: Tracing AIDS in Latin America* in his argumentation. See Meruane, Lina (2014). *Viral Voyages: Tracing AIDS in Latin America.* Trans. Andrea Rosenberg. New York: Palgrave.

[17] Murphy, Julian S. (1992). "The Body with AIDS: A Post-Structuralist Approach." *The Body in Medical Thought and Practice.* Ed. Drew Leder. Dordrecht: Kluwer Academic Publishers, 155-178, 157.

[18] Nolan (2018), 113.

[19] Jeffers (2002), 115.

[20] *Ibid.*

[21] Jeffers refers to the unveiling of various child abuse scandals in the 1980s and 1990s. In addition, many priests' frequent homosexual encounters also came to light at that time; see *ibid.*

[22] A media campaign in the 1980s in Australia, for example, produced a fear of contagion in the general population when it associated the figure of the Grim Reaper with risk groups it deliberately named, thereby making members of such groups social pariahs.

[23] Carregal-Romero (2016), 371.

[24] *Ibid.*

[25] Murphy, Julian S. (1992), 160. There are various films, novels and short stories dealing with AIDS as a threat to social life. *Philadelphia*, *The Hours* or *The Line of Beauty* are among the most famous examples.

[26] Carregal-Romero (2016), 357.

[27] *Ibid.*, 371.

[28] See *ibid.*, 361.

[29] Murphy, Robinson (2009). "The Politics of Rebirth in Colm Tóibín's 'Three Friends' and 'A Long Winter.'" *Irish Studies Review* 17.4, 485-498, 485.

[30] Carregal-Romero (2016), 360.

[31] Moreover, Eagleton stresses that the novel's "matter-of-fact portrayal of Declan's physical decay intensifies the horror of it without being contrivedly clinical [...]. The novel shows us discreetly what a practical, complicated matter dying is, how much logistics and paraphernalia it requires, and its unflinchingly exact style is a kind of respect paid to this" (Eagleton (1999), n. pag.).

[32] Various passages in the Irish constitution (1937) elaborate on the rights of families and tell of conservative gender roles and the influence effected by the Catholic Church: for instance, it defines the family as "the necessary basis of social order and as indispensable to the welfare of the Nation and the State" and defines the home as the proper place for women, claiming that the state has to protect "the institution of Marriage, on which the Family is founded" (Constitution of Ireland. Article 41 §2-3.1. Web. 14 March 2018.

<http://www.irishstatutebook.ie/eli/cons/en/html>). See also Carregal-Romero (2016), 354, for a short explanation of these cornerstones in the light of Catholicism.

[33] The almost complete absence of heterosexual men from the narrative is noteworthy. While Eagleton (1999) regards the banishment of Helen's husband, Hugh, and her children from the narrative as a flaw, such a 'removal' actually ties in with the centring of the margins by offering a counterpoint to a large proportion of Irish fiction in which the mothers are missing or silent (see Patten (2006), 270) while the fathers dominate the centre.

[34] Carregal-Romero (2016), 354.

[35] Nolan emphasises that "AIDS became a catalyst for rapid change across political, social, and cultural spheres" (Nolan (2018), 106). This aspect again points towards an allegorical reading.

[36] Jeffers (2002), 119.

[37] Walshe, Eibhear (2008). "'This Particular Genie': The Elusive Gay Male Body in Tóibín's Novels." *Reading Colm Tóibín.* Ed. Paul Delany. Dublin: Liffey Press, 115-130, 121.

[38] See Tóibín, Colm (2004). *The Blackwater Lightship.* New York: Scribner, 253 for various examples. Further references to this edition will be included in the text.

[39] Corber, John (2003). "Nationalizing the Gay Body: AIDS and Sentimental Pedagogy in *Philadelphia.*" *American Literary History* 15. 1, 107-133, 127.

[40] Canguilhem, Georges (1989). *The Normal and the Pathological.* New York: Zone Books, 92.

[41] Qtd. in *ibid.*, 91.

[42] *Ibid.*, 101.

[43] The Catholic Church preached abstinence or, for married couples, fidelity to remain healthy and to abstain from sinful behaviour. By implying that Declan could have contracted HIV from one of the members of Paul's Catholic gay organisation, the novel comments on the Church's hypocrisy, which was revealed by the above-mentioned scandals.

[44] Jeffers (2002), 114.

[45] See Carregal-Romero (2016), 369.

[46] Grosz, Elizabeth (1990). "The Body of Signification." *Abjection, Melancholia and Love.* Eds. John Fletcher and Andrew Benjamin. London: Routledge, 80-103, 81. This idea is stressed further by R. W. Connell's concept of body-reflexive practices which emphasise the central and active role of bodily experiences in human self-understanding. Connell, R. W. (2005). *Masculinities.* 2nd edition. Cambridge: Polity Press, 53.

[47] See Butler, Judith (1993). *Bodies That Matter: On the Discursive Limits of "Sex."* New York: Routledge, 3.

[48] Corber (2003), 109.

[49] The neighbours, however, briefly spot Declan and later talk to Helen and Lily, commenting on Declan's looks and hinting at their speculations about his sexual orientation. When they "realize that they had said too much too quickly" (Tóibín 246), the embarrassment is covered up by a more innocuous topic, but Helen stops talking to them altogether, which again points towards the interconnection of marginalisation and silence.

[50] Carregal-Romero (2016), 350.

[51] Jaworski (1993), 118.

[52] See Carregal-Romero (2016), 355.

[53] *Ibid.*, 362.

[54] See Carregal-Romero (2016), 365.

[55] *Ibid.*, 366.

[56] Eagleton emphasises that Dora, Helen and Lily, the latter two disunited by the death of Helen's father, "move edgily together over the body of Helen's brother Declan" (Eagleton (1999), n. pag.). This statement is reminiscent of the idiomatic expression 'over my dead body' and again alludes to the observation that Declan's body is marked by death and highlights transience.

[57] Carregal-Romero (2016), 359.

[58] Quinn, Deirdre (2008). "'French Letters': The Space of the HIV Body in Irish Television Broadcasting in the Mid-1980s." *Essays in Irish Literary Criticism: Themes of Gender, Sexuality, and Corporeality.* Eds. Deirdre Quinn and Sharon Tighe-Mooney. Lewiston: Edwin Mellen Press, 159-176, 164.

[59] Gay Byrne's *The Late Late Show*, which also features in Tóibín's novel, serves as a good example. See also Doyle O'Neill, Finola (2015). *The Gaybo Revolution: How Gay Byrne Challenged Irish Society*. Dublin: Orpen Press.

[60] Walshe (2008), 118.

[61] Corber (2003), 127.

[62] As Severiche points out, Larry refers to G.L.E.N (Gay and Lesbian Equality Network) and its invitation by Mary Robinson (2017), 123.

[63] Severiche (2017), 118.

[64] Jeffers (2002), 178.

[65] Walshe, qtd. in Carregal-Romero (2016), 350.

[66] Eagleton (1999), n. pag.

[67] Carregal-Romero (2016), 351.

Bibliography

Boller, Alessandra (2017). "Women, Violence, and Silence: Roddy Doyle's *The Woman Who Walked into Doors*." *Silence in Modern Irish Literature*. Ed. Michael McAteer. Leiden: Brill, 122-132.

Butler, Judith (1993). *Bodies That Matter: On the Discursive Limits of "Sex."* New York: Routledge.

Canguilhem, Georges (1989). *The Normal and the Pathological.* New York: Zone Books.

Carregal-Romero, José (2016). "The Cultural Narratives of AIDS, Gay Sexuality, and Family in Colm Tóibín's *The Blackwater Lightship.*" *Papers on Language and Literature* 52.4, 350-373.

Connell, R. W. (2005). *Masculinities.* 2nd edition. Cambridge: Polity Press.

Constitution of Ireland. Article 41 §2-3.1. Web. 14 March 2018. <http://www.irishstatutebook.ie/eli/cons/en/html>.

Corber, John (2003). "Nationalizing the Gay Body: AIDS and Sentimental Pedagogy in *Philadelphia.*" *American Literary History* 15.1, 107-133.

Doyle O'Neill, Finola (2015). *The Gaybo Revolution: How Gay Byrne Challenged Irish Society.* Dublin: Orpen Press.

Eagleton, Terry (1999). "Mothering." *London Review of Books* 21.20. 14 October 1999. n. pag. Web. 11 March 2017. <https://www.lrb.co.uk/v21/n20/terry-eagleton/mothering>.

Grosz, Elizabeth (1990). "The Body of Signification." *Abjection, Melancholia and Love.* Eds. John Fletcher and Andrew Benjamin. London: Routledge, 80-103.

Harte, Liam (2009). "'Tomorrow We Will Change Our Names, Invent Ourselves Again': Irish Fiction and Autobiography since 1990." *Irish Literature since 1990: Diverse Voices.* Eds. Scott Brewster and Michael Parker. Manchester: Manchester University Press, 258-271.

Jaworski, Adam (1993). *The Power of Silence: Social and Pragmatic Perspectives.* London: Sage.

Jeffers, Jennifer M. (2002). *The Irish Novel at the End of the Twentieth Century: Gender, Bodies, and Power.* New York: Palgrave.

Magennis, Caroline (2010). *Sons of Ulster: Masculinities in the Contemporary Northern Irish Novel.* Reimagining Ireland 26. Bern: Peter Lang.

McNay, Lois (1992). *Foucault and Feminism: Power, Gender and the Self.* Cambridge: Polity Press.

Meruane, Lina (2014). *Viral Voyages: Tracing AIDS in Latin America.* Trans. Andrea Rosenberg. New York: Palgrave.

Murphy, Julian S. (1992). "The Body with AIDS: A Post-Structuralist Approach." *The Body in Medical Thought and Practice.* Ed. Drew Leder. Dordrecht: Kluwer Academic Publishers, 155-178.

Murphy, Robinson (2009). "The Politics of Rebirth in Colm Tóibín's 'Three Friends' and 'A Long Winter.'" *Irish Studies Review* 17.4, 485-498.

Nolan, Ann (2018). "The Gay Community Response to the Emergence of AIDS in Ireland: Activism, Covert Policy, and the Significance of an 'Invisible Minority.'" *The Journal of Policy History* 30.1, 105-127.

Patten, Eve (2006). "Contemporary Irish Fiction." *The Cambridge Companion to the Irish Novel.* Ed. John Wilson Foster. Cambridge: Cambridge University Press, 259-275.

Quinn, Deirdre (2008). "'French Letters': The Space of the HIV Body in Irish Television Broadcasting in the Mid-1980s." *Essays in Irish Literary Criticism: Themes of Gender, Sexuality, and Corporeality.* Eds. Deirdre Quinn and Sharon Tighe-Mooney. Lewiston: Edwin Mellen Press, 159-176.

Severiche, Guillermo (2017). "The Political Embodiment of AIDS: Between Individual and Social Bodies in Colm Tóibín's *The Story of the Night* and *The Blackwater Lightship*." *Estudios Irlandeses* 12, 115-128.

Smyth, Gerry (1997). *The Novel and the Nation: Studies in the New Irish Fiction.* London: Pluto.

Tóibín, Colm (2004). *The Blackwater Lightship.* New York: Scribner.

Walshe, Eibhear (2008). "'This Particular Genie': The Elusive Gay Male Body in Tóibín's Novels." *Reading Colm Tóibín.* Ed. Paul Delany. Dublin: Liffey Press, 115-130.

--- (2015). "10 Milestones in Irish Gay Rights." *The Irish Times* 16 May 2015. n. pag. Web. 11 March 2018. <https://www.irishtimes.com/news/social-affairs/10-milestones-in-irish-gay-rights-1.2214151>.

Christoph Singer (Paderborn)

The Body Suspended in Time: Transience and Memory in the Work of Elizabeth Bishop and Leah Kaminsky

1. Introduction

To wait, etymologically speaking, is closely linked to suffering. This idea of suffering time lies at the root of the word 'patient'. 'Patience' and 'patient' both derive from the Latin 'pati' which means 'to suffer'.[1] Yet to express this temporal embodiment and the related experience of transience is a different thing altogether. The waiting room is an interesting setting that allows the intersections of space, time and well-being, as this is a place where, as Laura Tanner argues, "we are immobilized *in* and *as* our bodies".[2] In this intermediary and liminal space, the experience of transience, I would like to argue, is foregrounded.

In this paper I will compare two literary texts that attempt to make sense of the experience of transience. First, I will discuss Elizabeth Bishop's modernist poem "In the Waiting Room";[3] second, I will offer a comparative perspective in the form of an analysis of Leah Kaminsky's novel *The Waiting Room*.[4] Both texts share a number of themes. Most notably, they depict their female protagonists as dealing with their transient bodies and their perceived sense of being stuck in a certain space and time. What further connects both is their preoccupation with (embodied) memories as an essential part of their quest, aimed at making sense of their selves and identities. A comparison of both texts may be rewarding in their perception of the waiting room from two oppositional perspectives: The lyrical I of Bishop's poem, the six-year-old Elizabeth, faces an identity crisis while waiting for her aunt Consuela in a dentist's waiting room. The narrator of Kaminsky's novel, on the other hand, is a general practitioner herself, responsible for a small medical practice in Tel Aviv. Both characters, despite their differences in age and agency, are stuck in a transient state, a state that undermines any linear perception of time. Past, present and future constantly merge and become as transient as the bodies of the prepubescent girl in Bishop's poem and the pregnant doctor in Kaminsky's novel. After a short discussion of the waiting room as a place of warped temporalities, I will proceed with a comparison of both texts. Waiting and its spatial expressions and manifestations, I would like to claim, allow for an interesting focus on the experience of time while in a state of perceived transience. As such, the experience of transience manifests itself in a foregrounding and closer scrutiny of one's embodied identity.

2. Surveying the Waiting Room

The medical waiting room is essential to any health care system, yet it is mostly overlooked when it comes to scholarly discussion and academic scrutiny. Sociologist Gary Clapton, for example, argues that the

> waiting rooms and areas of general practice (GP) health facilities are places that nearly all of us will find ourselves in but the waiting experience is under-explored. What happens to our sense of self when we move between the outside world where we are citizens and these spaces where we become patients?[5]

Considering the impact of critical studies on the effect of institutions – think of Michel Foucault or Erwin Goffman – the disregard for the waiting room as a space is all the more surprising. After all, the waiting room is the antechamber of any kind of institution, be it an institution of business, of bureaucracy, or of health care. It is here where we find individuals who experience transience in its purest sense.

As a spatial remnant of the triage system, the medical waiting room was intended to quickly survey those in need and to sort them into groups, depending on the urgency of their respective needs. According to Iain Robertson-Steel, one of the earliest uses of the word was "originally applied to a process of sorting, probably around 1792, by Baron Dominique Jean Larrey, Surgeon in Chief to Napoleon's Imperial Guard".[6] This distribution of those who wait into different subgroups is reminiscent of waiting rooms in general. Waiting rooms highlight hegemonic temporalities by assigning a specific status to those in waiting: the 'sick', the 'unemployed', the 'stateless', depending on what they 'lack' and what kind of support they require. In this regard, Billy Ehn and Orvar Löfgren mention the power of administrations, quoting Walter Benjamin's argument that the "more life is regulated by administration, the more people will have to learn to wait".[7]

Whenever the seemingly predetermined course of quotidian life is interrupted by tragedy, failure or accidents, the most important spaces of waiting become manifest. Anna Secor argues that the resulting stories of waiting "provide a critical insight into the everyday sociospatial constitution of power – not despite but because of their banality".[8] To qualify Secor's statement, one should probably speak rather of a perceived banality, because what lies beneath these superficially mundane experiences can be quite existential for those in waiting.

While a waiting room may be able to provide a sense of community, more often than not it leaves the waiting subject alone, disoriented and dependent. In this regard, Leslie Rittenmeyer, Dolores Huffman and Chris Godfrey come to a rather damning description of waiting in the health care system. They argue that

> waiting is a fearful, turbulent experience and one in which the healthcare system affords patients, families and/or significant others little opportunity to have the power to influence time and outcomes. [...] For those who work in healthcare waiting is part of the culture, and is considered routine and normalized. For those who must wait the waiting is personal, fearful, and sometimes tortuous.[9]

As insightful their study may be from the perspectives of those in waiting, such a statement also articulates a dichotomy that may be discernible in health care systems that are running over capacity. Yet the problems at hand are often equally felt on the side of those that intend to help: administrative staff, nurses and doctors. The frustration and uncertainty, the agonizing sense of slowly passing time, the indeterminacy of the future, the frightful anticipations of what is to be expected, can lead to bouts of aggression from the people waiting. A psychological study conducted in Sweden, for example, reported that for nurses, "one of the psychologically toughest parts of their work was dealing with angry patients whose aggression mainly stemmed from their having had to wait".[10] The patients' aggression often results in insulting behaviour which "could include drastic, personal comments about their [the nurses] being ugly, fat, lazy, and so forth".[11]

Yet such a frustrating experience of time and space is not restricted to the ill, as Tanner argues: "the space of waiting casts even its healthy occupants outside the world of time and reference".[12] To illustrate this point, Tanner, a literary critic, refers to Jane Hamilton's novel *A Map of the World*,[13] where the narrator waits for days on end in a hospital in support of a friend whose child is in critical condition. The immobility and lack of productivity shapes her experience as follows:

> [I]n the lounge that had no windows, there was no signal to distinguish day from night [...]. Now and then, with the need to mark time, I listened for a change in the steady hum of the fluorescent lights [...]. Time and seasons were for others, for bankers and bus drivers, teachers and storekeepers. We would wait. We would wait, hour after hour in the subzero maroon-and-blue enclosure, with a rubber plant for oxygen.[14]

Another example that comes to mind when thinking about people who wait with others can be found in Raymond Carver's short story "A Small, Good Thing". The story follows a mother and father waiting for their eight-year-old boy to awake from a coma induced by a car accident.

Yet in spite of numerous examples, 'waiting room literature' is not a genre in and by itself. Literature, or narrative in a larger sense, always seems to have favoured the hero's journey over immobility and stasis. What happens, after all, when nothing happens? Everybody who has experienced the kind of uncertainty faced by a future that cannot be anticipated is acutely aware that in waiting, a lot happens. The predicate 'happens', however, is a misleading way to tackle the semantics of what is going on. Rather, one enters the realm of experience and embodiment. And this experience, in the words of Craig Jeffrey, can be perceived as a curse. As Jeffrey, who studies chronic and indefinite waiting, argues,

> But when people are catapulted out of their everyday lives, or when quotidian life radically alters for the worse, the sense of being caught up in a predictable and engaging set of activities that produce known forthcomings can break down and the present can come to weigh on the minds of the individual subject as a type of 'curse' or 'burden'.[15]

In a sense, waiting in the waiting room represents a particular kind of liminal stage. This is a situation that places the waiting subject quite literally in-between in spatial, temporal, and ontological terms. Spatially, the waiter is placed between the outside and the practitioner's room. Temporally, one is directed towards being admitted and treated. Ontologically speaking, if the nature and cause of one's ailments are uncertain, the prospective diagnosis can be a relief or terrifying. In that sense, Tanner is correct in her assessment that "the medical waiting room provides a space in which the seemingly 'immutable' categories [that is, the body as whole and incomplete, abled and disabled, normal and abnormal, functional and dysfunctional] are fraught, contested, or blurred".[16]

How can such a liminal experience in time and space be properly related? Is it possible to turn such an eventless state into a narrative? According to Tanner, the experience of a plotless state is essential to waiting in a waiting room:

> If the narrative of a life is structured around a series of experiences and activities that make up everyday existence, waiting represents the consumption of time without the creation of plot. In the waiting room, the force of time not only structures but to some extent constitutes experience, so that the temporal form of existence temporarily becomes its content.[17]

One helpful way, then, to productively reframe narrativity is provided by Monika Fludernik and her concept of experientiality. Fludernik states that traditionally, narrative comprehension "cardinally correlates with teleology, with the story producing or (being produced by) the stringencies of teleological design".[18] This is not to say that the experience and narration of illness precludes a teleological design; the opposite is true. The very telos placed implicitly or explicitly in illness narratives is the hope of attaining a state of well-being. However, such a process, as will be shown below, may be perceived as passive and eventless from the perspective of the ill subject. This feeling of passivity – that is, a sense of having hardly any influence on one's body and being overtly reliant on institutionalised help – may lead to the aforementioned perception of eventlessness.

Here Fludernik's concept of experientiality becomes helpful: "I had replaced the definition of narrativity as event sequence (traditionally based on the plot) with a conception of narrative that relies on representation *of*, and *by means of*, consciousness. In my model I defined narrativity as based on experientiality".[19] The key concept here is a shift from a narrative's temporarily, teleological and linear structure to a relation of how certain events are being individually perceived. In line with Fludernik's theory, the following (non-)literary texts are based on "conversational narratives in which the point of the story is not merely 'what happened', but especially what the experience meant to the narrator and what was the purpose of telling the story to the interlocutor".[20] Periods of waiting and of seeming inactivity may, however, be essential for the creation of a coherent and meaningful plot. For the psychologist Christine C. Kieffer, for example, the waiting room can be perceived as both: as a real space as well as a metaphorical expression of those periods of psychological treatment, when seemingly 'nothing happens' and no progress is being made. As Kieffer argues,

> Presentation of case material both at conferences and in journals tends to privilege the dramatic moment. In keeping with our operatic metaphor, we tend to wait impatiently for the arias and pay less attention to the background music from which it emerges—and which makes its own essential contribution to the aria's dramatic effect. In fact, rich exchanges such as the ones depicted were often interspersed with long periods (they could seem like an eternity!) in which I would be waiting in my consultation room for Carla to enter, which she finally would do, after a final crisp snap of a closing magazine. It should also be noted that the periods in which Carla defiantly sat in my waiting room were rich with connection and meaning for both of us.[21]

For Kieffer the moments of waiting allowed herself a time for reverie and introspection, while it allowed her client Clara to become active herself and to eventually transform stasis into a meaningful event. Strictly speaking in terms of narrative terminology, nothing happened, but regarding this moment of silence as meaningful rather than as suspended communication alerts us to the hidden layers of interstitial states, often regarded as waiting periods.

Thus, literature and narratives of the waiting room can help to illustrate these hidden layers and their meaning. Literature can also help to counter the idea of the body as an *epistemological deceiver*. Susan Bordo states that "Plato imagines the body as an *epistemological* deceiver, its unreliable senses and volatile passions continually tricking us into mistaking the transient and illusory for the permanent and real".[22]

It comes as no surprise, then, that literary texts that feature the theme of waiting or waiting rooms, medical or not, often translate this idea of transience from the story level to the discourse level. Joseph Conrad's *Heart of Darkness*, which places its protagonist and unreliable narrator in the company's waiting room – a theme echoed throughout the novel – is a case of early modernist deconstructions of linear time. William Earnest Henley's poem cycle *Hospital* begins with a poem called "Enter Hospital", which follows the lyrical I on his journey towards the hospital's dreary waiting room. What begins, formally speaking, as a classic Italian poem is quickly deconstructed in the cycle's second poem, called "Waiting". James Joyce's *Ulysses*, particularly the final Penelope episode, presents Molly Bloom's wait in the form of one uninterrupted internal monologue. Samuel Beckett's attempts at waiting 'plots' such as *Molloy*, *Malone Dies*, *Waiting for Godot* and *Endgame* took their associated genres to their respective breaking points. J. M. Coetzee's use of the present tense in *Waiting for the Barbarians* is as temporally disorienting as its employment in Joyce Carol Oates's short story "You". And W. G. Sebald's novel *Austerlitz*, to name one final example, does away in postmodernist fashion with any boundaries between fiction and reality. The different levels of narration, down to its lack of paragraphs, transform this Holocaust memoir in one uninterrupted stream of several kinds of consciousness. The novel's protagonist, Jacques Austerlitz, experiences one of his life's decisive moments in a waiting room, a place where memories, the present and the future merge into one:

> Memories like this came back to me in the disused Ladies' Waiting-Room of Liverpool Street Station, memories behind and within which many things much further back in the past seemed to lie, all interlocking like the labyrinthine vaults I saw in the dusty grey light, and which seemed to go on and on forever. In fact I felt, said Austerlitz, that the waiting-room where I stood as if dazzled contained all the hours of my past life, all the suppressed and extinguished fears and wishes I had ever entertained [...] and it covered the entire plane of time.[23]

3. Elizabeth Bishop's "In the Waiting Room"

Bishop's poem relates the experience of six-year-old Elizabeth, who is waiting in a dentist's waiting room for her aunt to return from the dentist. While waiting, triggered by a news report in a *National Geographic* magazine, she faces a short but acute identity crisis. Bishop's poem represents "the illusion of narrative clarity",[24] as Claire Bowen believes. Alicia Ostriker goes so far to argue that "In the Waiting Room" is a poem Bishop "waited a lifetime to write", and "in some sense, [the poet] has never left the room it describes".[25]

Bishop's poem single-handedly sets up and deconstructs a number of dichotomies: inside/outside, present/past, civilization/otherness, young/old, parts/whole. Hand in hand with this deconstruction of dichotomies, space, time and bodies in the poem are falling apart. As Catherine Cucinella contests,

> Bishop's "In the Waiting Room" clearly implicates the body in the process of becoming a gendered and active subject. However, the ontological crisis arises not only with the child's terror of "becoming a woman" and resolves not only with the power to call herself "Elizabeth." Rather, this moment of self-awareness occurs amid an overdetermination – an excess of the bodies, an awareness of those bodies, a moment of disembodiment, and finally, a return to the body.[26]

In the poem this 'embodied being' is very much concerned with bodies that are fragmented, grotesque and strange. This is illustrated by the photo story in *National Geographic*, the exotic content of which is focalised by the lyrical I as follows:

> A dead man slung on a pole
> "Long Pig," the caption said.
> Babies with pointed heads
> wound round and round with string;
> black, naked women with necks
> wound round and round with wire
> like the necks of light bulbs.
> Their breasts were horrifying. (lines 24-31)

Young Elizabeth's perception of these photos initially presents the African body as purely othered and savage. The cannibalism, strange babies, and black, naked women, with their 'horrifying breasts', evoke colonial texts like *Heart of Darkness*. Yet the dichotomy civilization/savagery is combined in the image of these 'savage' necks looking like 'civilised and domesticated' "light bulbs".

This negative perception of the body also affects those bodies that surround the lyrical I. The other waiters are only described in the form of synecdoches. They are reduced to

> shadowy gray knees,
> trousers and skirts and boots
> and different pairs of hands
> lying under the lamps. (lines 68-71)

This is reminiscent of Tanner's argument that "the waiting room emerges as a place in which 'the knowing body' fragments into a series of connected but ineffectual pieces".[27] A loss of control over the body and the self goes hand in hand with a rupture in the identity of the lyrical I. The lyrical I's moment of epiphany is reminiscent of the Lacanian mirror stage. Elizabeth realises in the waiting room that she is neither a whole being nor that she is in full control over her body. When she hears her aunt's scream from the dentist's office, she quickly realises that it "was me: my voice, in my mouth" (lines 46-47). This traumatic epiphany is located at the very centre of the poem: "But I felt: you are an I, / you are an Elizabeth, / you are one of them. / Why should you be one, too? / I scarcely dared to look / to see what it was I was" (lines 60-65).

This out-of-body experience unhinges the body's situatedness in space and time and the related subjective perspective. In Susan Bordo's words, "the only way for the mind to comprehend things as 'they really are' is by attainment of a dis-embodied view from nowhere".[28] Only in the last stanza, space and time, inside and outside, body and identity return to a stable, I-centred form:

> Then I was back in it.
> The War was on. Outside
> in Worcester, Massachusetts,
> were night and slush and cold,
> and it was still the fifth
> of February, 1918. (lines 94-99)

In a cyclical movement, the poem returns to its beginning. The precise mapping of space (Worcester, Massachusetts) and time (fifth of

February, 1918) echoes the beginning of a narrative with a clearly structured plot. I would like to claim that we encounter a narrative identity that collapses and has to reconstitute itself. We find the lyrical I depicted at the very moment of transience, between childhood and puberty, between a communal sense of self and identity, between past and present.

In the case of Bishop's poetry, one may be able to find meaningful connections between the poet's life and the expressions thereof. While I am still remiss to give in to an overtly biographical reading, it should be noted that Bishop suffered throughout most of her life from asthma, which brings Marilyn Lombardi to assume that "Bishop's imagination continually pursues the implications of her private battle for breath".[29] Bishop's constant fight for control over her own body, Lombardi argues, may be one of the reasons why her writing is so controlled and disciplined: "Her notebooks show just how closely she tended poetic control and a stoical and disciplined approach to discomfort. [...] Bishop published only ninety-five poems in her lifetime, each one a model of leanness and restraint".[30]

Again, such a biographical reading may be misplaced. Yet there is something to be said about the experience of being in the waiting room, a space that demands utmost control over one's thoughts, one's body and one's gaze. Waiting in such a place is certainly not a passive state; it is a performance of self-restraint, self-discipline and humility. As such, this is also a transitory state in epistemic terms, as Elizabeth proceeds from childhood's ignorance to a new sense of self and others. Humility in particular is a transitory state from ignorance to knowledge.

4. Leah Kaminsky's *The Waiting Room*

The themes introduced by Bishop are echoed in Leah Kaminsky's novel *The Waiting Room*, which begins with an epigraph taken from the final entry of Katherine Mansfield's journal: "We all fear when we are in waiting rooms. Yet we all must pass beyond them".[31] This fear and a sense of being stuck in a moment of transition lies at the heart of Kaminsky's novel and pertains not only to the novel's protagonist, Dina, a physician, but also to her clients. The idea of mental states and memory as a spatial construct is quite prevalent in the novel, as the following quotation illustrates:

> Dina's memory is filled with all sorts of other rooms too, her mind a kind of architectural haunted house, littered with icons of dusty cots, prams, toy rabbits, children's drawings, notebooks and vinyl records. Years of junk, piled high. Shelf upon shelf stacked with arguments, tears, lovemaking, music. (135)

The novel, set in Israel, is mostly related from the perspective of Dina. She is currently pregnant with her second child and struggles with her job, memories of her late mother, and the constant threat of terror in her new hometown, Tel Aviv. She finds herself at a point in her life where she feels stuck between a past she cannot let go, a present in a city she fears, and a future she is unable to anticipate. As a consequence, she is paralyzed by her experiences and hates the resulting self-image: "But more than that, she's sick of herself: the clichéd, cowering Diaspora Jew, always waiting for some catastrophe" (28). Dina is exasperated by her attempt to escape the overbearing influence of her late mother while retaining her mother's and her family's traumatic memories of the Holocaust. She perceives her grief like a physical pain:

> Her mother's presence is the phantom pain in a limb long gone. The loss is still so deep, so palpable. After her mother died, people offered platitudes like 'you have your whole life ahead of you' or 'your sorrow will ease with time'. (21)

Not only is her experience of this pain almost physical, she seems to be trapped in a transient state between past and present. The "platitudes" offered by the people around her, all of which are directed towards the future, do not manifest. Dina is as much stuck in a waiting room as are her clients. She is caught in the past, with visions of her mother's ghost haunting her while she is desperately searching for a new home. Her mother's anticipatory self is bound in a similar situation: "I know you are standing there, my daughter. You are hidden between the years that lie ahead, waiting for me to come, yet warning me not to leave. If I don't journey forward along these tracks, you will never be born. Then who will there be to tell my story?" (31). The waiting room that lends the novel its title is a space that is highly symbolic: "The tile in the centre of the waiting room has always been a little crooked, but last month it finally came loose, lifting up all the others around it. [...] According to Nilli, it is a Muslim custom to set one tile in the centre of a room slightly askew as a reminder of man's imperfection in the face of God" (61). Not only does the room represent man's imperfection and is as such already intended to humble the waiting subject's mind; on top of that, the waiting room is perceived largely as a passage and a space of transit, which by means of metonymical extension also defines the physician's job. The physician is the very instance that assigns – by means of diagnosis – a status to those in waiting; the physician is the one who helps the patients navigate this intermediate, transitory space and its peculiar temporalities. This change of status Katherine Young refers to as "realm-shift". In her study *Presence in the Flesh: The Body in Medicine* (1997) she argues that in the waiting room, "persons await realm-shift, and await too, the cues that tell them when to shift realms".[32] These cues are given by the related spaces and the staff at those spaces. In the novel, Dina's receptionist Yael has a clear understanding of the space she and Dina reside over: "Anyway, Yael thinks, a doctor's job description is rather like being purgatory's quack; the boatman who ferries people across to the other side, perched in a no-man's land, somewhere between the living and the dead. On the whole, she thinks, patients are idiots" (153).

Yet this job of assigning a status and of literally helping to change the patients' stories and narratives leads to an interesting contrast. Whereas the patients, as argued above, reside temporarily in a plotless and storyless state, those who are responsible for them have to carry the burden of these often unwritten stories. This is an experience the novel's protagonist increasingly struggles with. One example is that of a patient called Evgeni, who comes repeatedly to consult Dina, to no avail:

> When he first started coming to Dina she listened, held his hand, laughed at his jokes. She thought that she could make a difference in his life. But every visit is exactly the same. [...] They have been going around in circles for years now. Dina can recite the consultation word by word, and deliver her own lines, all the while thinking about what to make for dinner. (47)

Dina's mental absence during consultations leads to her frustration, and she fails to acknowledge that this ritualised meeting is more important to

Evgeni than the potential of a cure or of recuperation. In this situation she feels unable to further the patient's narrative, to transform a cyclical ritual into a linear story, with a beginning (illness), a middle (healing) and an end (health). Upon receiving a patient's test results, which confirm the diagnosis of cancer, she decides to withhold the news. She is literally unable to end the wait of her patient by telling her the dreadful news. Dina increasingly feels incapable of containing all of these narratives herself. She sees herself "becoming the doctor she never wanted to be – feels bloated with stories. They spill out from her onto the pavement as she walks down the street, and she seems to be losing pieces of herself along the way" (104).

This sense of fragmentation recalls Bishop's poem while expanding on the theme of impossible narration in the face of transient experiences. Dina perceives her psychological inability to contain and to deal with her patients' life stories in metaphorical terms that suggest a loss of physical control. Her body, she feels, is unable to hold what it contains, and it metaphorically gives birth to these narratives before they are ready to be born. Metaphorically, it is quite important that this perceived moment of lost control happens on the street, since the streets are the places that in Dina's memory of her hometown, Melbourne, are connected to traumatic silence and suppression: "Silence seemed to linger in the streets where Dina grew up. Melbourne was a city that absorbed the highest number of Holocaust survivors per capita after the war, outside of Israel" (111). In her quest to make sense of herself, the novel does provide her with an end that finally sees her leaving her self-imposed waiting room.

5. Conclusion

The idea of learning to wait, and more specifically of learning to wait in a specific space, to understand its rules, its norms, and the explicit and implicit requirements of this setting, is a powerful and recurring theme in the examples analysed above. In the waiting room, patients in their dependent state are forced to remain in a place of passage full of paradoxical elements. Here one waits alone, yet together with others. Here one is forced to remain as passive as possible, while – as we have seen in the texts discussed above – one experiences waiting as a highly active state. Here one may feel a certain loss of identity and loss of control, while the institution itself uses the waiting room to distribute and restructure according to certain physical as well as socioeconomic markers. The richer the patient or the more urgent the required help, the shorter the wait will be. I would like to end this analysis by quoting, in full, a poem by the late British poet Julia Darling, who, after a long fight against cancer, passed away in 2015.[33]

> Acute ears listen for
> the call of our names
> across the room of
> green chairs and walls.
> Our names, those dear consonants
> and syllables, that welcomed us
> when we began,
> before we learnt to wait.
> Call us to the double doors
> where the busy nurses go!
> Haven't we waited long enough?
> Haven't we waited beautifully?

Notes

[1] "patient, 1a." *Oxford English Dictionary*, June 2005, <http://www.oed.com/view/Entry/138820?rskey=HjJklp&result=1&isAdvanced=false#eid>. Accessed 30 July 2018.

[2] Tanner, Laura E. (2002). "Bodies in Waiting: Representations of Medical Waiting Rooms in Contemporary American Fiction." *American Literary History* 14.1, 115-130, 116, my emphasis.

[3] Bishop, Elizabeth (2008 [1976]). *Geography III: Poems*. New York: Farrar, Straus and Giroux, 3-8. Further references to this edition will be included in the text.

[4] Kaminsky, Leah (2015). *The Waiting Room*. New York: Harper Collins. Further references to this edition will be included in the text.

[5] Clapton, Gary (2018). "The General Practice Health Waiting Area in Images: Threshold, Borderland, and Place of Transition in the Sense of Self." *Forum: Qualitative Social Research* 19.1, 1-17, 2.

[6] Robertson-Steel, Iain (2006). "Evolution of Triage Systems." *Emergency Medical Journal* 23, 154-155, 154.

[7] Ehn, Billy, and Orvar Löfgren (2010). *The Secret World of Doing Nothing.* Berkeley: University of California Press, 35.
[8] Secor, Anna (2007). "Between Longing and Despair: State, Space and Subjectivity in Turkey." *Environment and Planning D: Society and Space* 25, 33-52, 42.
[9] Rittenmeyer, Leslie, Dolores Huffman and Chris Godfrey (2014). "The Experience of Patients, Families, and/or Significant Others of Waiting When Engaging with the Healthcare System: A Systematic Qualitative Review." *JBI Database Systematic Review Implement Reports* 12.8, 193-258, 218.
[10] Akerstrom, Malin (1997). "Waiting – A Source of Hostile Interaction in an Emergency Clinic." *Qualitative Health Research* 7.4, 504-520, 504.
[11] Akerstrom (1997), 509.
[12] Tanner (2002), 120.
[13] Hamilton, Jane (1999). *A Map of the World.* New York: Anchor Books.
[14] Tanner (2002), 122.
[15] Jeffrey, Craig (2008). "Waiting." *Society and Space* 26, 954-958, 955.
[16] Tanner (2002), 115.
[17] *Ibid.*, 123.
[18] Fludernik, Monika (2003). "Chronology, Time, Tense and Experientiality in Narrative." *Language and Literature* 12.2, 117-134, 120.
[19] *Ibid.*, 120. (Emphasis in the text).
[20] *Ibid.*
[21] Kieffer, Christine C. (2010). "The Waiting Room as Boundary." *JAPA* 59.2, 335-349, 340.
[22] Qtd. in Cucinella, Catherine (2010). *Poetics of the Body: Edna St. Vincent Millay, Elizabeth Bishop, Marilyn Chin, and Marilyn Hacker.* Houndmills Basingstoke: Palgrave, 18. (Emphasis in the text).
[23] Sebald, W. G. (2001). *Austerlitz.* London: Penguin, 193.
[24] Bowen, Claire (2008). "Frames of Reference: Paterson in 'In the Waiting Room.'" *Twentieth Century Literature* 54.4, 472-492, 484.
[25] Ostriker, Alicia Suskin (1986). *Stealing the Language: The Emergence of Women's Poetry in America.* Boston: Beacon, 72.
[26] Cucinella (2010), 59.
[27] Tanner (2002), 124.
[28] Qtd. in Cucinella (2010), 18.
[29] Lombardi, Marilyn May (1992). "The Closet of Breath: Elizabeth Bishop, Her Body and Her Art." *Twentieth Century Literature* 38.2, 152-175, 153.
[30] *Ibid.*, 162.
[31] Qtd. in Kaminsky (2015), n.p.
[32] Young, Katherine (1997). *Presence in the Flesh: The Body in Medicine.* Boston: Harvard University Press, 17.

[33] Darling, Julia (2015). "A Waiting Room in August." *The Guardian*. Web. 24 August 2015. <https://www.theguardian.com/books/2015/aug/24/the-saturday-poem-a-waiting-room-in-august>.

Bibliography

Akerstrom, Malin (1997). "Waiting – A Source of Hostile Interaction in an Emergency Clinic." *Qualitative Health Research* 7.4, 504-520.

Bishop, Elizabeth (2008 [1976]). "In the Waiting Room." *Geography III: Poems*. New York: Farrar, Straus and Giroux, 3-8.

Bowen, Claire (2008). "Frames of Reference: Paterson in 'In the Waiting Room.'" *Twentieth Century Literature* 54.4, 472-492.

Clapton, Gary (2018). "The General Practice Health Waiting Area in Images: Threshold, Borderland, and Place of Transition in the Sense of Self." *Forum: Qualitative Social Research* 19.1, 1-17.

Cucinella, Catherine (2010). *Poetics of the Body: Edna St. Vincent Millay, Elizabeth Bishop, Marilyn Chin, and Marilyn Hacker*. Houndmills Basingstoke: Palgrave.

Darling, Julia (2015). "A Waiting Room in August." *The Guardian*. Web. 24 August 2015. <https://www.theguardian.com/books/2015/aug/24/the-saturday-poem-a-waiting-room-in-august>.

Ehn, Billy, and Orvar Löfgren (2010). *The Secret World of Doing Nothing*. Berkeley: University of California Press.

Fludernik, Monika (2003). "Chronology, Time, Tense and Experientiality in Narrative." *Language and Literature* 12.2, 117-134.

Hamilton, Jane (1999). *A Map of the World*. New York: Anchor Books.

Jeffrey, Craig (2008). "Waiting." *Society and Space* 26, 954-958.

Kaminsky, Leah (2015). *The Waiting Room*. New York: Harper Collins.

Kieffer, Christine C. (2010). "The Waiting Room as Boundary." *JAPA* 59.2, 335-349.

Lombardi, Marilyn May (1992). "The Closet of Breath: Elizabeth Bishop, Her Body and Her Art." *Twentieth Century Literature* 38.2, 152-175.

Ostriker, Alicia Suskin (1986). *Stealing the Language: The Emergence of Women's Poetry in America*. Boston: Beacon.

"patient, 1a." *Oxford English Dictionary*, June 2005, <http://www.oed.com/view/Entry/138820?rskey=HjJklp&result=1&isAdvanced=false#eid>. Accessed 30 July 2018.

Rittenmeyer, Leslie, Dolores Huffman and Chris Godfrey (2014). "The Experience of Patients, Families, and/or Significant Others of Waiting When

Engaging with the Healthcare System: A Systematic Qualitative Review." *JBI Database Systematic Review Implement Reports* 12.8, 193-258.

Robertson-Steel, Iain (2006). "Evolution of Triage Systems." *Emergency Medical Journal* 23, 154-155.

Sebald, W. G. (2001). *Austerlitz*. London: Penguin.

Secor, Anna (2007). "Between Longing and Despair: State, Space and Subjectivity in Turkey." *Environment and Planning D: Society and Space* 25, 33-52.

Tanner, Laura E. (2002). "Bodies in Waiting: Representations of Medical Waiting Rooms in Contemporary American Fiction." *American Literary History* 14.1, 115-130.

Young, Katherine (1997). *Presence in the Flesh: The Body in Medicine*. Boston: Harvard University Press.

Elise Brault-Dreux (Valenciennes)

Who Cares for the Old? Old Age in Philip Larkin's Poems

1. Introduction

According to the *OED*, 'transience' is "the action or fact of soon passing away".[1] Passing away, which in common language euphemistically refers to dying, will here refer to an active process of living people in transit towards death. As the pace of time is objectively unchanged throughout one's existence, this end-of-life phase is, by nature, no more transient than earlier stages in life. It is the unknown yet absolutely inevitable event to which this phase leads that makes it singular, as well as the increasing vulnerability of the body at this stage. If time leaves no specific trace on the body, at old age its effects are visible as physical symptoms of frailty. Transience then becomes perceptible.

In her substantial and unprecedented study of ageing, *La Vieillesse* (1970), Simone de Beauvoir brings together old age and transience when she writes, "old age is not static; it is the full realisation and the extension of a process".[2] In other words, ageing *is* transience. For Vladimir Jankélévitch, old age is "a general entropy of time lived",[3] that is, a process of natural decay, decomposition, leading to a person's distinctive features disappearing. Though described differently, for both philosophers old age is a dynamic process that is wholly dependent on what precedes it: a linear process for de Beauvoir and a disorder for Jankélévitch.

In his poetry, Philip Larkin creates, sometimes quite transiently, images of deep old age, or the fourth age, of people incapacitated by their physical degradation. In other words, he makes visible people who are about to transgress into "the realm of invisibility"[4] and sketches "the corporeality of the ageing body".[5] But if old age is thus incarnated, it is generically so, in stock characters and by no specific, identified *persona*. Likewise, Larkin uses the word "old" without giving any age to determine what "old" means. He in fact relies on the collective

187

consciousness of his 1970s readers, or on what Chris Gilleard and Paul Higgs call "social imaginary"[6] – common images that come to mind when "old age" is mentioned: impotence, infirmity and corporeality and also, more simply, a "period in the chronology of a person".[7]

At a reasonably young age, Larkin declared that he "dread[ed] endless extinction".[8] With that in mind, I here want to examine the way he describes in his poetry, in a necessarily condensed and fleeting way, the transience of elderly bodies, which he seems to envisage at once as a linear process, like de Beauvoir, *and* as a chaotic one, like Jankélévitch. This form of *finite* transience can be analysed from different angles: biologically, poetically and socially.

The first part of the analysis will focus on Larkin's way of picturing old age as at once physical transience, paralysis, and a series of successive ruptures. I will then show how finite transience, still somewhat taboo in Western culture, is in fact "watched" in these poems – and "watch" here embraces seeing, comprehending and focalizing but also guarding, or even waking. Finally, I will address the question of care: How is biological and social transience cared for, both on the social and poetic levels? In other words, who cares for the old?

2. Old Age: Transience and Paralysis

The particularity of old bodies is the irretrievable process in which they are caught.[9] Unlike sick bodies that may be cured, old bodies cannot be made young again (or only deceptively so). And a body that cannot stand the test of time is a 'normal' body, however frail it may be. In other words, it is 'normal' to have a body that, because of old age, looks 'abnormal'. This is what de Beauvoir has called the "abnormal normality"[10] of old age.

Senescence, therefore, is a natural pathology,[11] a symptom more of mortality than of imminent death, for if the ageing body does give signs of upcoming extinction, it first and foremost signifies that it is alive, subject to time, and therefore mortal. In the late nineteenth century, the French doctor Jean-Martin Charcot noted that with age, "the physiological and the pathological states seem to mingle".[12] The question of whether one is ill because one is old or old because one is ill thus becomes unsolvable, and is further complicated by the frequent combination of undistinguishable pathologies in the old patient.

The title of one of Larkin's famous poems, "The Old Fools" (1974),[13] rests on this coexistence of 'normality' ("old") with 'abnormality' ("fools"). But this 'abnormal' mental frailty is, throughout the poem, clearly rooted in old age: They are fools – that is, pathologically deranged – because they are old. In another poem, "Hospital Visits" (1953), old age and death, these natural phases of existence, are staged in a hospital, the place for the pathological. The dying body is referred to as a "slowing-down body" (line 17), which points out the disjunction between objective time and the too-slow pace of the ageing body. This combination of 'normality' with 'abnormality', which weakens the frontier between age and pathology, is evoked by Larkin with images of both dissolution (transience as "passing away") and of rupture and paralysis (transience then coming closer to the idea of "crossing over"). A close examination of several of his poems actually reinforced this interdependence.

In "The Old Fools", Larkin's angry voice ponders what gives the old such a helpless and grotesque appearance. He starts his poem picturing bodies in a process of putrid dissolution:

> What do they think has happened, the old fools,
> To make them like this? Do they somehow suppose
> It's more grown-up when your mouth hangs open and drools,
> And you keep on pissing yourself, and can't remember
> Who called this morning? (lines 1-5)

Too senescent, the old fools are not the recipient of the questions but are reified, looked at, commented upon. Syntactically, they are rejected at the end of the first line, appositively both focussed on and segregated between two commas. The succession of provoking questions (others follow throughout the poem) points out the grotesque aspect of these bodies which have lost self-control – muscles are no longer fit enough to keep the mouth shut. Bodies are leaking: saliva and urine can no longer be held and take the whole body along in a general process of dissolution which reverberates in the syntax of "pissing yourself". Thus, by unexpectedly using a resultative verb structure, Larkin includes the whole self (including memory) in the "pissing" process. Jankélévitch's idea of old age as "general entropy" is here incarnated in these decaying "old fools" and chaotic (and creative) verb form. Later in the poem, this process of dissolution takes ontological dimensions when Larkin dehumanises the ageing bodies with unexpected predeterminations: "Ash hair, toad hands, prune face dried into lines – " (line 23). From the remains of a consumed material substance ("ash") to repulsive animality, features then become dryly organic and produce images of hybrid monstrosity that clearly dehumanise the old people. The dry "lines" of "The Old Fools" already appear in an earlier poem, "Skin" (1954):

> Obedient daily dress,
> You cannot always keep
> That unfakable young surface.
> You must learn your lines –
> Anger, amusement, sleep;
> Those few forbidding signs
>
> Of the continuous coarse
> Sand-laden wind, time [...]. (lines 1-8)

The skin, apparently disconnected from the human subject (it is a "dress"), is here displayed as bearing traces of ageing. The metapoetic "lines" make it a readable sign. The human self is dissolved into a sort of eroded message that is to be read, understood, and accepted, by dint of repeated reading and learning: "You must learn your lines". In the next two stanzas, Larkin glimpses dissolving identities, in transience, passing away. His poetic treatment of ageing skin makes it a sort of social accoutrement that wears out and becomes obsolete:

> You must thicken, work loose
> Into an old bag
> Carrying a soiled name.
> Parch then; be roughened; sag;
>
> And pardon me, that I
> Could find, when you were new,
> No brash festivity
> To wear you at, such as
> Clothes are entitled to
> Till the fashion changes. (lines 9-18)

The biological and social beauty of skin is eroded, passes away and falls out of fashion. The old people's social identity is thus seriously threatened.

In "Heads in the Women's Ward" (1972),[14] one of the rare instances where the old are *not* neutrally gendered, the women's femininity is threatened by a fleeting graphic image of "a bearded mouth talk[ing] silently / To someone no one else can see" (lines 5-6). Degendered, or in fact regendered, this male-female old person, synecdochically referred to by her prickly mouth, is, quite bluntly, losing her identity. This dissolution is further intensified by her dementia, which cuts her off from both her surroundings and herself. Such cognitive frailty is likewise evoked in "The Old Fools" as a loss of memory, therefore of one's own past, the basis of one's unique identity:

> Perhaps being old is having lighted rooms
> Inside your head, and people in them, acting.
> People you know, you can't quite name; each looms
> Like a deep loss restored [...]. (lines 25-28)

Ageing, then, as a dissolution of one's body, humanity and identity, somehow alienates the individual. Just like the apposition that syntactically segregates "the old fools" ("The Old Fools", line 1), ageing people are already no longer here – "That is where they live: / Not here and now" ("The Old Fools", lines 34-35). They are in transit towards other, so far unknown, biological and ontological conditions. They are indeed passing *away*, away from what they apprehend as their identity, away from their own and collective consciousness. This image of both dissolution and gradual distance takes us back to de Beauvoir's linear approach to ageing as the extension of a process. But one might here also use Andrew Blaikie's argument made in *Ageing and Popular Culture*. For him, "old people can un-become persons" as they pass towards very old age:

> the fact of such a transition implies a degree of failed intersubjectivity, referred to in the doubly meant phrase 'the un-becoming self'. Personhood requires the individual to have acquired physical, cognitive, and emotional maturity. Thus children become persons when they grow up. By the same token, the loss of any of these

> attributes means that old people can un-become persons (hence become un-persons) as they grow old.[15]

This idea of "un-becoming", of the disappearance of the individual's distinctive features, is actually not that far from Jankélévitch's entropic vision of ageing. Old people "un-become" in a process of successive sudden losses, more or less predictable ruptures and paralytic conditions. If death is the final passage, the ultimate rupture, it is preceded by sorts of rehearsals with abrupt moments of paralysis. Thus, transience no longer appears as "passing away", but more accurately as "crossing over", irretrievably passing from one stage to the next towards the final transit. In "The Old Fools", the old are "crippled" (line 9), caught in what Jankélévitch describes as "lethal geotropism".[16] Inertia creeps in and the body is gradually drawn to the ground, to its grave. The hopeless struggle against the final paralysis is heard in their breath, which is threatened by a potential sudden stop: one hears "the constant wear and tear / Of taken breath" (lines 39-40). In "To the Sea" (1974), a poem dedicated to the memories brought back to the I-voice by a sea scene, old people fleetingly pass through the pleasant holiday vision, as young people "wheel / the rigid old along for them to feel / A final summer" (lines 15-17). The striking effect of the unexpected epithet "rigid" magnifies the impression of a tense, definite paralysis. Physical vitality is weakened. In "Heads in the Women's Ward", such hardness and dryness are coupled with a tense poetic rhythm and coarse alliterations:

> On pillow after pillow lies
> The wild white hair and staring eyes;
> Jaws stand open; necks are stretched
> With every tendon sharply sketched […]. (lines 1-4)

Eyes are fixed. The open mouth, which in "The Old Fools" was too loose and grotesquely wet, is now depicted as though it were forced open. The echo of "stretched" and "sketched" evokes the tension of what appears as a stiff neck. The image of the stiff body (whose "tendon" is too sharply stretched), here constrained into what seems to us unusual positions, appears in "Hospital Visits" (1953) under another aspect, that of brittleness. This poem depicts a wife's daily visit to her husband who is dying in a hospital bed:

> Then one day she fell
> Outside on the sad walk
> And her wrist broke – curable
> At Outpatients, naturally. (lines 11-14)

The body fails and breaks. Here, "curable" brings to mind pathology. Yet the pathology derives from both the clumsiness and the frail bones of the ageing woman. If her wrist is later said to be actually "mending", it is still a "blithe bone" (line 20): a return to her former fit self is from now on impossible.

These images of rigidity and paralysis, of falls and bones broken, do not envisage ageing as a gradual transient process but as a series of ruptures. This is a quite common perception of ageing, in fact: the vision of the first white hair and the glimpse of the first wrinkle mark the sudden awareness of one's ageing process; menopause, too, abruptly ends female fertility, at a still-young age. Likewise, on a social level, retirement is a sudden disengagement that condemns the elderly person to social unproductivity and obsolescence and thus radically marginalises them from the working world. This entropic approach to ageing, which is caught in a linear process – or at least a chronological one – makes us see ageing as a finite transience. A series of transient ruptures, pathological but normal, that pave the way to the final, permanent rupture. Becoming aware of this transience, of one's existence as a mere "transient eternity",[17] is itself another major rupture. In his poems, Larkin actually prompts his readers' (sudden) awareness of transient eternity by putting before their eyes visible symptoms of life's transience. He therefore thematises the visual perception of ageing bodies.

3. Watching Transience

Larkin wrote his poems about ageing at a reasonably young age (between his thirties and early fifties). Old age is therefore not poetically rendered as an experience lived by the poet. For even if he says that he "dread[s] endless extinction",[18] no such dread finds any psychological equivalent in his poetry. Old age is rather the object of the poet's gaze. But in Western culture, the very old have tended to fall out of public vision. Their fight with death remains hidden, taboo, a source of unease and even threat. But Larkin, in these poems, tends to tackle this taboo.

According to the French historian Philippe Ariès, the twentieth century is characterised by a "refoulement de la mort hors du champ de la visibilité publique. [...] Réfugiée dans le secret de l'espace privé de la maison ou de l'anonymat de l'hôpital, elle ne fait plus signe"[19] – death is repressed, kept outside the public sphere, and remains private. Death, in common consciousness, becomes nothing, the void. This nothingness can barely be represented, for no sign corresponds to this black hole.

In "Hospital Visits", Larkin in fact does hide the man's dying body from the reader's eyes:

> At length to hospital
> This man was limited,
> Where screens leant on the wall
> And idle headphones hung. (lines 1-4)

The prominence given to "hospital" in the syntactic dislocation of the first two lines submits the subject – "this man" – to a helpless situation. The unusual verbal construction – "to be limited to hospital" – further objectifies him and reduces his horizon. "Hospital" suggests the pathological, while the presence of "screens" creates a form of suspense as they mysteriously wait for something to happen.

The reader is not allowed in the hospital room; only the wife is. Her function seems to be reduced to watching after she broke her wrist:

> Thereafter night and day
> She came both for *the sight*
> Of his slowing-down body
> And for her own attending,
> And there by day and night
> With her blithe bone mending
> *Watched* him in decay. (lines 15-21, my emphases)

The substantive "sight" alters the sense of action, as though the sight were only what the dying body put forth, but unrelated to the female watcher who thus seems estranged. The verb "watched" is here meaningful, as "ward" – hospital – etymologically derives from 'watching', 'guarding'. Here the dying body is watched. Paralyzed by pathologies (most likely due to age) in a place to which it is "limited", therefore held before being set free by death. Its biological, finite transience, then, is guarded in this ward, temporarily and spatially segregated. The next stanza marks the end of this guarded and watched transience:

> Winter had nearly ended
> When he died (the screen was for *that*). (lines 22-23, my emphasis)

A retrospective explanation for the presence of the screen leaning on the wall in stanza one is here provided. Death, then, as Ariès explains, is screened, hidden.[20] The body, which has completed its transit confined in a limited hospital room, is now a corpse, further enclosed behind screens. This mise en abyme – which foreshadows the coffin – is graphically marked by the parentheses. The deictic "that" in this one-line reference to death again places it at a remote distance. In this poem, then, death, which gradually creeps in, is enclosed in successive limited spaces that keep it away from the reader's eyes.

But this quite conventional treatment of death as something hidden is not a rule in Larkin's poetry. In "The Old Fools" the taboo of ageing and of verging on extinction is actually transgressed as old age is overexposed with abject references to "drool[ing]" mouths (line 3) and "crippled" (line 9) people who "piss themselves" (line 4). The taboo of incontinence is thus bluntly broken. The reader's comfort is likewise unsettled in "Heads in the Women's Ward", where body parts of women are also overexhibited when "jaws stand open; necks are stretched / With every tendon sharply sketched" (lines 3-4). Here again, in an extreme form of realistic close-up that verges on naturalism, the reader is forced to see too much of this decrepitude. While dying is culturally concealed, in Larkin's poetic vision drooling or dry mouths are indecently and helplessly open, uttering nothing, producing no meaningful sign.

However, in spite of these disturbing close-ups, the dying elderly nonetheless appear distant, generic, because of Larkin's own particular poetic stance. Larkin's poetic voice is characterised as ironic, or at least distant. This posture is verified when he broaches the issue of ageing. In "Hospital Visits", as we saw, the speaker does not enter the hospital room: "I don't know what was said" (line 8). "The old fools", too, though presented with repulsive details, are, like the other ageing figures in his poetry, generic, almost iconic. The distance is also conveyed in the focalisation when the speaker refers to their growing mental senescence:

> And these are the first signs:
> Not knowing how, not hearing who, the power
> Of choosing gone. *Their looks show* that they're for it. (lines 20-22, my emphasis)

This phenomenological approach places the old in the position of being observed, watched by the poet, but never wholly comprehended. One then reads, "*[p]erhaps* being old is having lighted rooms / Inside your head" (lines 25-26, my emphasis). Larkin avoids assertion, as he merely observes, speculates, and compensates for his cognitive shortage with a trope: the metaphor of the "lighted rooms" is a way of suggesting, evoking poetically, without asserting. Likewise, a little later the speaker says:

> This is why they give
> *An air of baffled absence*, trying to be there
> Yet being here. (lines 36-38, my emphasis)

The "air", just like "their looks" (line 22), is contemplated but does not yield to assertive declarations about old age. Death similarly remains unseen, as the speaker quite plainly declares,

> At death, you break up: the bits that were you
> Start speeding away from each other for ever
> *With no one to see*. (lines 13-15, my emphasis)

Advanced age and death, in fact, appear as a blind spot. Finite human transience is here, visible, transgressing the taboo with the presence and grotesque appearance of its symptoms, but at the same time, there remains a mysterious, invisible dimension. Gilleard and Higgs define this cognitive limitation as a "black hole":

> In thinking about the fourth age like this, we have drawn an analogy with a phenomenon from astrophysics, treating the fourth age as a 'black hole' about whose nature we can only speculate, restricting any attempts

at measurement or understanding to observing not the phenomenon itself, but disturbances around its 'event horizon'.[21]

This poetic distance from the dying process reads as a poetic adaptation, of what Larkin evokes in "The Old Fools" with the old people's own distant vision regarding their death. The old, though close to death, do not see it coming:

> [...] them crouching below
> Extinction's alp, the old fools, never perceiving
> How near it is. (lines 40-42)

The alp, which blocks the old people's clear vision of imminent death, stands for the taboo that tacitly blocks the poetic voice's assertion. The poet can merely speculate about what lies beyond the alp. But, however distant, remote, ungraspable, metaphorised, even objectified ageing may be, the old are still here, living, as heard in "the constant wear and tear / Of taken breath" (lines 39-40). Ageing people are no less living than any other adult – only the quality of life differs, altered by their declining vitality – but their ability to care for themselves is significantly damaged. This issue of declining independence is here and there fleetingly addressed in Larkin's poems with the underlying question around the notion of care: Who cares for the old?

4. Caring for Transience or Obsolescence

The natural but incurable physical frailty of the aged compels them to a state of dependence, which is hinted at in "The Old Fools" when Larkin refers to advanced old age as "the whole hideous inverted childhood" (line 47). "Old age" is thus an "inverted" version of childhood, an "un-becoming", especially negative in terms of what to expect from the future but otherwise similar to the early stage of life with regards to dependence. For with this phrase Larkin calls to mind images of incontinence, lack of control, and weakness; that is, conditions that necessitate someone needing care. Gilleard and Higgs synthesise precisely the parallel between both periods of life in relation to the issue of care: "Care is locked into the life cycle, shaping and being shaped by it. It decreases exponentially in the years following birth and increases in the years before death".[22]

In Larkin's poems, two types of care are present: one provided by relatives (based on kinship and moral ethics) and one regulated by a social institution, that is, the hospital. Both caring bodies deal with physical and social obsolescence, knowing at heart that any effort to fight this obsolescence would be absolutely pointless.

As Gilleard and Higgs rightly point out, the only property the aged still possess are their frail bodies, especially at the time when Larkin was writing. If the postwar period had improved the general situation, the aged were still often dying in rather impoverished conditions. That is what is implied in Gilleard and Higgs's reference to the old people's "cumulative incapacities and insufficiencies".[23]

In "To the Sea" the old pass through the poem twice:

> To lie, eat, sleep in hearing of the surf
> (Ears to transistors, that sound tame enough
> Under the sky), or gently up and down
> Lead the uncertain children, frilled in white
> And grasping at enormous air, or wheel
> The rigid old along for them to feel
> A final summer, plainly still occurs
> As half an annual pleasure, half a rite [...]. (lines 11-18)

Syntactically absent, those who "wheel" are a generic type of middle-age adult that bridges the transgenerational gap between the "uncertain children" and "the rigid old". The latter, given neither face nor voice, are inseparable from their wheelchairs that thus appear as a prosthesis for their sclerotic bodies. The care provided by their younger and fitter relatives, which may derive from a sense of family duty, appears as a routine, an unquestioned service. The use of "rite" transforms this "wheeling" into a traditional ceremony that is carried out in the microcosmic peculiar family circle. "Wheeling the rigid old", then, is part of the family ethic, which, at the end of the poem, even takes on an unquestioned moral dimension:

> Like breathed-on glass
> The sunlight has turned milky. If the worst
> Of flawless weather is our falling short,

> It may be that through habit these do best,
> Coming to water clumsily undressed
> Yearly; teaching their children by a sort
> Of clowning; helping the old, too, as they ought. (lines 30-36)

Again, the proximity within two lines of children and aged turn the generic middle-aged adult into the transgenerational carer for both young and old. The blunt end creates a poetic rupture strengthened by the intransitivity of "ought". The effect of this suspended "ought" is magnified by its position at the end of the sentence, where "to" might have been expected. While "should" would have introduced some subjectivity, "ought" suggests that caring for the old has now been interiorised by their relatives and is thus objectively, morally right.

This idea of moral family duty is also quite present in the first part of "Hospital Visits":

> Since he would soon be dead
> They let his wife come along
> And pour out tea, each day. (lines 5-7)

The awkward use of "since" conveys a too-systematic logic, and thus suggests that her dutiful daily visits are automatically authorised and, especially, mechanically carried out. As a wife, she unquestioningly visits him each day. This mechanical repetition returns in stanza three after we learn that she broke her wrist:

> Thereafter night and day
> She came both for the sight
> Of his slowing-down body
> And for her own attending,
> And there by day and night
> With her blithe bone mending
> Watched him in decay. (lines 15-21)

"Night" and "day" enfold the persona in a poetic chiasmus that conveys her being caught in the hospital routine. Her husband's death does not interrupt the routine:

> Winter had nearly ended
> When he died (the screen was for that).

> To make sure her wrist mended
> They had her in again
> To finish a raffia mat –
> This meant (since it was begun
> Weeks back) he died again as she came away. (lines 22-28)

The unsettling absence of any expression of grief is coupled with a sort of effacement of the individual before the institution. In other words, the functions of the hospital, embodied in a generic "they" ("They let his wife come along", "They had her in again"), takes precedence over the individual love duty or ethic. The widow is delivered into the hands of the institution, which cares for her now that she is socially obsolete: occupying her in making her do a certainly useless "raffia mat" further reinforces the transience of her social usefulness. The very end, "he died again as she came away", also signals that the hospital had protected her from the awareness of the blunt reality of her husband's death. Now out of this caring institution, she is truly facing death.

By the mid-nineteenth century there emerged the awareness of making old age a social political issue. Until then, care had been provided by the church, charities or, more frequently, by female relatives.[24] But as Michael Fine and Caroline Glendinning have pointed out, "research on 'care' has exposed to public gaze and to policy what hitherto has been assumed to be an unproblematic and 'natural' female activity".[25] The private sphere was therefore gradually replaced by state institutions. This movement of disengagement of the family in favour of that of the society, quite simply referred to by de Beauvoir as "une politique de la vieillesse",[26] is part of what Michel Foucault, in "Il faut Défendre la Société",[27] names "biopolitics", that is, a massive regulation of health by the state. The biopolitical power rests on a coordination of cure, of knowledge, a centralisation of information, and it involves rational, subtle mechanisms. The purpose of this power is to seek optimisation and regulate not individuals but a people ("la population"[28]) hence embraced as a scientific, biological and political issue. In Larkin's poems, biopolitics are subtly incarnated by the aforementioned anonymous collective "they" ("Hospital Visits", line 6, line 25).

In "Heads in the Women's Ward" (which is likely to be a place for poor old women[29]), the regulatory movement of the institution that guards the dying women is suggested in line 1: "On pillow after pillow lies / The wild white hair and staring eyes" (lines 1-2). The repetition of "pillow" conveys either the ward's organisation and optimisation of space (we may imagine rows of beds) or the recurring tasks of the unmentioned nurses who work mechanically, according to a predefined schedule. The nurses, then, are the invisible manifestation of the care policy of old age, of the anonymous biopolitical regulatory system that organises time and space and makes the whole institution efficient and profitable.

Now, going back to our initial question, "Who cares for the old", one may understand "care" less pragmatically but rather as a natural (that is, preeducational) inclination or compassion for the old. In that sense, does Larkin care for the old? To a reader who complained that "The Old Fools" was too "hard-hearted", Larkin replied,

> It is indeed an angry poem, but the anger is ambivalent: there is an anger at the humiliation of age (which I am sure you would share), but there is also an anger at the old for reminding us of death, an anger I think is especially common today when most of us believe that death ends everything. This is of course a selfish and cruel anger, but is typical of the first generation to refuse to look after its aged.[30]

Here, Larkin refers to the family disengagement, which he sees as the consequence of the old people reminding each of us of our own mortality. The worried mockery of the old "pissing themselves", the disturbing realism of the "jaws [that] stand open", and the sort of dramatic irony and lack of empathy towards the widow in "Hospital Visits" together convey Larkin's deliberate self-protective distance. At the end of "The Old Fools", the angry tone subsides to an almost excessively offhand tone: "Well, / We shall find out" (lines 47-48). "Well" flippantly, yet deliberately, puts an end to the reflection, and the inclusive pronoun "we", combined with "shall" (and significantly not "will"), which gives a fateful dimension to the process, retrospectively reveal that those who were portrayed as pissing and drooling fools are in fact each of us. Larkin thus first relies on the reader's repulsion, that is, on what de Beauvoir refers to when she writes that "la vieillesse des autres inspire une repulsion immédiate".[31] He then reminds his reader that this disgusting transience is natural. The sudden rupture of the realisation produced by the curt "Well, / We shall find out" somehow reads as a poetic translation of those moments of sudden awareness of ageing that turn transience into a series of ruptures – like when people spot their first white hair or wrinkle. The initially careless readers are suddenly forced to be aware that they are likewise transient. Larkin, then, cares for the old, all too aware that each of us is in a transient process of becoming old. There is in his poetry a peculiar form of compassion, but paradoxically somewhat distant. A compassion that involves hardly any affect, and no pity at all, but rather a sort of recognition (or prospective identification) of each individual's future condition.

5. Conclusion

The ageing people's transience, in Larkin's poems, is biological, social, and poetic. The old bodies pass through the poems as they pass through life, as "passengers or encumbrances",[32] either in dissolution or too rigid, and systematically vulnerable. No longer able to move, they are moved, wheeled, pushed. Their immediate environment moves around them and for them. Old age therefore appears as a series of irretrievable ruptures that Larkin makes visible. This finite transience is cared for by the poet himself as he endeavours to tackle the taboo of the representation of death, usually confined to the private sphere in our contemporary Western culture. He brings the rehearsals of death to the surface of his poetry, in different contexts (the women's ward, hospital, seaside, home), and, without any welfarist outlook nor any political ambition, forces the reader to wonder who, in our modern secular societies, really *cares* for *us* old?

Notes

[1] "Transience." *Oxford English Dictionary Online*. Oxford University Press, 2018. Web. 26 August 2018.
[2] De Beauvoir, Simone (1970). *La Vieillesse*. Paris: Galimard, 37, my translation.
[3] Jankélévitch, Vladimir (1977). *La Mort*. Paris: Flammarion, 191, my translation.
[4] Thomas, Helen (2013). *The Body and Everyday Life*. London and New York: Routledge, 116.

[5] Gilleard, Chris, and Paul Higgs (2013). *Ageing, Corporeality and Embodiment.* London and New York: Anthem Press, xi.
[6] Gilleard, Chris, and Paul Higgs (2016). *Personhood, Identity and Care in Advanced Old Age.* Bristol: Policy Press, 9.
[7] *Ibid.*, 1.
[8] Larkin, Philip (1983). *Required Writing.* London: Faber & Faber, 55.
[9] "L'irréversibilité et la continuité du devenir fini donnent en effet tout son sens à l'usure implacablement progressive qu'on appelle vieillissement" (Jankélévitch, 196).
[10] De Beauvoir (1970), 349, my translation.
[11] *Ibid.*, 599; Jankélévitch (1977), 192.
[12] Barry, Elizabeth (2015). "The Ageing Body." *The Cambridge Companion to the Body in Literature.* Ed. David Hillman and Ulrika Maude. Cambridge: Cambridge University Press, 132-148, 134.
[13] All poems quoted in this article are taken from Larkin, Philip (2012). *The Complete Poems.* Ed. Archie Burnett. New York: Farrar, Straus and Giroux. Further references to this edition will be included in the text.
[14] In a letter dated 18 May 1972, he writes, "My Mother is in a Nursing Home, not very well, which is a worry and very time-consuming: also starts up a chain-reaction of gloomy reflections on one's own account" (Larkin (2012), 492). This letter was written soon before the poem, which lets us believe that his mother's experience and, above all, his own experience of knowing her there must well have been a primary source of inspiration.
[15] Blaikie, Andrew (1999). *Ageing and Popular Culture.* Cambridge: Cambridge University Press, 193.
[16] Jankélévitch (1977), 196.
[17] *Ibid.*, 213.
[18] Larkin (1983), 55.
[19] "The repression of death outside public visibility. Because it now takes refuge at home or in the anonymity of the hospital, death is no longer visible". Ariès, Philippe (1983). *Images de l'homme devant la mort.* Paris: Seuil, 272.
[20] *Ibid.*, 272.
[21] Gilleard and Higgs (2016), 7.
[22] *Ibid.*, 91.
[23] *Ibid.*, 71.
[24] Fine, Michael, and Caroline Glendinning (2005). "Dependence, Independence or Inter-Dependence? Revisiting the Concepts of 'Care' and 'Dependency.'" *Ageing and Society* 25.4. Cambridge: Cambridge University Press, 601-621, 602.
[25] *Ibid.*, 603.
[26] "Politics of Ageing." De Beauvoir (1970), 257, my translation.

[27] Foucault, Michel (1976). "Il Faut Défendre la Société." *Cours au Collège de France* (1975-1976). Paris: Seuil.
[28] *Ibid.*, 162.
[29] In the early years of the twentieth century, "old age was also about segregation; all the old ladies were inmates in the same room, the women's ward" (Blaikie, 87).
[30] Motion, Andrew (1993). *Philip Larkin: A Writer's Life*. New York: Farrar Straus and Giroux, 425-426.
[31] De Beauvoir (1970), 51.
[32] Gilleard and Higgs (2016), 5.

Bibliography

Ariès, Philippe (1983). *Images de l'homme devant la mort*. Paris: Seuil.
Barry, Elizabeth (2015). "The Ageing Body." *The Cambridge Companion to the Body in Literature*. Ed. David Hillman and Ulrika Maude. Cambridge: Cambridge University Press, 132-148.
Blaikie, Andrew (1999). *Ageing and Popular Culture*. Cambridge: Cambridge University Press.
De Beauvoir, Simone (1970). *La Vieillesse*. Paris: Galimard.
Fine, Michael, and Caroline Glendinning (2005). "Dependence, Independence or Inter-Dependence? Revisiting the Concepts of 'Care' and 'Dependency.'" *Ageing and Society* 25.4, 601-621. Cambridge: Cambridge University Press.
Foucault, Michel (1976). "Il Faut Défendre la Société". *Cours au Collège de France* (1975-1976). Paris: Seuil.
Gilleard, Chris, and Paul Higgs (2013). *Ageing, Corporeality and Embodiment*. London and New York: Anthem Press.
--- (2016). *Personhood, Identity and Care in Advanced Old Age*. Bristol: Policy Press.
Jankélévitch, Vladimir (1977). *La Mort*. Paris: Flammarion.
Larkin, Philip (2012). *The Complete Poems*. Ed. Archie Burnett. New York: Farrar, Straus and Giroux.
--- (1983). *Required Writing*. London: Faber & Faber.
Motion, Andrew (1993). *Philip Larkin: A Writer's Life*. New York: Farrar, Straus and Giroux.
Thomas, Helen (2013). *The Body and Everyday Life*. London and New York: Routledge.
"Transience." *Oxford English Dictionary Online*. Oxford University Press, 2018. Web. 26 Aug. 2018.

Sara Strauß (Paderborn)

Ageing (Female) Bodies and Mortality in Eighteenth-Century Poetry

> Every Man desires to live long; but no Man would be old.
> Jonathan Swift

1. Introduction

The eighteenth century was a period when people were strongly interested in understanding the workings of the human body and mind. Against the background of new insights in the fields of science and philosophy and the emergence of clinical medicine as a discipline,[1] scholars and medical researchers were concerned with human anatomy and issues relating to health and disease over the life course. With an ever-present awareness of life's transience, a wish to extend the lifespan increased. Consequently, longevity became an ideal much aspired to. People tried to counter bodily decay so that the "management of the aging body became a visible means of exhibiting behaviours that conformed to hegemonic behavioural codes of [...] a progressive and polite Enlightenment society".[2] These behavioural codes manifest themselves in the discursive practices of promoting a healthy and youthful appearance as well as managing the transient body in order to attain a long life. Eighteenth-century society consequently experienced a dilemma between aspirations of immortality, the awareness of life's evanescence and the unavoidability of physical decline that gave rise to ideals of bodily self-restrictions. The present paper examines the representation of this dilemma in eighteenth-century poetry. It argues that the lyrical works of Jonathan Swift and Anne Finch, Countess of Winchilsea, unveil these efforts to improve the ageing body as vain and futile in view of the inevitable transience of human existence.

2. Managing the Transient Body: Eighteenth-Century Ideas of Ageing, Longevity and Mortality

"There was no word 'aging' in the eighteenth century, no specific word dedicated to describe the process of getting older".[3] Nonetheless, the period was "a cultural moment fascinated by embodied personhood, and [...] the aging body became a lens for investigating the nature of mankind and its relationship with society".[4] Against the constant threat of disease and mortality, the maintenance of health, youthfulness and beauty was seized on as a way to achieve a long life and prompted practices of bodily regulation. According to Norbert Elias, "the disciplining of the body was an important part of the 'civilizing process' in the eighteenth century".[5] Michel Foucault also cites the eighteenth century as a pivotal era when it comes to the evolution of modern mechanisms of discipline and punishment. He emphasises the highly contradictory nature of this cultural period: "The 'Enlightenment', which discovered the liberties, also invented the disciplines".[6] Following Foucault's line of argumentation, the ideal of managing the ageing body serves as an expression of the power exercised by the social body. In his study, Foucault differentiates "[three technologies of power] that face one another in the second half of the eighteenth century":[7] "the sovereign and his force, the social body and the administrative apparatus".[8] Society and discursive practices within society consequently play an important role in exercising power by setting and controlling standards of normality. It is through "sign [...] [and] representation"[9] that the social body promotes discipline and processes of (self-)regulation. Its influence is thus "distributed throughout the social space; present everywhere as scene, spectacle, sign, discourse; legible like an open book; operating by a permanent recodification of the mind of the citizens".[10] In such a way, the ideal of achieving a long life by improving one's body was "present everywhere as [...] discourse"[11] in eighteenth-century society.

The extensive distribution of this discursive practice can be exemplified by the proliferation of medical treatises that were no longer directed solely to professionals but increasingly addressed laypersons. Medical handbooks, booklets and self-help literature became affordable and thereby fashionable not only with the elite but also with literate people among the other classes.[12] A case in point is George Cheyne's

Essay of Health and Long Life (1724),[13] in which the physician advises on how to achieve longevity and avoid age-related problems, such as through fasting and changes in nutrition. In this way, medical treatises opened up the discourse to the general public about a possible prolongation of life through improving the body. As a result, "the idea of mortality as a curable condition [became] part of Enlightenment utopianism".[14]

The dissemination and wide reception of medical writing exemplifies that this health-related discourse was not regulated by the administrative apparatus but primarily by the social body itself.

> The social and economic changes of the Restoration had created, by the early eighteenth century, a class of patients more demanding of physicians. […] These people were well-informed about contemporary medical theory and practice […].[15]

Together with the growth of information and the increasing public interest in health issues and longevity, people constructed definitions of a 'normal' physical constitution and conduct that were linked to the ideal of youthfulness. As a matter of fact, Foucault points out that

> normalization becomes one of the great instruments of power at the end of the classical age. For the marks that once indicated status, privilege and affiliation were increasingly replaced – or at least supplemented – by a whole range of degrees of normality indicating membership of a homogeneous social body but also playing a part in classification, hierarchization and the distribution of rank.[16]

In order to affiliate themselves with social groups and to establish or maintain their position within the community, people strived to conform to the respective code of normality affirmed by each group. It is through these processes of normalisation that the social body exerts power and regulates discursive practices. As Luna Dolezal summarises Foucault's argument,

> in modern society an individual's behaviour is not regulated through explicit and overt oppression within an institution. Instead, control is achieved through standards of normality which are propagated through

vast and diffuse networks of power relations which infiltrate every corner of life.[17]

Consequently, the ideal of remaining in good physical shape affirms youthfulness as the standard of normality accepted in society. Then and now, young and middle age are connected with attractiveness, fertility and vigour, while old age is associated with illness, decline, dependence and death. Bernice Martin states that

> the celebration of youth is a persistent strand in European culture. [...] The binary opposite symbol is old age as *memento mori*. [...] [T]he sunken cheeks, withered dugs, and frosted locks are always deployed as symbolic reminders that old age is the threshold of death.[18]

The contrast between youth and old age or physical decay as *memento mori* also strongly features in Enlightenment poetry. The following analyses examine eighteenth-century society's ambivalent attitudes towards the ageing body that resulted from their normalisation of youthfulness and physical attractiveness and an increasing awareness of life's transience as represented in the works of Jonathan Swift and Anne Finch, Countess of Winchilsea.

3. Satirising Human Efforts at Disguising the Transient Body: Ageing in the Poetry of Jonathan Swift

Jonathan Swift's writing is characterised by a pronounced explicitness regarding physicality. Most evidently, Swift's satire *Gulliver's Travels* (1726) engages with corporeality from different perspectives, large- and small-scale, which unveil a misanthropic view on human self-fashioning. Moreover, Gulliver's third voyage to Luggnagg draws a disillusioning picture of longevity when portraying the fictional, immortal Struldbruggs and the severe mental and physical impairments they acquire as they grow old.[19] Similar to Swift's prose writing, his poetry stands out in its unforgiving realism when it depicts the body and its peculiarities in uncommon detail – not only for the eighteenth century but also for the present time.

In his satirical, scatological poems "The Lady's Dressing Room" and "A Beautiful Young Nymph Going to Bed" Swift contrasts the natural decline of the human body in the course of ageing and disease with the ideal of youthfulness. Through the graphic portrayal of the prostheses, clothing and cosmetics necessary to uphold the attractive outward appearance of Lady Cælia and the prostitute Corinna, both lyrical works give an inclusive account of the physical decay of a middle-aged woman. Age and gender, rather than class, function as defining categories here and reveal that the ideal of managing the ageing body permeates all social groups.

With regard to "A Beautiful Young Nymph Going to Bed", scholars have mostly interpreted this "extraordinarily outspoken, taboo-breaching poem"[20] as the epitome of Swift's misogynistic world view and have categorised it as "pornographic [being] about a whore".[21] Then as well as today, it is the female body that is expected to conform to a standard of normality more strongly connected to discursive practices of retaining beauty and youthfulness than masculine appearances. Sara Arber and Jay Ginn maintain that "[a]geist stereotypes about elderly people abound, but stereotypes of elderly women are particularly negative and demeaning".[22] Through Swift's "relentless recitations of the details of female grossness",[23] it is exceedingly often the female body that becomes the target of the author's satire. Yet, as D. J. Enright persuasively explains, "[i]rony's guns face in every direction".[24] As a result, satire is particularly effective when the aspects exposed and ridiculed are transferable from the object of satire to its audience and their own social context. Therefore, I argue that Swift's poems criticise the shallowness of eighteenth-century society as a whole, its vain ideals of beauty and youthfulness and the futility of its efforts at reinvigorating the transient bodies of both men and women. Beyond the female protagonists of Swift's lyrical works, it is especially the male suitors within the poems and the readership who are ridiculed in their voyeurism of a person's physical decline and their naïve disregard of the inevitable evanescence of their own existence. For instance, in "The Lady's Dressing Room", the voyeur Strephon has to pay a high prize for his unbidden entrance into Lady Cælia's dressing room: the insights into the true nature of the human body that he gains there "frighte[n]" and "disgust[]" him so much that the lyrical I ironically pities "poor *Strephon*[]" for being "punish'd [...] for his peeping".[25] The communicative situation of the lyrical work allows for comparisons between the experience of the poetic protagonist and the recipients of the scatological poems, who, while reading on, are confronted with "portraits of female intimacy designed to shock and revolt [...] through graphic, often grotesque, imagery".[26] Michael F. Suarez points out that "[t]he constructive content of the satires, therefore, is not directed towards Swift's 'villains' [the women satirised], but towards his audience".[27]

Consequently, Swift's irony works through the exaggerated portrayal of the female decaying body and its analogy to the male body. This analogy leads to the disillusionment that men are equally affected by transience as every living being is. As Penelope Wilson maintains,

> Swift's 'nymphs' [i.e., the female protagonists of the poems] do produce on their respective [suitors] effects nearly as dramatic as those feared by some cultures to result from contact with menstrual blood, but disillusion operates through a recognition of sameness, of shared excrementality, rather than through fear of otherness.[28]

Swift's hyperbolic depiction of bodily deterioration thus serves as a reminder of mankind's imperfection and the inevitable experience of transience, which is shared by every human being.

In "A Beautiful Young Nymph Going to Bed" the speaker describes a woman's procedure of removing her attire and corporeal accessories before retiring to bed. When undressing layer by layer, the poem's protagonist unveils the natural state of a body affected by ageing, poverty, poor hygiene and disease. The author thereby satirically contrasts society's normative standards of beauty and youthfulness with the blatant reality of people's outward appearance when it is deprived of any artificial attributes, like cosmetics, dress and jewellery, false hair, false breasts and teeth. Permitting the reader a voyeur's gaze into the intimate scene of the prostitute Corinna's disrobing after a hard day's work, the poem discloses what is usually concealed and refuted in public life. Corinna, alone in her private room at midnight, performs a ritual of unclothing and unmasking before she goes to bed. The full deterioration of her body gradually comes to the surface when she takes out enhancements that otherwise conceal its severe medical condition. With deepest dedication she "pick[s] out a Chrystal Eye, / She wipes it clean, and lays it by".[29] The discrepancy between Corinna's daytime appearance and her physical reality has a shocking effect on the reader when she takes out her glass eye and "wipes it clean" (line 12). Subsequently, she removes her false teeth and "With gentlest Touch, she next explores / Her Shankers, Issues, running Sores" (lines 29-30). In a mock-epic manner Swift describes the middle-aged woman's divergence from the socially expected and normalised standard. The rhyme scheme and the elevated style of language satirise the revolting actions necessary to recover Corinna's natural, transient state from her artificially enhanced appearance. Swift's elegant, sophisticated expressions, such as "smoothly" and "[w]ith gentlest Touch" (lines 16, 29), as well as eulogising the prostitute as a "young nymph" and a "lovely Goddess" (title, line 23) convey the woman's carefulness and her pure dedication to her actions as well as the pride she takes in her bodily accoutrements. These graceful evocations are in harsh contrast to the motivations for Corinna's delicate actions, that is, her body's decay caused by ill health, infections, ageing and defective organs. They conspicuously contrast Swift's otherwise informal and derogatory language with which he describes the woman's "flabby Dugs" (line 22) and how her cat "Puss had on her Plumpers p–st" (line 62). It is, thus, not only the theme of the poem that has caused it to be categorised in a group of scatological poems concerned with obscenity and excrements, but it is especially Swift's choice of vulgar language and imagery that may have led to this classification.

What creates a satirical effect is the combination of this obscene language and explicit content with the poetic style achieved through the prosodic form. The rhyme scheme, regular metre, syntactic parallelisms and alliterations result in an orderly structure and create a smooth melody and rhythm. The pair rhymes and iambic tetrametre repeatedly emphasise metaphors that are in ironic contrast to each other, such as when Corinna "next explores / Her Shankers, Issues, running Sores" (lines 29-30). By "explor[ing]" (line 29), the poetic protagonist indulges in an activity of close examination and contemplation, while the object on which she concentrates this action is something that is usually withheld from the public gaze. Swift, however, does not spare the reader the physical reality of the body's transience. Instead of mitigating or euphemising the woman's complaints, the speaker precisely specifies her wounds as chancres, which derive from venereal disease and usually affect the sex organs. The tricolon finds its climax in "running Sores" (line 30), which calls to mind pus-filled and infected wounds. Swift's explicitness about the transient human body creates a distancing effect on the readers, who regret their initial voyeurism. Consequently, Brean Hammond observes that "[t]here is a strange anomie produced, an alienation resulting from the utter absence of humanity, a weird silence".[30]

From the very beginning of the poem Swift plays with the reader's expectations, setting a peaceful scene and drawing upon associations with the pastoral imagery of "Nymph[s]" and "Shepherd[s]" (title, line 2). The poem's title, "A Beautiful Young Nymph Going to Bed", brings to mind associations with nature, peacefulness and vitality. It misleadingly suggests the poem to be an idyll or pastoral. As Hammond asserts, "the mock-pastoral opening of the poem is transgressive of literary decorum, an affront to literary convention but also to public decency".[31] Characterising Corinna as a young nymph, a goddess or spirit living in nature, arouses expectations of spirituality or otherworldly insights. Instead, as typical of the mock epic, it narrates the very human, mundane activity of retiring to bed. When witnessing this private, intimate process, during which Corinna's body returns to its natural, undisciplined state, the reader apprehends that no human body is spared from the effects of life's transience.

Similarly to Corinna's endeavours, "The Lady's Dressing Room" discloses that the owner of the room employs diverse means to conceal the true shape of her figure and the age of her skin. In Lady Cælia's absence the poem's protagonist, Strephon, "[steals] in and [takes] a strict Survey" of her private chamber (line 7), which reveals that the Lady's clean and controlled appearance results in fact from her many fine dresses, petticoats and, above all, a multitude of cosmetics and moisturising creams. Her used cloths, towels, combs and washbasin, by contrast, are covered in dirt and emit a blend of various smells. For instance, Strephon encounters

> A Paste of Composition rare,
> Sweat, Dandriff, Powder, Lead and Hair.
> A Forehead-Cloath with Oyl upon't,
> To smooth the Wrinkles on her Front:
> Here, Alum Flower to stop the Steams,
> Exhal'd from sour unsavoury Streams [.] (lines 23-28)

The substances Cælia leaves behind in her room convey that she tries to smoothen the visual traces of ageing on her face and cover unpleasant odours of the body and its excretions. Swift here strongly seizes on the imagery of smell to satirise the discrepancy between people's idealistic imagination of the human body and reality. The poet takes this to extremes when he dedicates a whole stanza to evoking the stench of burning grease as a metaphor for the scent emanating from the Lady's cabinet (see lines 99-114). When secretively inspecting Cælia's worn clothes and possessions stored in her chest, Strephon feels repulsed by the stench he is confronted with:

> So, Things which must not be exprest,
> When *plumpt* into the reeking Chest,
> Send up an excremental Smell,
> [...]
>   THUS finishing his grand Survey,
> The Swain disgusted slunk away. (lines 109-116, emphases in the text)

As a matter of fact, the poem only indirectly presents Lady Cælia through the "*[i]nventory*" the intruder provides of her chamber (line 10, emphasis in the text). This allows conclusions about her physical state without depicting it explicitly. Instead, the very absence of literal descriptions and the constant appeal to the reader's imagination creates ironic effects: "In such a Case, few Words are best / And *Strephon* bids us guess the rest" (lines 15-16, emphasis in the text). After all, the reader might imagine a scene worse than it actually is. The woman's outward appearance is not characterised, as Strephon's impression suggests, by missing hygiene, because she used her washbasin and the many means to clean and groom her skin. By contrast, all dirt may be left in the water and towels while Cælia herself is fresh and tidy.

The repeated allusions to the inexpressibility of the dressing room's poor condition ultimately result in an anticlimax: instead of observing the expected scandal, the audience realises that Cælia's body functions like any 'normal' body does. The emphasis on "[t]hings which must not be exprest [sic]" (line 109) ridicules Strephon's naiveté about natural human affairs and draws attention to the complexity of social norms and discursive practices. The poem's ironic twist, finally, achieves a distancing effect on the reader, who, guided by Swift's speaker (lines 119-144), condemns the intrusion into the Lady's most intimate sphere and the moral transgression it implies.

As in "A Beautiful Young Nymph Going to Bed", it is through the contrast between the orderly prosodic form and the obscene imagery as well as the formal and vulgar register that Swift's sarcasm unfolds. Thus, he stresses the protagonist's sensationalism and his attitude of taking himself too seriously by describing his endeavour as a "grand Survey" through which "[n]o Object *Strephon*'s Eye escapes" (lines 115, 47, emphasis in the text). As if in a position of authority, Strephon intends "to Make the Matter clear [and provide] [a]n *Inventory*" of the Lady's room (9-10, emphasis in the text). This imitation of official language ridicules the voyeur's self-importance. It thereby criticises the public's extensive interest in private affairs and the mechanisms of discipline exerted through the social body.

In both poems, Swift presents a woman's struggle with maintaining a decent body image. Yet Lady Cælia's more prosperous social position gives her access to a multitude of hygienic supplies and cosmetics. "The Lady's Dressing Room" is therefore less concerned with the medical aspects of ageing than with upholding the public impression of cleanliness and youthfulness. By contrast, in "A Beautiful Young Nymph Going to Bed" Corinna's increasing age and the absence of good sanitary conditions have detrimental effects on her health and economic situation. Earning a living from selling her body, she is dependent on her physical attractiveness and on concealing the consequences of life's transience.

It is through the explicitness about corporeal affairs and his transgression of literary and social conventions that Swift's criticism of eighteenth-century society unfolds. The irony employed in the two poems satirises people's high regard for outward appearance, their efforts at improving the body and the false pretence of youthfulness as a standard of normality. At the same time, the author ridicules the naiveté with which Enlightenment society strove for longevity and the ignorance with which people disregarded their own mortality. The series of scatological lyrical works sarcastically addresses the discrepancy between mankind's pride in its intellect and the harsh reality of its dependence on a body whose flaws, decay and deficiencies should serve as a constant reminder of the transience of human existence.

4. Bodily Transience in the Poetry of Anne Finch: Criticising Eighteenth-Century Discursive Practices towards Ageing and Gender

In contrast to Swift's scatological approach to the topic of life's transience and bodily decay, the poetry of Anne Finch, Countess of Winchilsea, is characterised by a contemplative, melancholic manner conveying highly psychological insights. Apart from her political poetry in favour of the Stuart monarchy, her writing reflects her high interest in medicine and chronicles (feminine) inward responses to life experience and to restrictive social and political traditions.[32] As such, her "poems [...] are situated in – and respond to – larger cultural debates about gender, language, and political authority".[33] Against the background of these debates, the poems selected for analysis here, "All Is Vanity", "Clarinda's Indifference at Parting with Her Beauty", "Melinda on an Insippid Beauty" and "The Unequal Fetters", address the topics of ageing, mortality and the transient nature of all existence. "Finch's works often bring together cultural and scientific overtones, re-reading traditional *topoi* in the light of contemporary medical discourse".[34] The unrelenting process of time passing and its effects on the human body play a central role in her multigenre work, particularly in the selection of elegies, philosophical poetry, and retirement and progress poems. Finch connects the passage of time to the natural life cycle, to a woman's attractiveness and thereby especially to feminist perspectives on the shallowness of late seventeenth and early eighteenth-century society. When she meditates on the importance that the public attributes to beauty and its loss, her lyrical texts frequently imply the discursive practice of enhancing the body and the senseless pursuit of longevity and immortality.

In her poetry Finch strongly evokes the ephemerality of the life cycle. She asserts that human existence is brief and therefore vain, fruitless and of no effect, as the poem "All Is Vanity"[35] suggests:

> How vain is *Life*! Which rightly we compare
>   To flying *Posts*, that haste away;
> To *Plants*, that fade with the declining Day;
>   To *Clouds*, that sail amidst the yielding Air;
> Till by Extension into that they flow,
>   Or, scatt'ring on the World below,
> Are lost and gone, ere we can say they were [...]. (lines 1-7, emphasis and format in the text)

From the beginning of the poem the speaker includes the addressee in her line of argumentation. Finch thereby presents the transience of life as a collective and shared experience of every human being. The lamentation "How vain is *Life*!" (line 1) is immediately followed by the adverb "rightly" and the generic pronoun "we" (line 1) so that the addressee is encouraged to identify with the speaker and the idea that life is "vain" (line 1). In order to point out the fleetingness and mutability of human existence, the speaker compares it to organisms that change quickly. The analogy to "flying *Posts*, that haste away" (line 2), that is, to couriers and post-horses, stresses the rapidity with which the course of life progresses from birth to death. Similar to the fast galloping of horses, the pace is unstoppable. The following comparisons, then, connect this fast process with the idea of decline and dissolution. The poem here employs metaphors for evanescence: "*Plants*, that fade with the declining Day" and "*Clouds*, that [...] / Are lost and gone, ere we can say they were" (lines 3, 4-7). In the case of plants and clouds the evolution of the life cycle is particularly visible. Through the effects of the weather and the seasons, they are always in the process of change. This is shown as a very lively, dynamic process since the objects are personified: they "fly", "haste", "fade", "sail", "flow" and "scatt[er]" (lines 2-6). It is through this imagery from nature that developments like withering, decay and loss are established as part of the undeniable, natural dynamics of life. In addition to these personifications, the anaphoric onset of the verses "To *Plants*, [...] To *Clouds*, [...] To *Autumn-Leaves*, [...] To rising *Bubbles*, [...] To *fleeting* Dreams" (lines 3-10, emphases in the text) underlines the vast number of evanescent, temporary elements which the human life course parallels in its impermanence.

In consequence of the fleeting, transitory aspect of life, Finch calls to mind the insignificance of human existence and criticises man's pride and self-importance. Employing a biblical allegory that man is just "Tenant to the Earth" (line 15), she characterises mankind as "weak" and "frail" (lines 15-16) and concludes that all "Hopes [...] and Desires" for achievement in life will ultimately be "disappointed [...] and frustrated" (line 20). According to Finch, it is only on their deathbed that people apprehend "*That Vanity's our Lot, and all Mankind is Vain*" (line 24, emphasis in the text).

Here and in the following, the poet takes advantage of the ambiguity of the words 'vain' and 'vanity'. She connects it to both the idea that mankind's existence is fruitless and of no effect as well as to man's senseless pride. Both types of vanity find their epitome in the high value people attribute to beauty. Finch, however, points to the short-lived nature of physical attractiveness:

> As Vain is *Beauty*, and as short her Power;
> Tho' in its proud, and transitory Sway,
> The coldest Hearts and wisest Heads obey
> That gay fantastic Tyrant of an Hour. (lines 109-112, emphasis in the text)

She reminds readers of the futility of beauty, since it is as transient as any phase of life. Hence, according to Finch, the passing of time eventually causes a loss of charm. Through the emphasis on the "short[ness] [of] her Power" (line 109), the poet here inevitably relates beauty to youthfulness. She thereby concentrates on the idea of physical attractiveness that corresponds to the standard of normality set by eighteenth-century society and its discursive practices. Although Finch does not overturn this normalised definition of beauty, she ridicules people's naiveté in attributing so much value to outward appearance. What's more, the verses reveal the discursive practice to permeate all groups, since it is supported by both "[t]he coldest Hearts and wisest Heads" (line 111). The power and coercion that the social body can exert through normalisation thus manifests itself in the fact that, despite all its transitoriness, the maintenance of beauty is experienced as the "Tyrant of an Hour" (line 112).

In contrast to the widely cherished ideal of managing the body in order to extend the length of one's physical attractiveness, several of Finch's poems also give counterexamples of protagonists who acknowledge the process of ageing and bodily decay. In "Clarinda's Indifference at Parting with Her Beauty"[36] and "Melinda on an Insippid Beauty"[37] Finch presents two views on ageing that discredit the importance attributed to beauty. Clarinda, who recognises the "[d]eparting beauty" of her mature body, accepts this condition "unconcern'd" (lines 3 and 35) as she does not see any merit in outward attractiveness: "And what, vain beauty, didst thou 'ere atcheive, / [...] that I thy fall shou'd greive [...]?" (lines 14-15). Instead, and in line with Finch's argument in "All Is Vanity", she considers an appealing body as the source of pride and vanity, which then intensify foolishness and thereby become a danger to wit (see line 25).

The relation between beauty and wit is addressed in more detail in "Melinda on an Insippid Beauty". Melinda again ponders on the inevitability of death and the "fleeting charm" (line 5) of outward appearance. The lyrical 'I' here, however, brings to mind the idea that prettiness is a transient state that can outlive the person through art: in paintings or in poetry. The normalised concept of beauty is thus extended from physical aspects to intellectual and moral gracefulness. Consequently, Melinda claims that her "polish'd thoughts, [her] bright Ideas" (line 8) will be transmitted to the subsequent generations through her poetry.

Finch's argument for the immortality of a poet's views and beliefs as conveyed through their poetry pays tribute to a long tradition in philosophical thinking and the arts. The subtitle reveals her poem to be an "imitation of a fragment of Sapho's" while many of William Shakespeare's sonnets also call attention to the transience of good looks and the social responsibility to pass on inward and outward gracefulness to the following generations through one's progeny or lyrics.[38] This idea about the continuity of moral and intellectual achievements is also expressed in "All Is Vanity" when the speaker demands that "*Wit* shall last" (line 165, emphasis in the text; see also lines 187-189) beyond a person's bodily decline and death.

As regards poetic diction, Finch's rejection of unnatural, artificially achieved beauty is also reflected in the "extreme plainness of [her] style".[39] Myra Reynolds argues in her introduction to Finch's poems:

> She seems always to seek for the simplest, plainest words she can find. [...] She has surprisingly few metaphors or similes. [...] It would, indeed, be difficult to find so large a body of work with less adornment.[40]

While metaphors and similes abound in works like "All Is Vanity", Reynolds is right in observing Finch's plain, simple language and the absence of adornment in the poems that criticise the futility of beauty and society's high regard for it. Reynolds continues to praise the writer's honesty in recording the simple facts of life:

> [B]ut now and then, when Lady Winchilsea is at her best, when her ideas are based on deep and rich experience, her honesty, her reticence, her

inability to say any more than just what she sees or feels, flowers out into an exact, lovely simplicity like that of the facts she records.[41]

Finch's simple, unrelenting and candid accounts of life's transience and the natural progress of time thus testify to the inescapability of ageing and bodily decay. As a result, her lyrics serve to remind her contemporaries that, despite all the medical and scientific advances of the seventeenth and eighteenth centuries, longevity and immortality remain an illusion.

What's more, Finch connects her observance of the fast passage of time and the inevitable loss of beauty to a feminist critique of the traditional, restrictive structures of seventeenth and eighteenth-century England. She criticises the disparate standards by which society attributes significance to the physical appearance of men and women. This especially unfolds in "The Unequal Fetters",[42] a poem published in 1713 that addresses inequality in marriage and social status:

> Cou'd we stop the time that's flying
>   Or recall itt when 'tis past
> Put far off the day of Dying
>   Or make Youth for ever last
> To Love wou'd then be worth our cost.
>
> But since we must loose those Graces
>   Which at first your hearts have wonne
> And you seek for in New Faces
>   When our Spring of Life is done
> It wou'd but urdge our ruine on[.] (lines 1-10)

The opening stanza again stresses the fast, unstoppable passage of time and points to the impossibility of "Put[ting] far off the day of Dying" (line 3). Finch here hypothetically imagines the chances of postponing death and maintaining youth throughout one's life. Yet she reveals this to be a mere fantasy, "since we must loose those Graces" (line 6) eventually. The use of the verb 'must' and the collective pronoun 'we' acknowledges the inevitability of the loss of youth and beauty. All efforts to improve the transient body in order to maintain health, good looks and a youthful appearance, such as through nutrition, medical aids, dress or cosmetics, thus prove to be futile and not "worth [their] cost" (line 5).

Despite the irrevocability of physical ageing for both genders, "The Unequal Fetters" emphasises the wide discrepancy between its effects on men and women and their status in society. Thus, Finch maintains that it is primarily a woman's loveliness and youth that attract men (see line 7). Upon the eventual loss of these traits in their wives, Finch argues, men tend to feel drawn to younger women (see line 8). Her poem criticises the double standards by which early eighteenth-century society assesses the roles of men and women: whereas extramarital relationships with younger women were a socially accepted form of adultery, since "Marriage does but slightly tye Men" (line 16), women of advanced age remained tied in the institution of marriage as "close Pris'ners" (line 17).

Similar to "All Is Vanity", Finch once more represents ageing and the inevitability of life's transience as a collective experience. Yet in "The Unequal Fetters", she contrasts masculine and feminine responses to this experience as well as public expectations of them. Hence, the speaker employs the collective pronoun 'we' to refer to all women and contrasts them and their behaviour towards men, addressed by 'you'. Moreover, the prosodic form of the poem also hints at imbalance and disruption. The five stanzas are composed of five verses each that alternate in length of seven and eight syllables. The stanzas' final verses further disrupt the rhythm of the poem by unexpectedly changing from trochaic to iambic metre. In a similar way, the rhyme scheme adds to this uneven structure. Thus, the fifth verse breaks the pattern of the preceding alternate rhyme when creating assonance with both the second and fourth lines. These breaks and ruptures call attention to the disparate social standards applied to feminine and masculine ageing. They can be seen as a critique of the prevailing discourse that, against all scientific evidence, established longevity as a gendered, masculine experience. As Heike Hartung explains:

> A concern with the prolonging of life is central to the eighteenth-century phenomenology of attitudes towards old age, and longevity itself is perceived as gendered [...]. Although demographic evidence for the eighteenth century shows that women tended to outlive men[,] [...] medical treatises insisted that only men were able to attain the utmost longevity.[43]

The breaks in the prosodic form of Finch's poem ironically reveal elderly men's attraction to youthfulness initially as a practice tolerated in public but eventually as an act of deluding themselves of their own ageing. At the same time, these inconsistencies disclose the initial hope to stop the passage of time as well as the fantasy of longevity and endless youth as an illusion. Paula R. Backscheider asserts that through the satirical undertones in Finch's work

> [...] she adeptly solves the problem of how women might appropriately write satire. Aiming at women as well as men, carefully controlling the tone and form, and playing the role of social reformer, she sets a useful example for later women poets.[44]

As such, the irony and the uneven structure of "The Unequal Fetters" disrupt the normalised standards and undermine the discursive practices prevalent throughout the late seventeenth and early eighteenth centuries.

To conclude, Finch's poems suggest the fast passage of time and the inevitability of ageing and bodily decline as a natural process. Her lyrical work – sometimes melancholically, sometimes satirically – addresses the transience of the human life course and criticises people's efforts at improving their bodies in order to fulfil the ideal of beauty and youthfulness as vain and senseless. Through her insights into the feminine experience of the life cycle, Finch not only ponders philosophical questions about the transience of all existence but also implies a critique of dominant political and social discourses and standards of normality. These characteristics of Finch's work exerted a wide influence upon eighteenth-century poetry and the following generations of poets, as Carol Barash emphasises:

> In her repeated – almost ritualistic – gestures of muted political opposition and collective, symbolically feminine emotional inwardness, Finch creates the patterns that will dominate female lyric poetry for the next century and a half.[45]

5. Conclusion

With their aspirations to attain longevity and the utopia of immortality Enlightenment society strongly promoted discursive practices of sustaining the transient body. In their poetry, Jonathan Swift and Anne Finch criticise the shallowness of normalising beauty and youthfulness as well as the double standards applied to feminine and masculine attitudes and behaviours towards ageing. Their lyrical works contemplate the fast passage of time and the shortness of the human lifespan as signs of the transience of all existence. Thus, they represent physical decline as a natural process that opposes artificially set standards of normality and satirise mankind's vanity in deluding themselves about their own mortality.

As such, Swift's scatological poems expose people's sensationalist interest in the effects of bodily decay that are usually withheld from the public gaze. At the same time, "A Beautiful Young Nymph Going to Bed" and "The Lady's Dressing Room" disclose how far people tend to deceive themselves and others through the use of bodily accessories. Through the mock-epic style and the ironic effects created throughout his satires, Swift ridicules his voyeuristic readers' disregard of their own ageing process.

By comparison, Finch's works convey philosophical insights and responses to the experience of life and the fast progress of time. She calls attention to the double standards for masculine and feminine ageing prevalent throughout society and thereby exposes the mechanisms of power the social body exerts through discursive practices.

In sum, the writings of both poets disclose processes of ageing and old age as integral parts of life. They thereby uncover the delusionary character of Enlightenment society's practices of managing the ageing body – a body that despite all efforts remains a symbol of the inevitability of human transience.

Notes

[1] See Kelly, Veronica, and Dorothea von Mücke (1994). "Introduction: Body and Text in the Eighteenth Century." *Body and Text in the Eighteenth Century*. Eds. Kelly and von Mücke. Stanford: Stanford University Press, 1-20, 10.
[2] Yallop, Helen (2016). *Age and Identity in Eighteenth-Century England*. Abingdon and New York: Routledge, 93.
[3] *Ibid.*, 2.

[4] *Ibid.*, 3.

[5] Elias, Norbert, paraphrased in Guerrini, Anita (2000). *Obesity and Depression in the Enlightenment: The Life and Times of George Cheyne*. Norman: University of Oklahoma Press, 100.

[6] Foucault, Michel (1995). *Discipline and Punish: The Birth of the Prison*. Trans. Alan Sheridan. New York: Random House, 222.

[7] *Ibid.*, 131.

[8] *Ibid.*

[9] *Ibid.*

[10] *Ibid.*, 129-130.

[11] *Ibid.*

[12] See Guerrini (2000), 96-98.

[13] See Cheyne, George (2016 [1724]). *An Essay of Health and Long Life*. (Classic Reprint). London: Forgotten Books.

[14] Hartung, Heike (2016). *Ageing, Gender, and Illness in Anglophone Literature: Narrating Age in the Bildungsroman*. New York and London: Routledge, 47.

[15] Guerrini (2000), 97.

[16] Foucault (1995), 184.

[17] Dolezal, Luna (2015). *The Body and Shame: Phenomenology, Feminism, and the Socially Shaped Body*. London: Lexington Books, 64.

[18] Martin, Bernice (1990). "The Cultural Construction of Ageing: Or How Long Can the Summer Wine Really Last?" *Aspects of Ageing: Essays on Social Policy and Old Age*, Social Policy Papers No. 3. Eds. Michael Bury and John Macnicol. Egham: Department of Social Policy and Social Science, Royal Holloway and Bedford New College, 53-81, 62, qtd. in Blaikie, Andrew (1999). *Ageing and Popular Culture*. Cambridge: Cambridge University Press, 29.

[19] See Swift, Jonathan (2003 [1726]). *Gulliver's Travels*. Ed. Robert Demaria, Jr. London et al.: Penguin, 191-198.

[20] Hammond, Brean (2010). *Jonathan Swift*. Dublin: Irish Academic Press, 149.

[21] *Ibid.*

[22] Arber, Sara, and Jay Ginn (1991). *Gender and Later Life: A Sociological Analysis of Resources and Constraints*. London et al.: SAGE, 1.

[23] Wilson, Penelope (2010). "Feminism and the Augustans: Some Readings and Problems." *The Essential Writings of Jonathan Swift: Authoritative Texts, Contexts, Criticism*. Eds. Claude Rawson and Ian Higgins. New York et al.: Norton, 784-794, 786.

[24] Enright, D. J. (1986). *The Alluring Problem: An Essay on Irony*. Oxford: Oxford University Press, 110.

[25] Swift, Jonathan (2010 [1732]). "The Lady's Dressing Room." *The Essential Writings of Jonathan Swift*. Eds. Claude Rawson and Ian Higgins, 603-606, lines 61, 116, 43, 120. (Emphasis in the text). Further references to this poem will be included in the text.

[26] McMinn, Joseph (2003). "Swift's Life." *The Cambridge Companion to Jonathan Swift*. Ed. Christopher Fox. Cambridge: Cambridge University Press, 14-30, 28.

[27] Suarez, Michael F. S. J. (2003). "Swift's Satire and Parody." *The Cambridge Companion to Jonathan Swift*. Ed. Christopher Fox. Cambridge: Cambridge University Press, 112-127, 115.

[28] Wilson (2010), 791.

[29] Swift, Jonathan (2010 [1734]). "A Beautiful Young Nymph Going to Bed." *The Essential Writings of Jonathan Swift*. Eds. Claude Rawson and Ian Higgins, 607-609, lines 11-12. Further references to this poem will be included in the text.

[30] Hammond (2010), 149.

[31] *Ibid.*

[32] For examples of Finch's political and medically oriented poems see Finch, Anne Kingsmill, Countess of Winchilsea (1974 [1713]). "Upon the Death of King James the Second" and "The Spleen." *The Poems of Anne Countess of Winchilsea*. Ed. Myra Reynolds. New York: AMS Press, 85-90 and 248-252.

[33] Barash, Carol (1996). *English Women's Poetry, 1649-1714: Politics, Community, and Linguistic Authority*. Oxford: Clarendon Press, 262.

[34] Natali, Ilaria (2016). *"Remov'd from Human Eyes": Madness and Poetry 1676-1774*. Florence: Florence University Press, 78. (Emphasis in the text).

[35] Finch (1974 [1713]). "All Is Vanity." *The Poems of Anne Countess of Winchilsea*. Ed. Myra Reynolds, 238-248. Further references to this poem will be included in the text.

[36] *Ibid.*, 111-112. Further references to this poem will be included in the text.

[37] *Ibid.*, 122. Further references to this poem will be included in the text.

[38] See, for example, William Shakespeare's Sonnets 1-6 and Sonnet 18 in Shakespeare, William (1975 [1609]). *The Complete Works*. New York et al.: Gramercy Books, 1191-1192, 1194.

[39] Reynolds, Myra (1974 [1903]). "Introduction." *The Poems of Anne Countess of Winchilsea*. Ed. Reynolds. New York: AMS Press, xvii-cxxxiv, xciv.

[40] *Ibid.*, xciii-xciv.

[41] *Ibid.*, xciv.

[42] Finch (1974 [1713]). "The Unequal Fetters." *The Poems of Anne Countess of Winchilsea*. Ed. Myra Reynolds, 150-151. Further references to this poem will be included in the text.

[43] Hartung (2016), 47.

[44] Backscheider, Paula R. (2005). *Eighteenth-Century Women Poets and Their Poetry: Inventing Agency, Inventing Genre*. Baltimore: Johns Hopkins University Press, 40.
[45] Barash (1996), 287.

Bibliography

Arber, Sara, and Jay Ginn (1991). *Gender and Later Life: A Sociological Analysis of Resources and Constraints*. London et al.: SAGE.
Backscheider, Paula R. (2005). *Eighteenth-Century Women Poets and Their Poetry: Inventing Agency, Inventing Genre*. Baltimore: Johns Hopkins University Press.
Barash, Carol (1996). *English Women's Poetry, 1649-1714: Politics, Community, and Linguistic Authority*. Oxford: Clarendon Press.
Blaikie, Andrew (1999). *Ageing and Popular Culture*. Cambridge: Cambridge University Press.
Cheyne, George (2016 [1724]). *An Essay of Health and Long Life.* (Classic Reprint). London: Forgotten Books.
Dolezal, Luna (2015). *The Body and Shame: Phenomenology, Feminism, and the Socially Shaped Body.* London: Lexington Books.
Enright, D. J. (1986). *The Alluring Problem: An Essay on Irony.* Oxford: Oxford University Press.
Finch, Anne Kingsmill, Countess of Winchilsea (1974 [1713]). *The Poems of Anne, Countess of Winchilsea*. Ed. Myra Reynolds. New York: AMS Press.
Foucault, Michel (1995). *Discipline and Punish: The Birth of the Prison*. Trans. Alan Sheridan. New York: Random House.
Guerrini, Anita (2000). *Obesity and Depression in the Enlightenment: The Life and Times of George Cheyne.* Norman: University of Oklahoma Press.
Hammond, Brean (2010). *Jonathan Swift*. Dublin: Irish Academic Press.
Hartung, Heike (2016). *Ageing, Gender, and Illness in Anglophone Literature: Narrating Age in the Bildungsroman.* New York and London: Routledge.
Kelly, Veronica, and Dorothea von Mücke (1994). "Introduction: Body and Text in the Eighteenth Century." *Body and Text in the Eighteenth Centur*y. Eds. Kelly and von Mücke. Stanford: Stanford University Press, 1-20.
Martin, Bernice (1990). "The Cultural Construction *of Ageing:* Or How Long Can the Summer Wine Really Last?" *Aspects of Ageing: Essays on Social Policy and Old Age*, *Social Policy Papers No. 3.* Eds. Michael Bury and John Macnicol. Egham: Department of Social Policy and Social Science, Royal Holloway and Bedford New College, 53-81.

McMinn, Joseph (2003). "Swift's Life." *The Cambridge Companion to Jonathan Swift*. Ed. Christopher Fox. Cambridge: Cambridge University Press, 14-30.

Natali, Ilaria (2016). *"Remov'd from Human Eyes": Madness and Poetry 1676-1774*. Florence: Florence University Press.

Rawson, Claude, and Ian Higgins (eds.) (2010). *The Essential Writings of Jonathan Swift: Authoritative Texts, Contexts, Criticism*. New York et al.: Norton.

Reynolds, Myra (1974 [1903]). "Introduction." *The Poems of Anne Countess of Winchilsea*. Ed. Reynolds. New York: AMS Press, xvii-cxxxiv.

Shakespeare, William (1975 [1609]). *The Complete Works*. New York et al: Gramercy Books.

Suarez, Michael F. S. J. (2003). "Swift's Satire and Parody." *The Cambridge Companion to Jonathan Swift*. Ed. Christopher Fox. Cambridge: Cambridge University Press, 112-127.

Swift, Jonathan (2003 [1726]). *Gulliver's Travels*. Ed. Robert Demaria, Jr. London et al.: Penguin.

--- (2010 [1732]). "The Lady's Dressing Room." *The Essential Writings of Jonathan Swift*. Eds. Claude Rawson and Ian Higgins, 603-606.

--- (2010 [1734]). "A Beautiful Young Nymph Going to Bed." *The Essential Writings of Jonathan Swift*. Eds. Claude Rawson and Ian Higgins, 607-609.

Wilson, Penelope (2010). "Feminism and the Augustans: Some Readings and Problems." *The Essential Writings of Jonathan Swift*. Eds. Claude Rawson and Ian Higgins, 784-794.

Yallop, Helen (2016). *Age and Identity in Eighteenth-Century England*. Abingdon and New York: Routledge.

Contributors' Addresses

Dr. Lisa Ahrens, Institut für Anglistik und Amerikanistik, Universität Paderborn, Warburger Straße 100, 33098 Paderborn

Dr. Alessandra Boller, Seminar für Anglistik (English Literary and Cultural Studies), Universität Siegen, Adolf-Reichwein-Str. 2, 57068 Siegen

Dr. Elise Brault-Dreux, Institut Sociétés et Humanités, Université Polytechnique des Hauts-de-France, Campus Mont Houy, 59800 Aulnoy-lez-Valenciennes, France

Dr. Sandra Dinter, Institut für Anglistik und Amerikanistik, Friedrich-Alexander-Universität Erlangen-Nürnberg, Bismarckstraße 1, 91054 Erlangen

Alexander Farber, M.Ed., Institut für Anglistik und Amerikanistik, Universität Koblenz-Landau, Universitätsstraße 1, 56070 Koblenz

Dr. Sarah Schäfer-Althaus, Institut für Anglistik und Amerikanistik, Universität Koblenz-Landau, Universitätsstraße 1, 56070 Koblenz

Julia Schneider, M.A., Institut für Anglistik und Amerikanistik, Universität Paderborn, Warburger Straße 100, 33098 Paderborn

Dr. Lena Schneider, Fachbereich II / Anglistik, Universität Trier, Universitätsring 15, 54286 Trier

PD Dr. Christoph Singer, Institut für Anglistik und Amerikanistik, Universität Paderborn, Warburger Straße 100, 33098 Paderborn

Dr. Sara Strauß, Institut für Anglistik und Amerikanistik, Universität Paderborn, Warburger Straße 100, 33098 Paderborn